AUTO DETAILING

I0619916

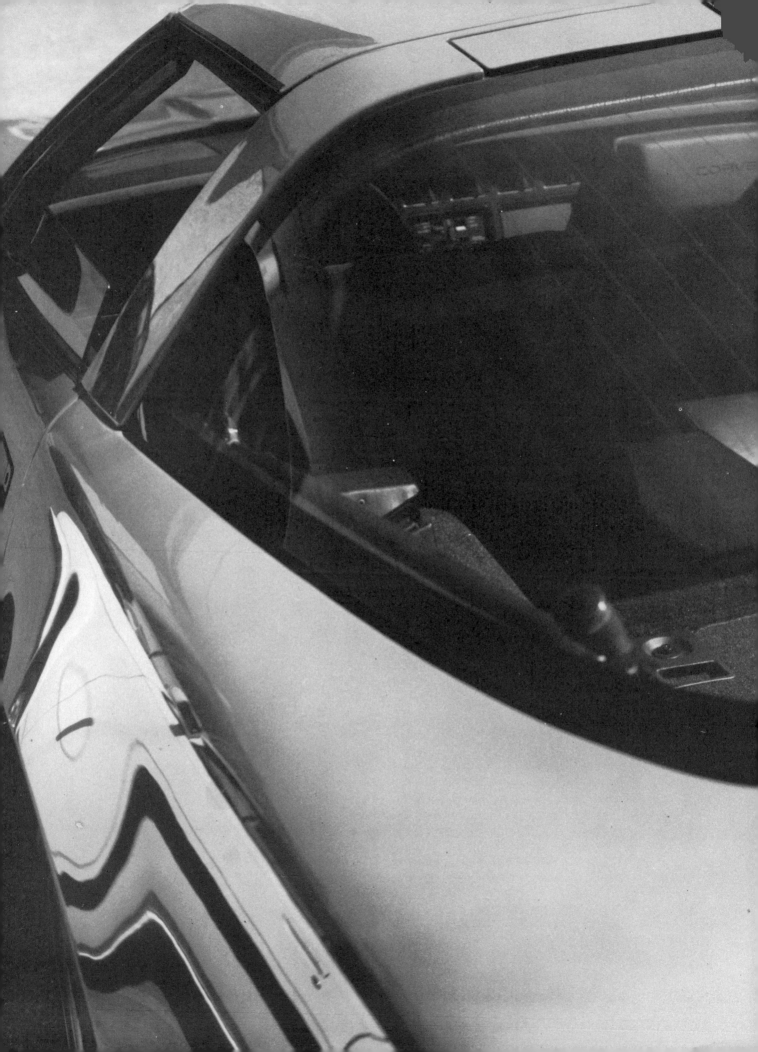

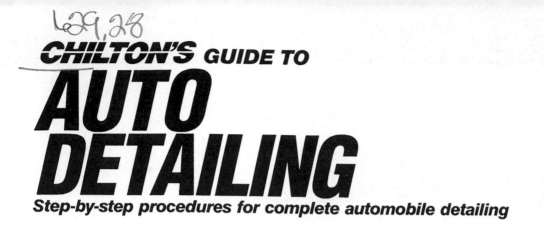

CHILTON'S GUIDE TO
AUTO DETAILING

Step-by-step procedures for complete automobile detailing

Sr. Vice President	Ronald A. Hoxter
Publisher and Editor-In-Chief	Kerry A. Freeman, S.A.E.
Managing Editors	Peter M. Conti, Jr. □ W. Calvin Settle, Jr., S.A.E.
Assistant Managing Editor	Nick D'Andrea
Senior Editors	Richard J. Rivele, S.A.E. □ Ron Webb
Director of Manufacturing	Mike D'Imperio
Manager of Manufacturing	John F. Butler

CHILTON BOOK COMPANY

ONE OF THE DIVERSIFIED PUBLISHING COMPANIES,
A PART OF CAPITAL CITIES/ABC, INC.

Manufactured in USA
© 1992 Chilton Book Company
Chilton Way Radnor, Pa. 19089
ISBN 0–8019–8394–0
Library of Congress Catalog Card No. 91–055224

1 2 3 4 5 6 7 8 9 0   1 0 9 8 7 6 5 4 3 2

CONTENTS

This book will guide you step-by-step to keep your car looking as new, inside and out, as the day you took delivery. That is what detailing aims to achieve: new car appearance throughout the life of your car.

In addition to thorough explanations and instructions for every detailing job you might need or want to do to maintain your car's showroom-new appearance, suggested products, materials and approximate times are provided for each job. An appendix lists currently available products both by the job performed and by automotive company recommendation.

Whether you consult the Appendix or the product lists accompanying each set of directions for the detailing you plan to accomplish, the choice of products is yours. And purposefully so. Some car owners with previous detailing experience may prefer one product over another. Others, with no particular preference, may pick and choose among products currently available from local auto supply or accessory stores. House brands may be available in some stores. Then, too, detailing products change, just as do cars, their finishes and materials. From time to time, new products will be introduced which are not listed here. For these several reasons, this book does not recommend any particular product except where it has a unique application. The lists are not all-inclusive: the products were selected because the manufacturer's instructions coincided closely with my directions in this book—directions I developed using a product with *similar* ingredients, procedures, and results. When in doubt, get a recommendation from your local automotive supply dealer.

Whatever detailing product you choose, it has but one aim: to help you to keep your car looking not only younger, but *new*. That, too, is the aim of this book.

"Detail" your car as the pro-detailers do? You can. This book tells you how, step-by-step, to do the things inside and outside your car—and under its hood and chassis—to retain its showroom-new luster and looks. Or, if your car is something less than showroom new, how to restore it to near-showroom good looks.

Regularly and properly detailed, your new car will always look new, inside and out. Detailed, it need never show its true age. Ten years and more down the road—or however long you keep it—your car's interior and its exterior paint job and chrome can be as flawless as when you first took delivery. Or, if yours is an older car, once you have restored it through detailing to all-but-new appearance, it need never show further signs of road wear or aging.

A Saturday miracle? No, a method, a calculated, step-by-step ways and means used by professional detailers to maintain a car's appearance—outside, inside, under the hood, and beneath the chassis.

Your neighbor's car which seems never to age and, if anything, to look *better* with age, is probably regularly detailed. So, for years, have been many luxury cars. And certainly so has every vintage car at an auto show that appears to have come from the factory only yesterday, although it came from the finish lines 10 years . . . 20 years . . . perhaps 40 or more years ago.

The secret is detailing.

"Detailing" is one of the hottest words in car care today. It is also one of auto care's most misused and ill-defined words. Although auto insiders have used pro-detailers—and known of their methods—for decades, most car owners are only just now discovering the miracle of detailing. It is the aim of this book to make you an insider to detailing and its methods. And, having done so, to guide you in detailing your own car.

By detailing your car yourself you can accomplish pro-detailer perfection at a fraction of the cost charged by professional detailers. Your largest investment is time: your own time. Investing your own time, rather than paying a professional detailer for his, enables you to afford to detail your car more often, say, two, three, or even four times a year. Detail it regularly, and your car will always retain its appearance and showroom good looks.

Doing it yourself makes sense—and dollars, too! And not simply the dollars you save over the high cost of shopping the detailing out to a professional. Regularly detailed, your car will almost certainly be worth more when you decide to trade it. The top trade-in prices quoted in the used car price books—the basis for pricing a used car—are for "clean cars." By definition a "clean car" is a detailed car.

Also, speaking of savings, if you detail your car regularly, you'll likely decide to keep the car you drive months, even years, longer, as many owners who detail do. One reason is pride—pride in the car you drive, which always looks good. Unlike most owners

CHAPTER 1

Detailing: More Than a Wash and Wax

Fig. 1.1 Classic Thunderbird meticulously detailed throughout its entire life looks factory-new after decades of road and show use. Detailing has helped boost the car's worth to far more than when it was delivered from the factory.

who pamper their cars the first few months and then allow them to fade and show age from neglect, you'll never need to tell yourself, "The old bus's paint job looks awful; I guess it's time to get rid of it."

Detailing frees you from costly "forced trade-ins" which keep many car owners forever in car hock. What forces many who neglect their cars to trade in prematurely and to buy new—thus assuming new debts and never-ending monthly car payments—is their car's appearance. But such trade-ins don't happen to a detailed car and its owner. For owners of cars regularly detailed, appearance is seldom the reason for trading in or up. You trade in—your detailed car fetching a premium "clean car" trade-in price—when and if you choose.

Detailing preserves a car's costly irreplaceables: its original factory paint job and interior. No matter how expert or costly a repainting, it can never duplicate the original factory finish. Nor can interior upholstery and finish be duplicated, again no matter how expert the redoing. Detailing preserves both the interior and the exterior in original, near-factory-perfect condition.

To put detailing in basic dollars and sense perspective: A few dollars and hours regularly spent detailing your car preserve an investment which may have cost you $10,000 to $30,000, and perhaps much more. That same few dollars and hours of detailing investment frees you from the necessity of a costly re-

Fig. 1.2 Another oldie with that fresh-from-the-factory look. Detailing can add years of life and super looks to the paint job, too.

painting ($300–$2000) or an equally costly reuphol-
stering ($500–$2000) which, whatever their cost, can
never equal the factory originals.

Detailing protects your investment by stretching
out car life. Plainly and simply, a detailed car costs you
far less to own. And, over the long haul, figuring all
costs, far less to drive.

Most owners, probably you among them, want
to—and often must, by financial necessity—keep their
cars longer. All costs considered, few today can afford
to trade in or up every two or three years, as was done
regularly in the past. In those "other days," when people kept their cars only a few years, they passed their
neglect on to the next buyer. There was less reason to
keep up a car's appearance, inside and out. Today,
there are plenty of reasons for keeping up your car's
appearance. And what does it is detailing. Almost all
of today's persuasive reasons for detailing to maintain
long life involve the "M" word: *Money.*

The facts speak for themselves. The ever-rising
price of new cars (today, an average $16,000 base
price), their far better quality than a decade ago (rust-
out and engine failure have been all but eliminated),
and today's long-term financing (often 48- to 60-
month), which leaves little trade-in equity even after 3
or 4 years of payments, have persuaded many to keep
their cars longer. In 1971, the average age of cars on
the road was about 5¾ years. Today, the average is
almost 7½ years. All of these factors make detailing an
attractive and relatively inexpensive way to preserve a
car's worth and appearance; in short, to preserve your
automotive investment. Detailing is economy car care.

A detailed car is also a potentially safer, lower-
maintenance car. The reason is obvious: when your
car is showroom clean, especially under the hood and
beneath the chassis, little problems—such as leaks
(fuel, oil, water), worn hoses and fan belts, and dangerously misaligned tires—are easily spotted before
they become major and costly problems.

Yet, oddly, although auto detailing and detailers
have been around for decades (mostly around the
used car lots), only recently have most car owners
made "detailing" an everyday word in their automotive
vocabularies.

"Detailing" has crept into our vocabularies before
it has crept into any of the world's basic dictionaries.
None of them, at this writing, has gotten around to
defining "detailing," although likely they will soon correct the omission. However most, in defining what
doing something in "detail" entails, come close—
although inadvertently—to defining what detailing is.

*The Random House Dictionary of the English Lan-
guage, Second Edition, Unabridged,* defines "detail" as
"attention to or treatment of a subject in individual or
minute parts." As for "detailer," the same widely re-
ferred to source of definitions seems oddly stuck in the
nineteenth century. It defines a "detailer" as "a manufacturer's representative who calls on customers . . .

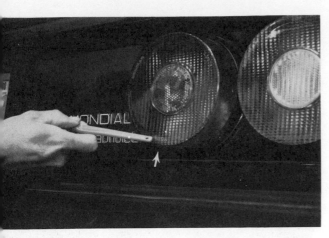

Fig. 1.3 A minute car wax smudge on a taillight lens gets attention from a serious detailer.

Fig. 1.4 The toothbrush is a favorite tool of the pro-detailer.

and visits stores to monitor sales and replenish stock." In the horse-and-buggy days, maybe, but not today when the horses are under the hood and the "buggy" sports a gleamingly painted exterior, topped by a protective layer of clearcoat.

With no help from such official sources, then, we'll have to define "detailing" ourselves. "Detailing" is the maintenance or restoration of automotive good looks, inside and out, through the application of advanced techniques, appropriate materials, and hands-on doing. What detailing is *not* is simply a wash and wax. You add luster to your car's exterior with an application of wax, but you will not have achieved the mirror-finish characteristic of a detailed car's exterior. You can bring a shine to a dull paint job with any number of one-step cleaner-waxes (which clean and wax in one easy step), but one-step luster is *not* detailing—or what detailing can achieve. Detailing is nothing less than the precison restoration or maintenance of automotive excellence, inside and out. And under the hood and chassis as well.

For all its buzzword virtues, detailing's heritage is something less than virtuous. The earliest detailers—and some of them still work the used car lots—would be more correctly called cover-up artists. With paint, polish, a steam cleaner, and consummate skill, they made the used lots' ailing oldsters seem years, if not miles, younger. Deftly, they touched up body nicks, steam-cleaned and repainted tired engines, gave the rusty radiator a shiny new black-paint exterior, and erased years of wear from upholstery. Such superficial "detailing," yesterday as today, is plain and simply a cover-up. What's covered up are a myriad of real or potential mechanical faults, ebbing horsepower, a road- and weather-worn paint job, and miles and years of wear and tear.

"Sure," says a used lot owner, "we use detailers. If we didn't, not many of our 5- to 7-year oldsters would move off the lot. When a detailer finishes with an engine that shows 80,000 miles on its odometer, that engine looks practically new. I mean, it's been steam-cleaned and spray-painted. So have the radiator, rocker covers, manifold, air cleaner, and even the hoses. When a potential customer lifts the hood (something we encourage prospects to do), he sees a gleaming "new" engine. The prospect concludes that if the previous owner was so meticulous about the engine, he must have been meticulous about the entire car throughout its life. What the customer doesn't know is that the car's been detailed—and only hours before he or she lifted the hood. Detailing builds buyer confidence and sales. Without detailing, there wouldn't be much of either on my lot."

"Detailing," declared automotive writer-editor Michael Lamm in *Motor Trend,* in describing used lot detailing, ". . . masks a car's true condition and history."

Not only are such detailing lot-practices deceptive, they are short-lived. That, and where they concern

Fig. 1.5 At self-service carwash places some car owners merely wash their cars. One sign of a detailer: the car's hood and trunk are open and the owner is painstakingly at work.

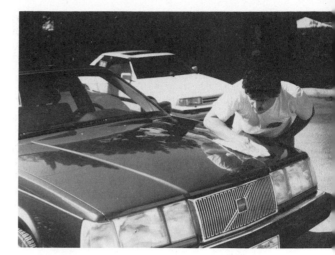

Fig. 1.6 Detailers carefully scrutinize the car's finish while they polish it, checking for nicks, scratches, and the first signs of oxidation.

black-painting worn tires and hoses, potentially dangerous.

The cover-up as practiced on used car lots is not detailing because true enhancement of a car is not its purpose. It is cosmetic subterfuge. Within days or weeks the cosmetics wear off and fade away. But not before the dealer has pocketed his asking price: a far higher price than he would have realized without cosmetics.

Witness the best of pro-detailers at work and you don't observe a cover-up, but rather the application of advanced products and techniques which enhance, and largely restore, what was originally there: paint, chrome, vinyl, and leather.

But while detailing can strip years from an older car and regain or preserve a newer car's original looks, it can seldom completely erase years of neglect. For while detailing can "restore" much of any car's original sheen and shine, detailing is not, in strictest terms, "restoration." Restoration implies refinishing and reconstruction—in short, body work and repainting.

Detailing, by constrast, is enhancement: the close-as-possible renewal of a car's original showroom appearance.

Above all, detailing is about pride: the pride you'll feel at the wheel of a "looker," a finely detailed car you're proud to own and prouder to drive. And then there's the fun factor. No doubt about it, a clean car is more fun to drive. And a super-detailed car? Super fun to own and drive.

Fig. 1.7 This person is a "wheel cleaner," but most likely not a detailer. Missing from his work are the tools and products generally needed to upgrade cleaning to detailing, such as cotton swabs and special alloy polishes.

Fig. 1.8 The well-manicured look of this complex exterior belies good detailing by its owner or a pro.

The "secrets" of professional detailers are subtle. While some pro-detailers concoct cleaning and sprucing-up formulas of their own, probably the vast majority use products right off the local auto stores' shelves, products as easily available to you as to the professionals.

Most pros, of course, buy their detailing products—from buffing pads to polishes—in professional-size quantities from distributors who make it their business to supply large-volume users. And a few manufacturers formulate products designed solely for use by professionals (their use usually requires professional skills and equipment). Yet even these formulators generally offer some of their products to weekend detailers through auto supply stores and home centers.

In dozens of interviews for this book with pro-detailers, most admitted that few, if any, of the wash formulas, polishes, chrome cleaners, and waxes they routinely use were "proprietary"—that is, formulas of their own making. And, as such, "secret."

Says a pro with decades of daily detailing experience. "Really, detailing's only real 'secret' is plain hard work. That, and knowing what works best and fastest."

That pro-detailers often use the same brands of products available to weekend detailers should come as no surprise. Today's auto finishes—inside and out—are going high-tech. In the past decade, and continuing, whole new "systems" of finishes have largely made the old finishes obsolete. And with them, many products which worked in the past, but don't work as well, or at all, on the new finishes.

Most revolutionary of the new finish systems is clearcoating, in all of its varieties. Clearcoat finishes require a whole new family of detailing products and new detailing techniques.

Professional detailers are not chemists, paint technicians, or fabric makers. Nor do they claim to be. The developers of the new exterior and interior finishes and materials are technical experts. They are lab people rather than rack people. Seldom can even the best pro-detailer's self-made formulas match the products researched, formulated, and car-tested by the major manufacturers of detailing products.

Recently, as one example, Nissan introduced for its *Infiniti* luxury car a new fluorine-based clearcoat finish which the carmaker said would need no waxing for years. But, while it might not need waxing, the new clearcoat required, as do all clearcoats, special care and special products to administer that care.

Chemists from one of the most respected manufacturers of detailing products in the United States worked closely with DuPont's chemists, who had developed the fluorine-based finish, to formulate products designed to maintain its beauty and assure its long life. This product maker has a full-scale lab of its own. It staffs chemists specialized in car-care products. Nissan and DuPont approved the products specially formulated for the new clearcoat. Result: Nissan issued a

CHAPTER 2

Secrets of Detailing Pros

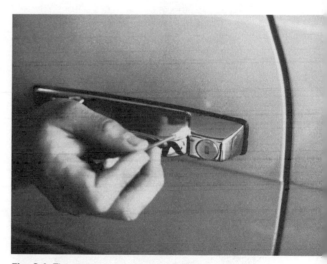

Fig. 2.1 *The cotton swab is one of the "secret" tools of pro-detailers. (Hint: Use a toothpick to dislodge dirt buildup in crevices even a swab can't get into.)*

maintenance bulletin to its dealers and to independent detailers recommending that *only* the new fluorine-compatible detailing products be used on the *Infiniti*—until some other product maker came up with products as compatible with the finish (which is likely to happen). It is unlikely that a detailer's own cleaning, polishing, and waxing formulas could work on the special clearcoat finish as well as laboratory-formulated products.

Are there, then, any "secrets" that the weekend detailer can learn from the pros?

The answer: a resounding "plenty of them."

The pros' *real secrets* are the how and when—and in what order and with what tools—to apply what products to best protect, beautify, and preserve a car, inside and out.

Following are interviews with some of America's top pro-detailers. Step-by-step, they reveal the "how" of detailing it right, safest, quickest—and best.

Restoring Good Looks to Exterior Paint

Cahalane: Every three to four months, more often if you have the time, you glaze and wax it.

Q: Glaze it first?

A: Before you wax it, yes. To detail it right, which means restoring the paint's true, deep color, it's a two-step job. Glaze first, then wax.

Q: It's not a one-step job, as most car owners do, using any of the quick, one-step cleaner/waxes the auto supply stores sell?

A: No, two steps. The auto stores sell the right stuff, of course, and not simply one-step products. But you've got to know what to buy.

To understand why it's a two-step job, you've got to understand what causes even a car's clean paint to look dull, hazy, and discolored.

It's not dirt but scratches. Minute—all but microscopic—scratches you can scarcely see. Actually, you can usually see them if you look closely. The purpose of the glaze—which can vary, depending on the type, from a clear, water-like to a tan or brown creamy liquid—is to fill in the scratches. Filling in the scratches brings the paint's color back—restores it—to where, hopefully, it was right out of the factory.

Q: The pre-waxing glazing step is simple?

A: Yes. You apply it—I hesitate saying "rub it on"—with a super-soft rag. I use a diaper. Then you carefully rub if off.

Q: After glazing, you wax it?

A: You must. The glaze simply fills in the scratches and enhances the color. Glaze doesn't protect the paint or the clearcoat, the final protective finish common to most factory paint jobs today. In fact, if after glazing you didn't wax, and you took the

Mark **Cahalane** is one of the nation's top professional detailers. His business, Auto Art, based in Manhattan Beach, California, doesn't advertise. Not even a sign hangs in front his modest shop. Yet hundreds of car owners have for more than 20 years beaten a path to his door. They drive some of the world's most expensive and exotic cars. Seldom is the waiting line shorter than three months. When Cahalane is ready to detail your car, he phones you to bring it in. The cost for detailing a car inside and out: $125 and up. Here, Cahalane discusses some of the most crucial steps in restoring good looks to any car's paint job.

Fig. 2.2 Mark Cahalane is one of the West Coast's top professional detailers. For more than 20 years he has detailed some of Southern California's most expensive and exotic cars.

car out in the sun, in an hour's time the glaze would be gone, taken right off by sunlight.

Q: So, in effect, waxing protects the glaze first and the finish almost secondarily?

A: That's right. When you glaze, as every car owner should and as every reputable pro-detailer does, the wax does double duty: protects the glaze and protects the paint.

Q: But all this involves time and a lot of work. Suppose a car owner shortcuts: waxes, as most owners do, but skips glazing?

A: Oh, you'll get a shine, all right. But nothing like the mirror-finish when the car was new—and nothing like the restored good looks even an older paint job can have if you glaze it first.

We're talking about keeping up a car from the day you take delivery. Detailing can do a lot for a car that's been neglected. But the basic idea in detailing is not restoring a neglected car, or bringing it back as close as possible to its original appearance. Rather, it's to keep a car up so that it *never* looks bad.

Q: Doing that, a car can look good virtually forever?

A: Absolutely. Ten years down the road it can look very nearly as good as the day you bought it.

Q: But suppose there are visible nicks and places where the paint needs touching up? Is that beyond the average car owner's skill?

A: It's within nearly anyone's skill, assuming the places you want to retouch are small. And providing you get a touch-up paint that color-matches what's on the car. Neither is really difficult—either finding a color-matched paint or, once you have it, touching up the spots.

Q: Where would a car owner find an exact-match paint for his or her car?

A: From the dealer where you bought the car . . . or from one of those stores, specialized to auto paints—and most larger cities have them—which can batch up a quart or so of the original color for any car. All you have to give them is your car's "Paint Number," which is on the car somewhere. Your owner's manual should tell you where. And some paint matches are also available from local auto supply stores (see Fig. 8.6, "Locating Your Car's Factory Paint Code").

Q: So let's consider the doing—retouching a single, typical little place that needs retouching. Not, of course, a sizable area. *That* calls for repainting, not retouching—right?

A: Right. Before you glaze, but after you've washed and dried the car, you dab a little paint—very little on the first try—on the spot. I prefer to use a very small, high-quality artist's brush, *not* the applicator brush that comes with most bottles of retouch paint. It's a good idea, by the way, to use masking tape to mask off the retouch area. The

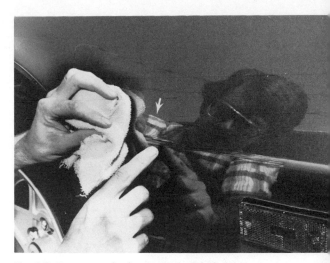

Fig. 2.3 *The secret of a flawlessly detailed finish is glazing, a critical step that comes after washing and before waxing. Glaze fills in microscopic scratches (arrow) and buffs to a high gloss (which in most cases must be protected immediately with wax).*

second step in retouching explains the reason for the masking.

Q: So retouching is a process that involves several steps?

A: Yes. It's not something you get done all at once. In fact, you let that dab spot dry for a full week. Then, remasking around it if your tape isn't still there, you carefully, lightly, sand over the spot using very, very fine—say, 600 grit or so—*wet* sandpaper.

Q: Using very fine wet sandpaper—which is really not a sandpaper, but a super-fine emery paper—is the same technique used by fine furniture finishers to achieve a super-smooth finish on furniture?

A: The same technique, yes.

And after sanding, you very gently rub out the retouched place, using rubbing compound, a very fine abrasive that erases any scatches in the retouched place that might have been left by the super-fine wet sandpaper.

Your masking tape, of course, remains in place, the tape being masked in very closely to the spot you've retouched, so you can sand and rub out the spot without mistakenly sanding the paint around it—which, of course, you don't want to do. Doing that, you'd scratch the body paint and botch the job.

Q: And after rubbing out the wet sandpaper's minute scratches in the retouched spot?

A: Well, after super-smoothing the retouched place with the rubbing compound, you can glaze and polish the car. That retouched spot will just blend in, the nicked place disappearing as though by magic.

Q: Until somebody next to your car on a parking lot puts another nick in your paint job?

A: Like housecleaning, you never really finish with retouching.

"Prepping" It: Detailing's All-Important First Steps

Q: When you say "prepping," you mean "preparation"—something the at-home detailer should do *before* glazing or waxing his or her car's exterior?

A: Yes. Preparation, what pro-detailers call "prepping," is the single most critical and important phase of *exterior* detailing, without doubt.

Q: In some of your columns in professional detailing magazines, you list "prepping" first—ahead of glazing, ahead of polishing, and ahead of waxing.

A: Ahead of them all, yes. Prepping is the first step—really several steps—leading to final exterior detailing.

Some, I know, consider prepping and final detailing as merely different steps—prepping being the first steps, and final detailing being the con-

Stephen Grisanti is one of detailing's acknowledged experts. A regular columnist for *Professional Carwashing & Detailing* magazine, he is president and founder of Classic Shine Auto Fitness Centers, based in Greenwich, Connecticut. A veteran of more than 14 years' hands-on detailing experience, his franchised Classic Shine Auto Fitness Centers currently operate in four states—New York, New Jersey, Connecticut, and Massachusetts. Here he discusses "prepping," a vital series of first steps that should take place *before* you glaze or wax.

Fig. 2.4 Stephen Grisanti, founder and president of Classic Shine Auto Fitness Centers.

cluding steps—of professional-quality detailing. Most professional detailers, as myself, see prepping as a distinctive series of make-ready steps that are *essential* for any quality detailing job.

Now, I concede that some pro-detailers, as well as "do-it-themselfers," may skip some prepping steps. That's their choice. But failing to properly prep a car's exterior—and that includes beneath the chassis and under the hood—can be costly.

Q: In time and results?

A: In both. Prepare the exterior properly, and you can cut overall detailing time by an hour, perhaps two hours. Sometimes more. Prepare it right, and you also end up with a first-class detailing job and a car you can be proud of. Skip prepping and the result of a lot of hands-on work is apt to be only so-so. We aren't talking here about a fair-to-middling, quickie detail job. We are talking about a super professional job.

Q: Detailing results that a car owner can achieve, if he or she goes about it right?

A: Absolutely.

Q: Well, then, how would *you* define "prepping."

A: I'd rather use an analogy. Prepping a car is analogous to a woman taking off all of her makeup at night. You want to strip off all of a car's exterior makeup. That's a perfect prep: when there is nothing, no dirt or grime, left anywhere on the car. Only then is it ready for final detailing—for glazing, polishing and waxing.

Q: And where do you begin prepping?

A: The very first thing to do in prepping, before you get down to "cleaning" anything, is quickly to hose down, with water, the car's exterior, but not the tires or, if it has one, the vinyl or convertible top. You don't wet those areas because you want them dry when you begin prepping there.

Q: And after the initial wet-down?

A: Start at the wheels. While we use some proprietary products, I'll mention the types of products that are available in most auto supply stores.

Q: Let's go step-by-step through the prepping routine.

Wheels, wheel wells, and tires

A: For prepping the tires' black rubber or whitewalls, use an all-purpose household cleaner. A very strong household cleaner/degreaser can be used to degrease the engine.

Spray the cleaner on a tire *and* into its wheel well. Sure, you may have to get down on hands and knees to reach the inner recesses of the wheel well. Then move to the next tire, letting the cleaner "work."

Then get to work on the tires' rubber with a tire brush made especially for prepping rubber.

Most auto supply places carry them. The tires, you'll discover, are really dirty, right up to their treads, and beyond. Some pro-detailers neglect that portion of a tire. You shouldn't, not if you're intent on prepping it right.

You can use the same tire brush to prep the wheel wells. Why do the wheel wells? Because they are usually very dirty and they're visible. *That's* reason enough for prepping anything.

In some black tire and wheel well areas you may need to use steel wool and all-purpose cleaner. A better combination, especially for prepping whitewalls, is steel wool and soap, as found in household steel wool cleaning pads.

For most other prepping jobs (other than tires), where you want only a minimum of abrasiveness, use *very fine* steel wool. Triple-0 (000) steel wool is usually the prepping choice.

Q: Among very fine steel wools, the triple-0 is mid-range on the abrasive scale?

A: Yes. Three grades of steel wool are commonly used by pro-detailers. All are extremely fine. They range from double-0 (00), the "coarsest" of very fine steel wools readily available, to quadruple-0 (0000), the gentlest, with triple-0 (000) falling between these two. Even though all three are minimally abrasive, compared to other types of detailing abrasives, there is a distinct gradation in their abrasiveness. I consider the double-0 too abrasive for most prepping jobs. The quadruple-0 is so minimally abrasive that you have to work too hard to achieve any results at all. The abrasive happy medium is the triple-0; therefore, mid-range triple-0 steel wool is our steel wool of choice—a choice born of detailing experience.

A play-it-safe mildly abrasive combination is triple-0 steel wool and all-purpose cleaner. It's the right and safest combination for prepping wheels, whether solid or spoked, and whether magnesium, steel or aluminum.

But on well-chromed (not the cheap stuff) wheels, and "straight-through" wheels—where the metal (steel, aluminum or magnesium) is solid straight through, and where there's no paint—we also use a weak but effective hydrochloric acid solution followed—after 10–15 seconds to let it work—by a water rinse. You can buy hydrochloric acid at most home centers. Cut it 7 to 1. That is, dilute it, mixing a solution that's 1 part acid to 7 parts water. Or, from auto supply stores, you can buy equivalent products under various labels (see box).

Q: What about the *toothbrush* as a wheel and tire prepping tool?

A: No doubt about it, the toothbrush is still prepping's best cleaning tool, but it is not usually used for tires and wheels. And especially not if you're

---

Wheel Cleaners

Car Brite Wire Wheel Cleaner
CSA Premium Gold
Eagle 1 All Finish Wheel Cleaner
Eagle 1 Wire & Chrome Wheel Cleaner
Eagle 1 Mag Cleaner
Entire Whitewall and Wheel Cleaner
Espree Mag Wheel Cleaner
Espree Mag Wheel Cleaner & Polish
Espree Wheel Magic (for painted, clear-coated, plastic, sculptured mag and wire wheels)
Espree Wire Wheel Cleaner
Mothers Mag & Aluminum Polish
Mothers Wheel Mist
OxiSolv Wire Wheel Cleaner
PRO Aluminum & Mag Polish
PRO Professional Wheel Cleaner
The Treatment Mag and Aluminum Wheel Cleaner
The Treatment Mag and Aluminum Polish
Turtle Wax Wheelbrite (for all wheels/hubcaps)
Turtle Wax Wheelbrite Wire Wheel Cleaner
Turtle Wax Wheelbrite Mag Wheel Cleaner

cleaning in and around the tires' raised lettering, if your tires have them.

A toothbrush hasn't surface area enough to clean tire letters efficiently. What does is a medium-soft wire brush made especially for cleaning tire "type." The brush and a little all-purpose cleaner make quick work of tire "type" prepping, helping to rid the letters of every last vestige of dirt and road grime.

When it comes to toothbrushes, get the kind with soft to medium bristles, not hard bristles. Also, you want a toothbrush that's well bristled, without a lot of gaps. To get into wheel crevices, nylon toothbrushes work well, too.

Q: Are any other brushes used in prepping?

A: An *engine brush,* for removing stubborn engine grease after we've hit the engine with all-purpose cleaner or solvent, and a *prepping paint brush,* for getting into body paint crevices where there's a buildup of wax.

The prepping paint brush, used strictly on paint, is a wooden-handled brush with very soft bristles made of horsehair. It looks like a paint brush, only it's designed for prepping and detailing. Most makers of the horsehair brushes claim they won't scratch paint. Actually, they sometimes will unless you use them very carefully, and with minimum pressure and action as you brush out whatever you're brushing—usually wax that's caked between two painted surfaces or in the crevice between chrome strips and the car's body. Some auto supply stores carry the horsehair brushes.

Q: And next you prep the engine?

Engine and engine compartment

A: After the tires, wheels, and wheel wells, the engine compartment, yes. Since you're planning to cover engine cleaning and detailing elsewhere, here I'll just highlight engine compartment prepping.

First off, we "baggie"—put a plastic bag or plastic wrap over—the distributor cap and, if they're installed, the car's alarm system components, including the wiring, to keep water and solvent out. We don't cover the spark plugs or, generally, anything else underhood. For one thing, on today's newer cars you can't reach the spark plugs. They're hidden deep under a raft of accessories. And we don't warm up the engine before beginning the engine compartment prep, although some detailers recommend that you do.

In engine/engine-compartment prepping we want to clean things completely, getting at the last smidgeon of grime and grease. You can use spray-on all-purpose cleaner or any of the spray-on degreasers, or both. And you'll probably have to go over a dirty engine several times. We generally do.

As for what's on the underside of the hood—the material bonded to the underside of the hood—use common sense. Fiberglass, which is often found on the hood's underside in older cars, won't come clean. And, if it's insulating material, leave it alone—and keep it dry. The foam hood-undercoating on many newer cars can and should be cleaned. A quick look and maybe a touch usually tell you what the underhood material is and whether it's cleanable. Probably the majority of hood material is insulation and should be left alone.

First, shoot the engine compartment with an all-purpose cleaner. Follow that with an engine degreaser. You'll notice this is in reverse order from what some others recommend. The degreaser—available at auto supply stores—is basically a strong, all-purpose engine cleaner. In prepping, the engine degreasing solution has just one use: to rid the engine and its accessories of grease.

Having degreased it once, do the same thing—for most engines—a second time. Both cleaning solutions are spray-applied, either from a spray bottle or from an aerosol can, if that's what the solution comes in. The more forceful the spray, the better the cleaning. The spray jet, alone, helps break up grease, especially in engine and compartment nooks, crannies, and crevices. And most engine compartments have a lot of them.

With the degreaser and all-purpose cleaner working, we go over all the greasy places with a stiff-bristled *engine brush* made for engine cleaning, available at auto centers.

Finally, using clear water, we rinse and wash the engine and engine compartment. A garden hose will do. Set it to deliver medium water volume, or even less; then adjust the nozzle to deliver the least water you can with maximum force, making a kind of jetstream.

Most pro-preppers use a *pressure washer*. They're fairly expensive, but possibly worth your investment if you intend to prep and detail your car regularly through the years. The beauty of a pressure washer—especially when prepping the engine—is that it delivers very little water but a lot of air pressure, so you don't risk dousing the engine, particularly its spark plugs and electronics, with more water than you absolutely have to. In engine prepping, more water—or more of anything else—isn't necessarily better.

Once the engine's rinsed, air blow it dry—say, with your household vacuum's blower end. Use rags to sop up any puddled water.

Will the engine start, even though you haven't protected the spark plugs? Usually, it will. If it doesn't on the first try or so, let it sit while you complete the prepping and do the finish-detailing: glazing, polishing, and waxing. By then, dried out, the plugs will fire, and so will the engine. We experience very little trouble with engine starts after engine prepping.

Q: And now to the car's unders, beneath the chassis—right?

Prepping the underside

A: Prepping the underside, yes. Actually, it's a pretty quick job because, first, it really doesn't show and, second, all you're really doing is ridding it of any buildup of grease and road debris. There's no need to hike the car on a lift or even to jack it up to get underneath, as some few preppers do—or to first drive the front wheels up on a curb, a kind of concrete "jack" that some claim gives easier access to the underside. ("Curb jacking" risks throwing the wheels, especially the front ones, out of line.)

It's enough, usually, just to spray the underside with all-purpose cleaner. But do it systematically—working prone—all the way around the car. Then, with a forceful water stream from a hose or a pressure washer, rinse it well.

Q: Suppose the car has a convertible or vinyl top?

Convertible or vinyl top

A: The top's the last major prepping step, usually, before prep-washing the car.

Remember, we didn't wet the vinyl/convertible top or wheels when we initially wetted the rest of the car. So the top is dry. We want it dry because water or any wetness would dilute the strength of our prepping solutions.

For a vinyl roof, dust it with a powdered household cleaner. Dunk a soft-bristled brush in all-purpose cleaner and scrub, working the powder into the vinyl. The brush's bristles, the abrasiveness of the powdered cleaner, and the strength of the all-purpose cleaner do a phenomenal job. That's really all it takes to prep the vinyl.

Apply the powdered and all-purpose cleaners in a slurry. Do half the roof, that is, one side at a time. Draw an imaginary line down the vinyl roof's center. Stand on a stepladder so you can reach to the center and scrub just the side you're prepping. Avoid wetting the other half, because you want it dry, for reasons mentioned previously, and you want to prevent cleaner from dripping on the paint on the far side of the car.

When you've finished the first half, flood it with water. (In the whole process, you use a lot of water to prevent streaking the paint.) Then move to the roof's other half. On white vinyl roofs you'll likely have to repeat the process.

Many vinyl roofs are inset with emblems, usu-

▌▌CAUTION: Don't let the abrasive slurry you've created drip down on the body's paint. It's abrasive and, chemically, a rather strong solution. Drips can cause streaks in the paint. Keep the paint hosed down and wet. Immediately wash off any cleaning solution that reaches the paint.

ally the carmaker's emblem. Use a soft-bristled toothbrush dipped in the all-purpose cleaner, and maybe a little of the powdered cleaner, to get into the emblem's recesses.

You treat convertible tops the same way. As with white vinyl tops, if the top is white, expect to do it twice to prep it right.

Q: What about the chrome?

Prepping chrome

A: Well, there are plenty of good chrome cleaners around. But a water-wetted steel wool and soap pad cleans chrome about as well as any of the prepared cleaners. The steel wool and soap pad won't scratch the chrome, providing you use the usual steel wool caution: light pressure. Just be careful not to stray over into painted areas when using steel wool of any kind. Or, you can use triple-0 steel wool. But it's so fine that it cleans chrome more slowly—and thus requires more doing—than the soap/steel wool pads.

There is, however, one considerable caution when it comes to chrome: avoid anything even remotely abrasive when cleaning some of the English chromes, such as the Jaguar's, or fake chrome, which is either paint and not chrome at all, or very thinly chromed metal.

Chrome on many cars manufactured in England—"English chrome"—is extremely fine, elegant-looking chrome. It is not as shiny as the chrome on most American-made cars because it is electroplated differently. The Jaguar is one of the most difficult cars to prep, partly because of the special treatment its chrome requires. No abrasive material or liquids should be used. Even a little abrasiveness can scratch some English chrome. Clean it with a very mild, nonabrasive liquid chrome cleaner. Steel wool, no matter how fine its grade, is an absolute no-no.

Q: There's only one major prepping chore left— washing the car?

Prepping the paint

A: In prepping, do *last* what most driveway detailers do first—wash the car, which means its paint.

We're talking about a hand-wash, of course. And you're the washer. In prepping, avoid— except, perhaps, for engine degreasing—the commercial carwashes. Few, if any, give the time or care required to properly prep-wash a car.

Actually, the easiest part of prepping is washing.

There are two washing situations you should be aware of:

1. If the car is already waxed, you want to use a very mild soap so as to remove the dirt from the wax, yet not remove the wax from the paint.

Fig. 2.5 Step 1 at a self-service carwash is a soapy water wash. (A point on which detailing pros are unanimous: Don't subject your car to commercial carwashes.)

Fig. 2.6 Step 2: Using the self-service bay's heavy suds dispenser (brush or sponge), "float off" the dirt. Most experts say to begin at the top of the car when doing self-service sudsing.

2. If you plan to polish and wax the car once it has been prepped—the usual case, actually—you could use a stronger soap solution, such as a carwash soap. Why? Because you don't care if the wax is removed since you intend to rewax. There are several fairly strong and effective carwash soaps available.

My recommendation is to use a very mild soap—dishwashing detergent or a liquid hand soap, diluted in a bucket of water. Apply generous amounts of the soapy solution—the more solution, the better—with a clean, terry cloth towel or a lamb's wool washing mitt.

The soapy wash water acts as a kind of lubricant. It makes your wash towel or mitt slippery, easing it, without scratching, over the paint. In many cases, water and toweling alone would adequately prep-clean the car's finish. The soap solution's main job is to prevent the towel or washing mitt from scratching. So use lots of the soapy solution. And continually keep dunking your towel or mitt in the clean soap solution.

Wash top to bottom. Some preppers, I know, do just the opposite, wash bottom to top. One reason for washing top to bottom is to avoid the dirtiest area—the bottom molding, which often is streaked with road tar—until the very last. This keeps your wash water clean and free of grit, which might turn the wash solution abrasive.

As for road tar? Run your fingers along the bottom molding's underside and, beneath it, the rocker panel, which is the bottommost panel, between the front and rear wheels. If you feel little bubble-like raised places, it's probably road tar. It comes off like butter using a bug and tar remover (see box). Saturate a rag in the remover and run it over the tar bubbles. Presto, they're gone!

Fig. 2.7 Step 3: Keep working suds lower, paying special attention to the lower area of the exterior, including front and rear bumpers, wheels, and wheel wells.

Tar and Bug Removers
CSA Tar & Bug Remover
Cyclo Bug & Tar Remover
McKay Tar & Bug Remover
No. 7 Tar & Bug Remover
PRO Bug Remover
Turtle Wax Bug & Tar Remover
Ultra Shine Tar Remover & Motor Degreaser
Westley's Bug & Tar Remover

Fig. 2.8 Step 4: Allow 2 minutes of your alloted 5-minute wash cycle for a thorough rinsing.

Fig. 2.9 After completing the wash cycle, move to the carwash's drying/vacuuming area.

George Nojima is founder/president of Keystone Body Shop, Inc. (in Santa Monica, California), whose custom paint jobs can cost $1000—and up. Here he talks about repaint jobs and how to make them last longer.

Washing done, hose down the car. Then thoroughly dry it with a synthetic chamois. Genuine chamois stiffen and harden after a few uses. The synthetic kind doesn't.

Q: We've spent considerable time going through prepping, step-by-step. How long should prepping take, start to finish?

A: A lot less time than it takes to describe the doing. After a prepping or two, and with a little hustle, and with everything ready to go (the right brushes, cloths, and products at hand), you should be able to whittle the prepping time down to 30–45 minutes. The engine compartment, for example, shouldn't require more than 15 minutes or so to prep if you've got your equipment lined up and ready.

But even if, the first few times, you spend a couple of hours prepping—and you very well might—that's often time saved when you get down to glazing and waxing.

Besides, as one radio ad says, a clean car—a properly prepped one—is a happy car. And so is its proud owner.

Treatment and Care After Repainting

Q: In some instances, detailing involves repainting part, even much, of a car. Is there a right way to prolong repaint life?

A: Well, that begins with preparation *before* you paint, because 99% of a good repaint job is preparation. Once an area is repainted, either with a base color or with a base color overlaid with a clearcoat, you let it dry two weeks, at least, in warm weather; longer if the weather is rainy or damp. Then you give the new paint area a "color sanding."

Q: That's the treatment that enhances the new paint's color and shine, and helps to prolong repaint life?

A: Yes. That's the purpose of color sanding. We go over the repainted area with 1000–1200 grit wet-dry sandpaper. First, we thoroughly wet the painted area. Then, very lightly, using the 1000–1200 grit paper, which is extremely fine, we very carefully, very *lightly*, hand sand the area. All the time we keep wetting—and keep wet—the area we're color sanding.

Color sanding removes any small surface defects—roughness called "nibs"—in the paint or clearcoat. Then, we thoroughly rinse the sanded area and remove the excess water with a squeegee.

Q: And after that?

A: We apply a mildly abrasive rubbing compound, selecting one that is only slightly more abrasive than the wet 1200 grit paper. That done, we wax the area. We use, although it may seem odd, a boat wax—a wax used on fine boats—that is nonabrasive and helps to preserve the paint or clearcoat.

The result is an extremely fine paint finish with high shine and luster. And a finish with wax protection.

Q: Still, the car owner needs to wash and rewax the car periodically, especially its repainted areas?

A: Absolutely. To retain and prolong repaint life a car should be washed, preferably by hand, at least once a week. And, periodically, say every six months, rewaxed.

Most owners make the mistake—especially with a repainting job—of not keeping their paint clean. Washing reduces oxidation, which gradually dulls and eventually degrades the repainted finish. If you wash the car regularly, and periodically rewax it, a refinish with conventional paint or clearcoat will retain its new-paint appearance for years. And, certainly, for repainted finish, for five years and far longer.

Q: Still, no matter how good a repainting, it is never as good or as long-lived as a factory paint job?

A: There's no way, the second time around, to duplicate the factory's original paint. That's why detailing is so important: it preserves the unduplicable factory paint—and prolongs the life of repainted areas as well.

Fig. 2.10 George Nojima, founder and president of Keystone Body Shop, Inc., of Santa Monica, California.

Masking: One Secret of Good Detailing

To detail it right, you need to mask it right.

Masking involves covering up the parts of the car immediately adjacent to the area or parts you're working on. The cover-up avoids damage to paint, chrome, fabric, or other materials or parts you're not detailing at the time.

One thing is sure, however: it's often easier, and makes better sense when possible, to remove a part for detailing rather than leave it in place and mask around it.

Masking, while it takes time, is easy. You merely cover the immediate parts or body areas you're not currently detailing with paper (newspaper works fine). Use masking tape to hold the paper in place.

If you use wide enough masking tape—say, 1 to 2 inches wide—you can sometimes protect surrounding areas with the tape alone, provided you work carefully. If painting is involved, *always* mask around your spray area with paper, *never* with tape alone.

Masking tape, available at auto supply stores, paint stores, and home centers (see box for some possible brand choices), is inexpensive. At some discount places a 40- to 60-yard roll of 1-inch wide masking tape costs less than $1. Masking tape usually comes in ½- to 3-inch widths. For narrower ¼- to ⅛-inch widths, used for some specialized detailing jobs, you'll have to look harder, or ask a store to order them for you.

Masking tape is a unique and highly useful product, one seemingly made for detailing. Most masking

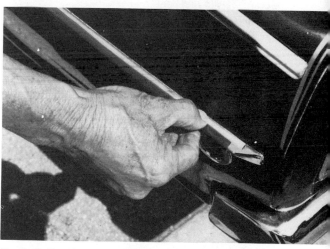

Fig. 2.11 Your thumbnail can be a dewaxing "tool" to remove trim wax from places no other tool can reach (but be careful not to scratch the finish).

Masking Tapes
Manco Auto Masking Tape
Manco Auto Seat Repair Tape
Shurtape
3M Masking Tape

tape is an industrial grade of crepe paper bonded to a natural and processed rubber adhesive.

While all masking tapes may look alike to the average buyer, the tape comes in several grades. Toughest are several *industrial grades*, including high-temperature industrial tape that can withstand temperatures to 300°F, as well as a variety of exotic solvents and solutions. *Utility grades*, while good enough for most auto detail masking, aren't as thick as industrial tapes and have less strength. Industrial grades, with better adhesion, are less likely to allow paint to bleed through them. Bleed-through can ruin the very areas that masking and masking tape are meant to protect.

At least one major maker of masking tapes produces a slightly higher-grade (and slightly more expensive) tape for car detailing. As a tape designed for automotive applications, including detailing, it is usually found in auto supply stores, rather than in paint stores. This same maker advises against leaving masking tape in place (especially on body paint) for longer than 24 hours. If left longer, removing the tape could—depending on the condition of a car's paint—remove some finish.

Masking, avoided by some pro-detailers because it is time-consuming, has many detailing applications, some of which are described in the following paragraphs.

Touching up paint. When you're touching up chipped, nicked places in the car's paint, you mask around each place you want to touch up to protect the surrounding finish.

Polishing chrome body molding. It's all but impossible to do a thorough job of polishing chrome body molding without masking, because the molding's edges come in contact with the body paint. If you're polishing the molding with steel wool, an abrasive, masking is mandatory because steel wool can scratch and abrade the paint.

If, on the other hand, you're using any of the many available auto chrome polishes, you probably can get by without masking. However, if you don't mask you face a tedious cleanup problem: the polish's residue is difficult to remove from the molding's edges and from the adjacent painted surfaces. Then, too, while auto chrome cleaners won't harm body paint, others may. To play it safe, mask.

Spray-painting small body areas. Any body-area painting requires masking immediately adjacent to where you intend to spray-paint. Overspraying is inevitable, no matter how expert you are with a spray can or paint spray. The slightest breeze or draft puts tiny particles of sprayed paint where you don't want it. Masking all around your work area protects the surrounding area from overspray.

How far around any particular job should you mask? That depends on the area you're working on and on environmental conditions—a breeze blowing through a garage work area, for instance. If what's blowing is a mere whiff of breeze, wide enough masking can protect what needs to be protected. If anything much more than a zephyr is blowing, hold off spray-painting. No amount of masking—short of covering the entire car—can protect it against overspray. Given decent environmental conditions, for many detailing jobs involving spray painting, masking a minimum of 3 feet all around the work area is a good rule of thumb.

Often, masking width depends on what—and how—you're detailing. Suppose you're repainting a sun-faded canvas convertible top. Some canvas recoloring products are applied with a cloth or brush. Masking 2 feet around the top should be enough. Other canvas recoloring products are sprayed on. Add a foot of masking—making it 3 feet all around—to prevent overspraying.

Detailing small parts.   If you're cleaning door handles, roof light fixtures or similar small parts, masking to protect surrounding areas makes sense.

Detailing intricate parts.   Masking lets you do detailing jobs you can't afford to have done by professionals. If you keep your car longer than do most owners, inevitably some painted parts—in particular painted wheel covers and grillwork—will need to be repainted. The doing involves extensive and precision masking, involving an hour or more of labor, for which a paint shop or pro-detailer would necessarily charge—often, a lot more than you'd be willing to pay. However, if you do the masking yourself you can achieve pro-detailing results for little more than the cost of a spray can of paint, a roll of masking tape, and your time.

Most auto masking is simple and quick. Let's say you want to repaint a rubber or synthetic front bumper and you need to protect the car's front and grille. You merely cover the area behind the bumper with newspaper or masking paper (a heavier grade paper used by body shops) and fix the paper in place with masking tape.

Or perhaps you want to steel-wool and brighten chrome stripping along one side of your car. After the car is washed and thoroughly dry, you run 1- or 2-inch wide masking tape along each side of the chrome. The "running" must be precise. The tape must cover every bit of body paint adjacent to the chrome molding.

To achieve this masking accuracy, you may have to lift and reset the tape several times as you go. Or, patch in a piece of masking tape here and there to achieve perfect no-paint-showing masking. Because no painting is involved, thus there's no risk of overspraying, an inch or two width of masking tape protection either side of the molding should sufficiently protect the body paint without addition of masking paper.

The most perfection-oriented custom-detailers (whose client-cars are often the exotics) routinely mask the lower few inches of canvas convertible tops, forming a mask-barrier between the car's finish and the canvas. Reason: when waxing the finish, it's all but impossible not to get some on the lower edges of a canvas top, where it meets the body. Wax is very difficult to remove from canvas; in fact, often it cannot be removed without leaving a permanent stain.

For precise masking where car parts curve, or for masking small parts or places, use narrow (¼- to ¾-inch) tape, which bends and adheres more precisely to rounded and small surfaces. Once masking tape is accurately placed, run your fingers along it, firming the adhesive bond.

When the detailing is done and the paint or cleaners are thoroughly dry, remove the tape slowly, a piece at a time. Avoid hurriedly ripping tape off, which risks damage to the painted surface.

While most auto masking is simple, there are some masking jobs that are difficult and time-consuming.

Rejuvenating wheel covers—common to many older cars, but found on some late models, too—is a job that involves the kind of time that can cost quite a bit unless you do it yourself. Depending on the complexity of wheel cover design, masking wheel covers can be among the most tedious—but most rewarding—jobs faced by home detailers.

Consider the wheel cover masking and repainting illustrated on these pages. The process involves (1) initial cleanup/polishing of the wheel covers' chrome; (2) masking their 44 once-black-painted areas, each separated by a chrome strip; (3) masking their center insignia; (4) spraying the areas to be painted with primer; (5) spray-painting a new color over the primer; (6) wet-sanding between each dried coat of primer and finish; (7) stripping off the masking paper and tape; and, finally, (8) spraying the entire wheel cover—chrome and painted areas—with three coats of clear gloss lacquer to protect the new paint and to seal the chrome against oxidation and dulling.

Masking all four wheel covers can take more than four hours of careful masking. The process of applying spray primer, paint, and protective clearcoat lacquer, plus wet-sanding, can span two to three days, with ample time between spray applications for thorough drying. The finished job: as expert as any professional detailer's. In fact, however, few pro-detailers could—or would—afford the time involved. Nor could the average car owner afford a pro-detailer's probable bill for the work—likely no less than $50 per wheel cover, or $200 for detailing all four. (The author ac-

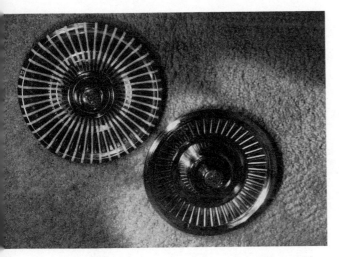

Fig. 2.12 The chrome is in good condition and is masked. The black worn areas will be repainted.

complished the entire job on a kitchen countertop for less than $15.)

On small jobs—as wheel covers—spraying is quick, with each spray-can pass involving only a few seconds. Fumes are minimal. Nonetheless, should you work indoors, you've got to use caution (see box) and common sense.

Below is a step-by-step explanation of how wheel-cover detailing—including time-consuming masking—should be done.

> **❗❗ WARNING:** Even limited indoor spray-painting with lacquer and enamel can be dangerous, even explosive, without proper ventilation. Any nearby flame—as that of a gas range or furnace pilot light—can ignite paint fumes. Spray-can painting should be done out-of-doors or in some well-ventilated place (a basement or garage shop), well away from pilot lights or other ignition sources. In addition, do not smoke or allow anyone else to smoke nearby while you spray-paint.

1▶2▶3

STEP-BY-STEP:

Masking and Detailing Wheel Covers

Time required: *1:15*
  1 hour 15 minutes per wheel cover, not including drying times for various steps

Materials needed:
  Masking tape: ¾- and ¼-inch widths
  A few sheets of 8½- × 11-inch typing paper
  Artist's knife
  Chrome cleaner/polish
  Steel wool (grade: 00, very fine)
  Wet sandpaper (600 grit)
  Auto primer paint
  Auto enamel
  Clearcoat

> **❗❗ CAUTION:** Follow all the directions on a product's label carefully. Product manufacturers want their products to work for you and your car because they want you to become a repeat buyer. Label directions aim to make the product perform as well as it can for you, so it pays to follow the manufacturer's step-by-step instructions.

Steps:
1. Clean and polish each wheel cover's chrome—strips, rim areas, and insignia—restoring the chrome's good looks.
2. Now the tedious masking begins. Use two widths of automotive masking tape: ¾-inch for general masking, and ¼-inch for masking the thin chrome strips and the chrome "rim" that surrounds the areas to be painted.
3. Run a single strip of ¼-inch tape very accurately atop

Aerosol Paints (body, chassis, wheels, touch-up, etc.)
Krylon Car Color
Krylon Van & Truck Spray Paint
Mar-Hyde Supreme Van & Truck Spray Paint
Mar-Hyde Supreme Roll Bar & Chassis Coating
Mar-Hyde Supreme Screamers (fluorescent colors)
Mar-Hyde Supreme Metal Flake
Mar-Hyde Supreme Chrome Aluminum
Mar-Hyde Supreme Silver & Gold Metallic
Mar-Hyde Touch-Up Paint
Mar-Hyde Lacquer
Plasti-kote Body Shop Paint
Plasti-kote Car Color Touch-Up
Plasti-kote Classic Lacquer
Plasti-kote Competition Colors (Metal Flake, Candy Apple, etc.)
Plasti-kote Import Car Color Touch-Up (also in bottles)
Plasti-kote Steel Wheels/Gold Wheels Paint
Plasti-kote Super Urethane
Plasti-kote Truck Color
Rust-Oleum Auto Primer
SEM Killer Color Fluorescent

Spray-on Lacquers/Urethanes/Acrylics
Autoglym Engine Lacquer (acrylic lacquer designed for engine compartment components, such as wiring, plastic parts, hoses)
Car Brite Clear Acrylic Engine Paint
Krylon Acrylic Spray Coating
Mar-Hyde Supreme Lacquer
Plasti-kote Classic Lacquer
Plasti-kote Clear Acrylic Spray
Plasti-kote Super Urethane
Zynolyte Spray Lacquer (clear)

the center of each raised chrome strip and overlap on the rim areas (Fig. 2.13). Finger pressure firms each strip's edges over and around the raised strip. Use the same precise procedure on each of the many divider chrome strips.

4. Next, accurately apply ¼-inch tape to the round edges of the rim sections. Mask the rim in small sections to ensure accuracy and to achieve, overall, a circular and unbroken run of tape (Fig. 2.14). This precision work done, the wider ¾-inch tape completes the outer rim masking.

5. Remaining to be masked is each wheel cover's cone-like center, topped by a chrome insignia. For each, use a sheet of 8½- × 11-inch typing paper. Round one end with scissors. The rounded paper edge is taped to the masked inner rim and the paper worked into a cone-shaped covering, configured to the wheel cover's

Fig. 2.13 Masking tape (¼-inch-wide) is pressed over the chrome spines to protect them from paint spray. Spine masking must be done accurately.

Fig. 2.14 Tape is run in a circle along the inner edge of the painted area. Overlapping short sections of tape helps to achieve a nearly perfect circle. Tape is pressed firmly over and around the chrome to prevent paint from bleeding into masked areas.

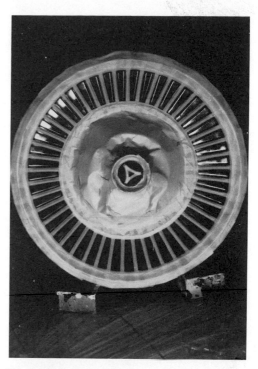

Fig. 2.15 *Masking is completed.*

Fig. 2.16 *Wheel cover sits on wooden blocks in front of a plastic drop cloth; it has been thoroughly masked and is ready to be sprayed with primer.*

center cone. Once the paper cone is finished and taped in place, trim it (with the artist's knife), exposing the wheel cover's raised center and insignia. Cover any areas of the insignia not to be painted with short strips of ¼-inch masking tape. Firm them to the cut upper edge of the paper cone.

6. Finally, lay strips of ¼-inch tape atop the insignia. Press in place along the insignia's raised sides. Use the artist's knife to trim any tape that intrudes into insignia areas that are to be painted.

7. With all of the wheel covers' chrome masked, and only areas to be painted exposed, clean the to-be-painted areas with a household cleaner/degreaser. Allow to dry. Then sand with 600 grit wet sandpaper.

8. Next, spray on the primer. After each quick spray pass allow a drying time of 15 to 20 minutes. Over the next hour, apply two to three coats of primer.

‖ CAUTION : Never use spray-on paints or degreasers in a closed-in area in which there is any danger of a stove or furnace pilot light—or any flame—igniting the product's fumes or spray. Also, don't smoke or permit anyone else to smoke nearby when you are using such products.

9. When the primer is thoroughly dry (overnight), wet sand and allow to dry (Fig. 2.17); then do a first spray pass with the auto enamel (Fig. 2.18). In all, three to four passes, spread over a day's time, completes the painting. Allow the paint to dry overnight.

10. When completely dry, carefully—sometimes inch by inch—strip off the masking tape (Figs. 2.19 and 2.20). Revealed is brilliant chrome surrounding the new paint—and, all in all, a perfect, professional-looking job: no overspray, no missed places, no flaws caused by faulty taping (Fig. 2.21).

11. To complete the detailing and to ready the wheel covers for installation, thoroughly spray-coat each with three protective layers of clear gloss lacquer. Allow the

Fig. 2.17 *Flat gray primer coat that has dried overnight is lightly sanded with 600 grit wet-sanding paper.*

Fig. 2.18 First of several finish coats is sprayed over sanded primer coat.

Fig. 2.19 When finish paint is dry (allow 18–24 hours) the masking tape is stripped off carefully to avoid removing any paint.

Fig. 2.20 Masking tape covering chrome spines must be taken off one strip at a time.

Fig. 2.21 The restored wheel cover is reinstalled on the wheel. It has been expertly detailed by a do-it-yourselfer, and its good looks put the not-yet-detailed tire rubber to shame.

lacquered covers to dry for 24 hours. Finally, wax with 100% carnauba wax.

The result of the painstaking masking and detailing: like-new wheel covers. And, as you might also conclude, a job to be proud of, one well worth the time and effort.

Tips from the Pros

Paint retouching

Shortcut. If there's a nick or chip in the finish and you haven't time at the moment to retouch it with color—or you feel you don't have the skill for a color retouch—but you want to protect it from rusting, dab a little clear nail polish or clear touch-up paint on the spot. You won't hide the nick, but you'll discourage rust.

Retouch paints. Don't trust the color match of any retouch paint, including those available at auto stores or from car dealers. Test the paint's color match on some small, unnoticeable place on the finish. Let it dry thoroughly before deciding whether or not it matches your car's finish.

Black is by far the easiest color to retouch and match, followed by white.

Don't attempt to retouch metallic paint. Its "match" depends on tiny metallic particles being held in suspension in the paint. Considerable skill, a controlled painting atmosphere, and spray-painting techniques are necessary for properly retouching metallics. Applying metallics with a brush is also almost always doomed to failure. The "retouch" will likely end up looking worse than the original nick or scratch.

Interior detailing

Leather upholstery. All leather is not the same. There's a considerable difference between European car leather (the way it's dyed and treated) and leather in, say, a Cadillac. Leather used by English and Italian car makers, for example, is of a higher quality than most furniture leather. A good deal of the leather in U.S.-built cars is coated with a plastic.

Euro-leathers are usually very deep grained. One problem: their dyes, especially those used in English luxury cars, are often extremely sensitive to various cleaning products. Use the wrong cleaner and the dye will come off.

Use only soft brushes and soft cloths when cleaning any leather, whatever the car. Only a few time-tested leather cleaners are on the market (see box). Saddle soaps, once the standard products for cleaning leather, are generally no longer nearly as good or nearly as safe to use on car leather as some newer leather-specialized products. Your car's maker may even recommend specific leather-cleaning/maintenance products. If you use a toothbrush to get into the leather's crevices and seams, use an extremely soft-bristled one.

Shampooing car carpets. Manual shampooing gets car carpets and carpeted floor mats reasonably clean, but never as clean as when they are mechanically shampooed and, as important, mechanically dried with professional equipment. Almost all pros use an *extractor,* which has the ability to pull ("extract") rinse water from carpeting. Extractors are often built into carpet-shampooing machines and into home shop wet/dry vacuums. You can rent a carpet-shampooing machine with extractor at most grocery stores. Or, at very little cost, arrange to drive your car and its rinse-water–soaked carpeting to a local carpet cleaning place and let someone there use the shop's powerful extractor to quick-extract, and thoroughly dry, your car's carpet-

Fig. 2.22 Protectants are easy to apply: simply rub or spray on, wait a few minutes, then wipe off.

Leather Cleaners/Protectants
Armor All Leather Care
Autoglym Leather Care Cleaner
Blue Coral Leather & Vinyl Conditioner (cleans, restores, protects)
Connoisseur's Choice Cleaner
Connoisseur's Choice Protectant
Eagle 1 Creme Leather Care & Conditioner
Hide Food
Leather Clean
Leather Lotion
Lexol-pH Balanced Leather Cleaner
Lexol Leather Conditioner and Preservative
Meguiar's Vinyl/Leather/Rubber Cleaner/Conditioner
Scotchgard Leather Protector
Westley's Leather & Vinyl Cleaner

Fig. 2.23 A protectant can correct minor scratches on dull plastic and put a sheen on it.

Fig. 2.24 Protectant is generally swabbed on and then removed using a soft towel.

Fig. 2.25 Protectant helps highlight hidden recesses in the dashboard and instrument console.

ing. With professional equipment, the whole process probably won't take more than 5 to 10 minutes.

Cleaning headliners. Be especially careful cleaning the headliner, which is the material that lines your car's ceiling. Whereas you can confidently scrub fabric seats with plenty of shampoo and water, doing the same with the headliner can cause the glue that holds it to the ceiling to come unglued. Result: a saggy headliner that usually requires an expert to repair.

Although detailing's golden rule is "If it can be cleaned, clean it," bend the rule for the headliner. Usually, it doesn't get as dirty as the rest of the interior. Cleaning it gently, with a minimum of liquid, every second or third time you detail the interior keeps things glued and in place.

"Things to do" checklist

It's easy to miss doing something because, in a thorough car detailing, there are plenty of things to do. Pro-detailers work from a "things to do" list. As they finish doing one detail item on the list, they check it off and move to the next. A checklist is especially important for do-it-yourself detailers who may do the exterior one weekend, the interior the next, and the engine compartment weeks later.

While a checklist can be quite extensive, because detailing can involve a number of "things to do," following is a simple checklist used by a leading pro-detail shop.

Detail Checklist

Exterior

Exterior paint ☐

Vinyl or convertible top ☐

Tail pipe ☐

Body chrome ☐

Wheels/tires ☐

Hubcaps/wheel rims/wheelcovers ☐

Wheel wells ☐

Windows/mirrors ☐

Windshield ☐

    Others: ☐

☐

☐

Special attention

Remove wax/cleaner from cracks ☐

Remove/clean behind license plates ☐

Retouch nicks/chips ☐

    Others: ☐

☐

Underhood/under-chassis/trunk

Engine compartment ☐

Under-chassis ☐

Trunk ☐

Gas filler pipe/area ☐

    Others: ☐

☐

Interior

Vinyl/fabric/leather ☐

Carpeting/vacuum/shampoo ☐

Door jambs ☐

Windows/windshield/frames/mirror ☐

Dashboard/instruments/panels ☐

In-car electronics ☐

Headliner ☐

Floor mats ☐

Ashtray ☐

Pedals/foot ☐

Controls/hand ☐

    Others: ☐

☐

☐

Whether you're about to give your car its first—and your first—detailing experience, or you're by now an experienced driveway detailer, you've got to plan ahead. You do, that is, if you want to do the job with the least effort, for the most lasting effect, and in the shortest time. Above all, you want to make the doing fun, and the results—when you stand back to admire your gleaming handiwork—something you can be proud of.

Fun? Washing, drying, glazing, waxing, and shampooing? It can be, if you plan ahead. That may mean *segmenting the job*—doing it piecemeal, as your time allows; *prioritizing*—working today on what *really* needs attention (the car's exterior, let's say), while putting off less urgent detailing for another day; and, before you start, *acquiring the supplies you'll need* for the job.

First, size up your car so you can segment the total job into detailing bite sizes. The sizing up has a lot to do with the condition of your car. If you car's odometer shows 20,000 miles and this is its first detailing, expect the total job to take more time. But once you've detailed it, further detailing—in the weeks and months ahead—will most likely take relatively little time. After a car's first real detailing, the upkeep is easier. And it often gets even easier with each increment of detailing. For starters, any car regularly detailed is easier to keep up with small increments of detailing. Besides, once you get the hang of the job, detailing becomes a less time-consuming routine. Detailing, which is car-keeping, is much like housekeeping. If your kitchen floor hasn't really been scrubbed and waxed since you moved into the place, the first thorough floor cleaning takes time. After that, if you keep things up, the doing is much easier.

Strategies

Here are some tested strategies for sizing up and setting up the job, before you begin:

One job at a time. Pick what needs to be detailed first (interior, exterior, vinyl top—and only later underhood or under-car). If this is your first detailing experience, don't attempt to detail the entire car, inside and out, in one session.

Set priorities. Almost certainly, if this is the car's first detailing, the exterior will get top priority. This is because every additional day of neglect risks permanent damage to the finish. Among exterior finish destroyers: atmospheric pollutants, strong sunlight, and such "natural" fallout as bird droppings and tree sap.

Piecemeal or whole-hog? While most driveway detailing can be done piecemeal, doing just part of any detailing segment and finishing the job later, at least one segment—detailing the exterior finish—must be

CHAPTER 3

Before You Begin the Job

Fig. 3.1 Before you begin, decide what you have time to detail right. For example, grooming four wheels correctly can take over an hour.

Fig. 3.2 For your car and your detailing abilities, where does detailing end and "restoration" begin? The average car owner should not attempt to repaint large areas of the car's exterior.

Fig. 3.3 Consider adding a little customizing. For example, you might think about adding a vinyl top and play around with some mock-ups such as these. (You can specify the design, but leave the actual doing to a qualified top shop.)

started and completed in a single session. Once the car is washed, you usually apply glaze, which sunlight will quickly dissipate unless, immediately afterward, you wax the car. In short, washing the car one day, glazing it the next, and waxing it the day after won't work.

But virtually all other detail segments can easily be piecemealed. For example: You can steam-clean underhood but not finish detailing or painting for a day or so. You can shampoo and dry the rear seats and leave the front seats for another day. You can detail just the dashboard and its accessories one day and do the rest of the interior molding and trim later. You can detail the headliner and do the rest of the interior later. In fact, in an emergency—say, something spilled on the upholstery—you can detail just the one spill-stained bucket seat and detail the other seats at a more convenient time.

Allot time for each segment.   How much time should you allot for each major detailing step? Much depends on the model of car (obviously, some are larger and some more complex to detail than others); whether it has been previously and regularly detailed, or long-neglected; whether you do all the work at home (for ex-

Fig. 3.4 You may decide to do the exterior one day and the interior at a later time.

Fig. 3.5 You may want to detail the two dirtiest areas of the car—underhood and under the chassis—in one messy session.

ample, washing, vacuuming, steam cleaning) or do some of it at a coin-op or commercial carwash; and how fast, skillfully, and steadfastly you work.

As an example, for a midsize, well-cared-for car whose finish is in good condition and whose engine and compartment are not super-dirty, here are some approximate time allotments for major detailing segments:

Exterior (wash, clean/polish, glaze, wax)	3–4 hours
Exterior trim, including wheels and tires	1–1½ hours
Interior carpeting, upholstery	2 hours
Interior trim, windows	1 hour
Underhood (steam-clean)	10–30 minutes
Underhood (detailing, but not painting)	1–2 hours
Underhood (painting, finish detailing)	1–1½ hours
Under-chassis (steam clean)	30 minutes
Trunk	20 minutes
Vinyl top (clean only)	20 minutes
Vinyl top (renew, including masking)	1 hour
Miscellaneous	2 hours

Start to finish. If, as the estimate above indicates, it will probably take you at least 3 hours to wash, glaze, and wax the finish, starting the job late in the afternoon with dusk all but upon you doesn't make sense. You'll wind up working in the dark, or at least in something less than full light. By the same measure, if you do the car out-of-doors, you want to avoid detailing the finish in strong sunlight. Exterior detailing should be done in the shade, or when sunlight is muted.

If you live in the snowbelt, you'll probably have to do wintertime detailing in the garage, if you have one. Or, better yet, in some heated, well-lighted protected

Fig. 3.6 *Decide what to take off the car before detailing and what to leave on. For example, it is all but impossible to detail beneath a rack such as this.*

place. Detailing indoors eliminates problems with sunlight—and also the problem of hurrying to finish a crucial step before nightfall. (Purists, however, contend that only natural light shows up minute flaws and swirls in exterior finish.)

Wherever and whenever you decide to start a detailing segment, make sure you have time and light enough to finish what you begin. And be alert to the weather. Nothing is more discouraging—or futile—than getting halfway through exterior detailing only to have a rainstorm drown the job.

System or individual products. Decide whether you want to assemble products for yourself or go with a "system". When it comes to buying detailing products, you can buy any combination of brands of waxes, polishes, and cleaners—or you can "buy a system."

Product-maker "systems" specify the step-by-step use of a particular maker's products. Clearly, this is an astute marketing strategy because, by specifying only its own products, the particular maker encourages purchase of its brand over other brands. But for do-it-yourself detailers, product systems take much of the guesswork out of picking and choosing among the myriad products on any auto supply or home center's shelves.

Product systems offer home detailers several major advantages: (1) all of the step-by-step products have been formulated and tested to produce a desired result; (2) all system products are compatible with one another; (3) a system's step-by-step instructions and products eliminate errors a home detailer might make in selecting and using products at random.

However, "system" products are not necessarily the least expensive you can buy for any given detailing job. Also, for many segments of detailing, any of numerous household products may produce equal results, and at considerably lower cost. And system-recommended products may not be as readily available at auto supply stores as non-system products.

!!**CAUTION**: Read product labels carefully before you buy or use a product. For example, if you prefer 100% carnauba wax, be sure that the label states "100% carnauba"—not something like "contains carnauba" or "formulated with carnauba."

An example: A brand name product producer markets a three-step (and three-product) system for cleaning, shampooing, and stain-proofing fabric car upholstery. Several non-system products, purchased separately, will do the same job. So will any of a number of household upholstery cleaners and shampoos available at supermarkets. Generally, the non-system upholstery cleaners cost less than the system's brand products. But, using the system products, you are assured that each of the products is chemically compatible with the others in the system and that they were formulated to work together to achieve a promised result.

Products and supplies.   Before you start work on any detailing segment, make a quick list of the supplies you'll need. Have them at hand before you start. Running down to the auto supply store or supermarket for something wastes time. And if you use the car you're detailing for transportation, you risk botching the job.

‖ **C A U T I O N :** Detailing products are meant to be applied, not inhaled. Many spray-on products warn against inadvertent inhalation. When applying, work in a well-ventilated place, preferably out-of-doors. If detailing your car's interior, assure adequate ventilation by leaving doors and windows open.

But don't buy things you'll need for detailing you plan to do in the future. Having the supplies you'll need for a future detailing segment can be a mistake. Why? The temptation to do only a halfway job on the first segment and to get, prematurely, to the next. Suppose you're detailing the exterior but also have out shampoo, buckets, and brushes for detailing the interior fabric upholstery. Certainly the temptation, for most, is to hurry along the exterior detailing and squeeze in the fabric cleaning.

When Not to Detail a Car

If you've had your car repainted or have purchased a recently repainted used car, hold off detailing it until the new paint is thoroughly—and safely—dry. Some additional precautions for owners of newly refinished vehicles:
- *Avoid* polishing or waxing your vehicle for 90 days.
- *Avoid* extreme temperatures.
- *Avoid* wiping the finish with a dry cloth.
- *Avoid* commercial car washes for 90 days.
- *Avoid* spilling chemicals such as antifreeze or coolant on the finish.
- *Avoid* scraping snow or ice from the finish.

During the first 90 days after a new paint job, you can wash the car with mild detergents and cool water—providing you wash it in the shade. Heeding the warnings listed above can mean longer life and beauty for any newly applied car finish.

Fig. 3.7 Teaming up for detailing gets the job done more quickly—and makes it more fun.

Fig. 3.8 Each member of the team has specific detailing chores.

Fig. 3.9 A dated detailing reminder tells you when you last detailed the entire car and when it should be detailed again (usually every 6 months).

Pro-Detailer 3-Month Schedule

Function	Week 1	2	3	4	5	6	7	8	9	10	11	12
Wheels:												
Clean	•	•	•	•	•	•	•	•	•	•	•	•
Detail	•			•				•				•
Tires:												
Clean	•		•		•			•		•		
Detail	•		•		•			•		•		
Car Wash:	•	•	•	•	•	•	•	•	•	•	•	•
Finish Restoration:					As Needed							
Wax:												
Carnauba (spray)	•			•				•				•
or												
Carnauba (liquid)	•							•				
Glaze and carnauba (paste)	•											•
Trim Detailing:	•			•				•				•
Interior:												
Glass/clean and polish	•			•		•		•		•		
Vacuum	•	•	•	•	•	•	•	•	•	•	•	•
Spot clean					As Needed							
Clean: leather and vinyl	•			•				•				•

Average Car Owner 3-Month Schedule

Function	Week 1	2	3	4	5	6	7	8	9	10	11	12
Wheels:												
Clean	•			•				•				•
Detail	•			•				•				•
Tires:												
Clean	•			•				•				•
Detail	•			•				•				•
Car Wash:	•	•	•	•	•	•	•	•	•	•	•	•
Finish Restoration:					As Needed							
Wax:												
Carnauba (spray)	•			•				•				•
or												
Carnauba (liquid)	•							•				
Glaze and carnauba (paste)	•											•
Trim Detailing:	•			•				•				•
Interior:												
Glass/clean and polish	•			•				•				•
Vacuum	•			•				•				•
Spot clean					As Needed							
Clean: leather and vinyl	•			•				•				•

Identifying Car Plastics

Advanced do-it-yourself detailers sometimes tackle rejuvenation jobs for which they need to know what kind of material they're working on. Identifying the material can be a key in selecting the right detailing product (usually, some type of rejuvenation finish). Happily, a growing number of carmakers now stamp plastic parts with a letter-code—a "plastic symbol"—which identifies the type of plastic the part is made of. Here's a list of the most common plastic letter-codes, the plastic they identify, and where the plastic is commonly used on cars:

Plastic Letter-Code	Type of Plastic	Typical Parts
ABS	Acrylonitrile butadiene styrene	Trim panels, dash panels
E/P, EPM	Ethylene propylene	Impact strips, body panels
PC	Polycarbonate	Bumpers
PE	Polyethylene	Washer tanks, batteries
PP	Polypropylene	Interior trim, finder liners
PUR	Thermoset polyurethane	Bumper covers/panels
PVC	Polyvinylchloride	Interior soft trim, exterior soft filler panels
TPO	Thermoplastic olefin	Exterior body panels
TPUR	Thermoplastic polyurethane	Bumper covers

C H A P T E R 4

Exterior: Restoring Its Good Looks

If all you want is a shine, you can have it.

Wash the car or run it through a carwash. Apply car wax or one of the cleaner/wax combination products. Buff with a clean cloth. The finish will shine— but it won't be "detailed."

For some car owners, a shine is enough, because, as the miles and months and years go by, they forget the mirror-brilliance and vibrant color perfection of their car's finish when it was fresh from the factory. However, that "wet look," as though the finish had been applied only moments before, was probably a key reason they bought the car!

Detailing aims to do nothing less than recapture, insofar as possible, a car's showroom look. And to restore the factory-fresh "wet look" to its finish. A mere wash and wax won't do it.

To understand why not is to understand how to refresh and restore its showroom look: how to *detail* its finish.

Two progressive afflictions, oxidation and scratches, first dim, then dull, and finally degrade a car's finish, as described below.

1. Oxidation. Oxidation is a chemical reaction between atmospheric pollutants and the paint's pigments. The oxidation of conventional car paint (and, to a lesser extent, the newer clearcoat finishes) creates an ever-growing layer of scum on the paint's surface. In conventional finishes, the scum is "dead paint": the oxidized top color layer of paint. In clearcoat finishes, what's oxidized is the see-through protective top layer of the clearcoat. Unless the finish is regularly detailed and the scum removed, the oxidation layer thickens and builds and dulls the paint.

Waxing does not remove the oxidation. It merely covers it up. No amount of waxing alone can recapture oxidized paint's original color or vibrancy. Only detailing can.

2. Scratches. Look closely at your car's finish. Better, examine it with a magnifying glass. The finish— whether conventional or clearcoat—is cross-hatched by a myriad tiny scratches. Wear and tear from many sources—from carwash brushes to wind friction— cause car paint scratches. Whether in conventional paint or in the top layer of clearcoat, scratches have the same effect: they opaque the paint, bending (refracting) light rays from their normal straight paths. The result is ever-diminishing clarity. (Pro-detailers call clarity *DOI—Distinction of Image*.)

Waxing does not remove or correct a finish's light-refracting hairline scratches; however, detailing can. Detailing removes the oxidation, the finish's "dead paint." Doing so, it uncovers and exposes a fresh, original color layer once covered and obscured by oxidation; or, in the case of clearcoat, removes what

Fig. 4.1 A mirror-like reflection denotes superior detailing.

amounts to a film that blurs its see-through clarity. Detailing also removes or fills in the light-bending scratches and, with oxidation removed and scratches filled in, protects the revitalized finish from further oxidation or scratching.

Detailing Products

You can pick and choose from dozens of car products formulated to remove the oxidized paint layer, fill in the scratches, and protect the revitalized paint or clearcoat from further degradation. Here is how finish detailing products are generally classified:

- Oxidation removers (in order, from the most abrasive to the least abrasive): rubbing compounds, polishing compounds, cleaners, and polishes.
- Scratch removers: polish and glaze.
- Scratch fillers: glaze and sealer.
- Finish protectors: wax.

If, reading various product labels, you're confused as to what is a "cleaner" and what is a "polish," to say nothing of "compounds," you aren't alone. Even their makers only hazily differentiate between "cleaners" and "polishes."

There is, however, a critical difference between the four types of oxidation-removers. The critical difference is their degree of abrasiveness. Whatever their type, most oxidation removers contain grit, a sandlike abrasive that acts much like sandpaper to remove surface imperfections. Oxidation is a surface imperfection.

Polishes, cleaners, and compounds

In detailing your car's finish, start with the least abrasive, a *polish*. (So fine are some grits used in the polishes and cleaners especially formulated for clearcoat finishes, which cannot tolerate abrasion, that they produce a paste that is not abrasive in the usual sense.) If polish doesn't remove the oxidation, progress to a slightly more abrasive oxidation remover, a *cleaner*. If you are absolutely convinced that something even more abrasive is needed to remove badly oxidized finish, usually found on long neglected paint jobs, use the even more abrasive product, a *polishing compound*—but use it with great care and with minimum application pressure so as not to cut right through the finish and down to base metal. *Rubbing compounds* are so abrasive ("aggressive," in detailing lingo) that they should probably only be used by pro-detailers and paint shop experts. Improper use of such products puts your paint job at risk.

Glazes

Often a watery, sometimes transparent liquid, glaze has two primary jobs: to fill in tiny scratches and, buffed, to produce a brilliant shine. Glaze is applied with a clean, nonabrasive 100% cotton cloth and allowed to dry. The glaze dries as a haze, which is buffed to a lustrous shine. Buffed semi-wet, either by hand or machine, glaze often produces an ultimate shine—a shine which, almost immediately, must be protected by wax. If left unwaxed, glaze and its benefits are quickly dissipated by sunlight.

Sealers

Sealers perform and are applied much like glaze. The chief difference between a sealer and a glaze is the visible effect on the finish. Glaze gives the finish a higher luster than does sealer. However, sealers generally do a better job of enhancing a finish's depth of color and reflective clarity (DOI). Like glaze, most sealers lose their effect unless protected by wax.

Wax

Wax, in car detailing, has four important functions: (1) it protects the newly exposed fresh paint or clear-coat layer; (2) it protects the scratch-filling glaze or sealer; (3) it produces a brilliant, mirror-like shine; and (4) it weather- and waterproofs the finish (see "Restoring Good Looks to Exterior Paint," in Chapter 2).

What about combination products which claim to do two, even three, things in one step? Among combination products are cleaner/waxes, sealer/waxes, polish/waxes, and wash/waxes. Most combinations are easy and quick to apply, but the combinations seldom if ever do either job as well as do single-purpose products. Exceptions may be some sealer/glazes and some cleaner/polishes. Both partners in these combinations do essentially the same job.

If it's simply a shine you want, the combinations may deliver it—and in considerably less time than the sequential application of two to four single-purpose detailing products. However, if you want your car's finish to be the best it can be—detailing's ultimate promise—stick with single-purpose products.

Before you begin detailing the finish, you need to know whether your car has a *conventional* finish (the kind of paints all cars were painted with, until recently) or the newer *clear-coated* finish (see "A Master Detailer Discusses Clearcoat Finishes," in Chapter 4). Abrasive polishes and cleaners, as previously noted, must never be used on clearcoat finish. Abrasives can permanently scratch the clearcoat, destroying its see-through clarity.

If you are unsure whether your car's finish is conventional or clearcoat, ask the dealer from whom you bought the car. A quick test of the finish may also help you to decide: With a nonabrasive cloth, apply wax or a mild polish to a few inches of finish in some out-of-sight place. Rub firmly but gently. If finish color comes off on the cloth, the car probably has a

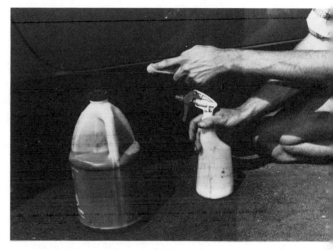

Fig. 4.2 Among the handiest tools for detailing is an inexpensive plastic spray bottle. Filled, a pint-size bottle weighs only a little more than a pound.

‼ CAUTION : If you are in doubt about whether your paint job is conventional or clearcoat, treat it and detail it as though it were clearcoat finish. Use only products whose labels specify that they may be used on clearcoat finish.

conventional finish. If no paint shows on the cloth, the finish is probably clearcoat.

One last decision remains before you set to work. Should you randomly select various finish-detailing products, such as cleaner, polish, glaze, and wax? Or should you use a step-by-step, product-by-product detailing "system" (see "Tech Tip: Paint Restoring Systems," in Chapter 12) as formulated and tested by the various product makers? While finish restorative systems invariably use only a particular maker's products, these maker-recommended products—and their step-by-step application—all but guarantee superlative results. The systems take the guesswork out of product selection and help you avoid finish-damaging mistakes.

---

1 ▶ 2 ▶ 3

STEP-BY-STEP:

Detailing the Exterior

Washing

Time required: *1:00*
 30–60 minutes

Materials needed:
 soft, 100% cotton cloths (as terry towels, diapers, or T-shirts that have been washed and treated with a fabric softener) or soft sponges
 garden hose with spray-adjustable nozzle
 large bucket (at least 2-gallon capacity) for mixing car-wash solution
 carwash solution (see box); follow product instructions for mixing

Three basic rules about washing: (1) do not wash and detail your car in the sun; (2) in extremely cold weather, do your washing and detailing indoors (preferably in a heated place); and (3) work only on a cool car (hand-test the car's surface temperature before you begin).

While carwash products will remove most oil and grease stains, road tar—which may smudge a car's lower parts—may need special effort and special products. First, try an all-purpose cleaner, such as dishwashing detergent. Stubborn, dried tar and grease can be removed with special tar removers (see box), but they also remove car wax. Specially formulated tar cleaners are available from most car dealerships.

Steps:
1. With hose's nozzle adjusted to medium spray, thoroughly wet car's finish, washing off loose grit, dirt, and pollutants.
2. Soak towels thoroughly in sudsy carwash solution. Use minimum application pressure. The sudsy solution acts as a lubricant between your wash cloth and the car's finish. The aim is to loosen surface dirt and pollutants, float them off the finish, and hold them in suspension

---

Washing/Cleaning Chemicals and Soaps
Armor All Car Wash
Blue Coral Car Wash Gel
Blue Coral Car Wash (powder)
Blue Coral Blue Poly Wash
Blue Coral Carnauba Wash Wax
Car Brite Industrial Fallout Remover (pre-wash concentrate)
Car Brite OK Car Soap (liquid)
Eagle 1 Car Wash & Wax Conditioner
Finish 2001 Car Wash
Liquid Crystal Ultimate Car Wash
Liquid Glass Wash Concentrate
Meguiar's Car Wash & Conditioner
Meguiar's Deep Crystal Soft Wash Gel
Meguiar's Hi-Tech Wash
No. 7 Car Wash (powder concentrate)
Nu Finish Car Wash
PRO Super Car Wash
Pro Grade Condition 1 Professional Car Wash
Rain Dance
The Treatment Spray N' Glow
Turtle Wax Minute Wax Silicone Car Wash
Turtle Wax Pro Grade Condition #1 Professional Car Wash
Westley's Acid Rain & Water Spot Remover
Westley's Car Wash
Zip Wax Car Wash

Tar and Bug Removers
CSA Tar & Bug Remover
Cyclo Bug & Tar Remover
McKay Tar & Bug Remover
No. 7 Tar & Bug Remover
PRO Bug Remover
Turtle Wax Bug & Tar Remover
Ultra Shine Tar Remover & Motor Degreaser
Westley's Bug & Tar Remover

within the solution. Floating them off prevents them from scratching the finish. Dunk the cloth frequently in your bucket of washwater to get rid of suspended, potentially abrasive particles. Work with a clean, sopping wet cloth, heavy with solution. While application in a circular motion is easier, and for most detailers more natural, a forward-backward motion is better because it does not leave circular swirl marks in the finish.

3. Some pro-detailers wash the dirtiest parts—wheels, wheel wells, and lower body area—first. Others start at the roof, then move to the hood and the trunk lid, doing wheels and fender wells last.

4. Pay particular attention to hard-to-reach places: areas behind the bumpers, hood edges (you may have to raise the hood to reach them), wheel wells, wheel spokes, front and taillight assemblies.

5. Rinse well with a medium spray from the hose, flooding areas to float particles off.

6. Dry with clean, nonabrasive cotton cloths, preferably terry towels, or with a soft chamois or sponge.

Quick-dry tip: Drive around the block. Air and wind will get rid of excess rinse water, especially in hard to dry places as the radiator grills, vents, and emblems. But don't drive so far as to dry the finish. Some moisture must remain to prevent spotting during final towel-drying.

As you dry, be sure not to let any water droplets remain, because they'll leave spots in the finish. Don't neglect to dry bumpers, wheels, and chrome. If any dirt comes off on your drying cloth, you didn't wash the finish well enough.

Removing oxidation

Time required: *1:00*
> Approximately 1 hour (somewhat longer for larger cars and cars with clear-coated finish)

Materials needed:
> 2 clean, nonabrasive 100% cotton cloths (one for applying cleaner or polish, the other for buffing/removing the product)
> cleaner or polish (see box)

If the finish is heavily oxidized, use a good cleaner; use a polish if the finish is only moderately or marginally oxidized. Whatever the product, make sure its label specifies it's to be used (1) for your car's type of finish (conventional or clearcoat, or both) and (2) for the way you want to apply it (manually or by buffing machine, or both). There are many cleaners available for either conventional or clearcoat finishes (see box). Read labels carefully to determine what is appropriate for your car's finish.

Polishes, cleaners, sealers, and glazes, when manually applied, are allowed to dry only up to the point of being "nearly dry"—then they are wiped and buffed. Allowing any of these products to dry completely before rubbing them off and buffing the finish risks the possibility of abra-

Polishes/Cleaners
Autoglym Exhibition Polish
Auto Wax All Weather Polish
Car Brite Super Seal
Clear Care
Eagle 1 Ultra Fine Scratch Remover & Polishing Compound
Finish 2001
Liquid Crystal Automobile Polish
Liquid Glass Polish/Finish
Meguiar's Deep Crystal Deep Gloss Polish
Meguiar's Heavy Duty Car Cleaner
Meguiar's Hi-Tech Cleaner No. 2 (clearcoat or conventional finishes)
Meguiar's Professional Machine Cleaner No. 1
No. 7 Auto Polish
Nu-Finish Liquid Car Polish
Nu-Finish Soft Paste Car Polish
PRO #1 Polish
PRO Progold
PRO Troubleshooter
3M Prep-Team Liquid Polish
Turtle Wax Pro Grade Condition #2 Professional Cleaner
Turtle Wax Pro Grade Condition #5 Professional Swirl Remover
ZEP Quick Gloss
ZEP Zeperfex

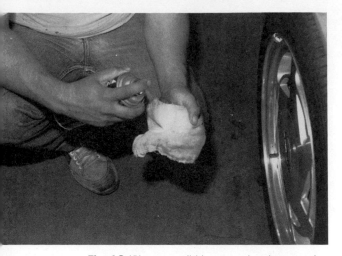

Fig. 4.3 *Wet your polishing rag rather than spraying cleaner on wheels and tires. You'll use cleaner more effectively and generally do a better job with a cleaner-soaked rag than with a spot-wetting technique.*

sive "chalking"; that is, the tiny particles of hard, dried product can, themselves, become abrasives.

Steps:

1. Apply cleaner or polish to a 1-foot-square area with a clean, nonabrasive, 100% cotton cloth. (Experienced detailers usually work on somewhat larger areas.)
2. Use the preferred back-and-forth motion if you can; use a circular motion if you must. Apply only enough cleaner or polish, and buff with only enough pressure, to remove oxidation. Stop frequently to observe results. When oxidation is removed from a conventional finish, the newly exposed color layer shows deep, original color; a clearcoat finish relieved of oxidation has renewed, see-through clarity. Guidelines for buffing conventional finishes and clearcoat finishes appear below:

Conventional finish. Since you're working directly on pigmented paint, expect some color to come off on your rag. You are working to remove only the oxidized, dead paint, and to expose a fresh layer; when deep-toned, fresh paint shows, *stop*. You want to remove as little paint as possible. Removing more than necessary will only thin the pigment layer, not improve its color.

Clearcoat finish. To remove the oxidized top layer of clearcoat, follow the procedure given for conventional paint—but be aware that clearcoat can be tricky. Because you aren't working on color pigment, but rather on the finish's transparent protective paint, no color shows on your cloth. You must therefore stop more frequently to observe results. When the clarity of the clearcoat has been restored and the deep-toned color underlying the clearcoat shows through, *stop*. Further application of cleaner or polish will needlessly remove good clearcoat, reducing the clearcoat's protective thickness.

‖ C A U T I O N : (1) Before you use any product on clearcoat finish, carefully read the product's label. Use no product unless its label specifies that it is safe to use on clearcoat.

(2) Old cloths from your household rag bag may be good enough for dusting the furniture, but not for cleaning and polishing your car's finish. Use only clean, soft, 100% cotton cloths, preferably pre-washed with a fabric softener. Anything else risks scratching your car's finish—especially clearcoat finish.

3. When a small area has been cleaned and buffed, move to an adjacent small area. Doing one small area at a time reduces the chances of the product thoroughly drying and abrasively "chalking." Typically, pro-detailers clean and polish one-half of the hood at a time.
4. Work carefully around insignias, headlights, taillights, moldings, crevice areas, and the "opening" edges of doors and trunk—places where cleaner or polish, if allowed to dry thoroughly, will be tedious to remove.
5. Hand-buff to a high gloss.

Glazing/sealing

Time required: *0.45*

Materials needed:

> clean, nonabrasive 100% cotton cloths (a clean cloth for applying glaze and a clean cloth for buffing/removing the glaze)
> glaze or glaze/sealer (see box)

Closely inspect the cleaned, oxidation-free finish and note where hairline scratches are most severe. Glaze and/or sealer fills in minute scratches and is buffed to a high shine. The finish's ultimate shine depends on the shine you buff into the glaze or sealer, not on the shine of its final wax protective coating. Glazes buff to a high luster; sealers generally do not buff to as high a luster, but they produce deeper-toned color.

If you use glaze, use a single-purpose product; if you choose to use a sealer, use a combination product, such as a glaze/sealer (see box). Single-purpose sealers have other finish corrective uses not discussed in this book.

Steps:

1. Apply successively to small finish areas with a clean, nonabrasive 100% cotton cloth. (Some detailers prefer cheesecloth.)
2. Allow to semi-dry to a haze. Buff to a high gloss.
3. If you can't achieve a high gloss, reapply glaze or sealer/glaze and buff again.

Waxing

Time required: *1:00*

> 1 hour (for a single application)

Materials needed:

> soft, nonabrasive 100% cotton towels or cloths
> wax (see box)

Waxing after application of glaze or sealer is essential to protect the glaze from dissipation by sunlight and to achieve ultimate depth of color in conventional finishes and ultimate clarity in clearcoat finishes.

There are a few exceptions to this wax-after-glazing rule. Some glazes do not require wax protection; however, these glazes must be reapplied frequently—too frequently to suit most driveway detailers. Most glazes of this type are used to super-shine show cars or cars being entered in a concours competition (in which cars are judged on their excellence of appearance).

For a long-lasting wax job the best choice is carnauba. The wax, derived from the Brazilian carnauba palm, is nature's hardest wax, providing hard, long-lasting finish protection. Carnauba also has the highest melting point of any natural wax. It remains protective even at temperatures of 200°F. During summer's hottest days, in the hottest regions (as the southwest), a black painted car left in the sun can reach such elevated temperatures.

Glazes/Sealers

Auto Wax New Car Glaze
Auto Wax Sealer Glaze
Car Brite Super Seal
Car Brite Crystal Shine (clearcoat/base-coat glaze)
Eagle 1 Ultra Glaze & Sealer
Meguiar's New Car Glaze
Meguiar's Sealer & Reseal Glaze
Mothers California Gold Sealer and Glaze
Pro Grade Condition 3 Professional Sealer Glaze
3M Final Glaze
3M Imperial Hand Glaze
3M Imperial Machine Glaze
3M Prep-Team Light Duty Compound and Glaze
TR-3 Resin Glaze
Turtle Wax Pro Grade Condition #3 Professional Sealer Glaze
ZEP Auto Glaze

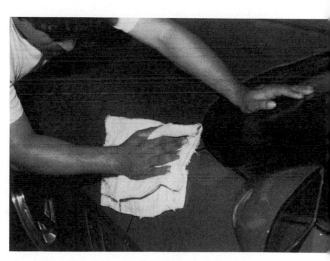

Fig. 4.4 Rub glaze or wax with a straight, not circular, motion. Swirl marks—circular blotches in a newly glazed or waxed finish—are most often caused by machine buffing. However, hand-buffing can cause them, too.

Waxes/Pastes/Pre-Waxing Cleaners

Armor All Car Wax (paste and liquid)
Autoglym Liquid Hardwax
Auto Wax Auto Magic E-Z Wax Paste
Blue Coral Carnauba Premium Paste
    Wax
Car Brite Butter Wax
Car Brite Crystal Finish (clearcoat/base-
    coat wax)
Car Brite Easi-Off (carnauba paste wax)
Car Brite Ultimate (carnauba creme
    wax)
Eagle 1 Cleaner/Wax (pre-wax cleaner/
    wax restorer)
Eagle 1 Carnauba Paste Wax with
    Cleaner
Eagle 1 Non-Abrasive Carnauba Paste
    Wax
Harly Carnauba Wax
Liquid Glass Pre-Cleaner
Meguiar's Deep Crystal Carnauba Wax
Meguiar's Hi-Tech Yellow Wax (liquid)
Meguiar's Yellow Paste Wax
Mothers California Gold Carnauba
    Paste Wax w/Cleaner
Mothers California Gold Carnauba
    Cleaner Wax
Mothers California Gold Pre-Wax
    Cleaner
Mothers California Gold Pure Carnauba
    Wax
PRO Carnauba Cream Wax
PRO Fallout Remover
PRO Yellow Wax
Rain Dance (paste and liquid)
Rain Dance Wash + Wax
Rally Car Wax (liquid and cream)
The Treatment Pre-Wax Cleaner and
    Conditioner
The Treatment Pre-softened Carnauba
    Wax
Turtle Wax Car Wax
Turtle Wax Carnauba Wax
Turtle Wax Plus with Teflon
Turtle Wax Pro Grade Condition #2
    Professional Cleaner
Turtle Wax Pro Grade Condition #4
    Professional Yellow Wax
Turtle Wax Super Hard Shell Car Wax
Turtle Wax Super Hard Shell Silicone
    Car Wax
Westley's Acid Rain & Water Spot Re-
    mover (cleans, conditions surface for
    waxing)
ZEP Industrial Fallout Remover
ZEP Pro Finish (carnauba wax)

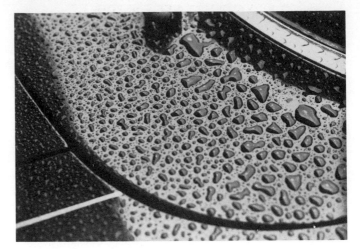

Fig. 4.5 Water should bead up like this on a well-waxed finish.

!! CAUTION : Waxing is seldom a one-step operation. Far better to apply a thin coat of wax initially, then buff it, then apply a second thin coat. The first merely gets into the "pores" of the finish; the second fully overcoats the finish.

Choose a carnauba paste wax over a carnauba liquid wax. The paste contains a slightly greater percentage of carnauba. Spray-on waxes contain considerably less carnauba because the formula must be thinned to spray. With the paste, it is also easier to apply the wax in a very thin layer, which gives best results and which buffs easiest to a super shine. Two thin wax applications with buffing in between is usually the best approach for long-lasting results. Properly applied, carnauba wax may continue to protect your finish, depending on climate and other conditions, for as long as 3 to 6 months—and sometimes longer. The hood and the roof—body areas that receive lots of sun—may need waxing more frequently.

Steps:
1. Apply successively to small areas of the finish (best: areas of about 1 square foot) with a *damp* 100% cotton cloth. A terry cloth towel that has been laundered in fabric softener is the best applicator.
2. With back-forth motion (or circular motion, if you must), apply a thin, even layer of wax.
3. Buff with a clean nonabrasive cloth. Repeat until the finish is completely waxed and buffed to a brilliant shine.

Cleanup. Wherever cleaner or wax has hardened in crevices (on door edges and the like), remove it with a cotton swab or a *used, soft-bristled* toothbrush. Also recommended: a soft paintbrush, its bristles trimmed to about a 2-inch length, which can get into the smallest places—such as insignias and where molding meets the body's sheet metal.

Detailing vinyl and convertible tops

See Chapter 11, "Renewing Vinyl and Convertible Tops."

Polishing chrome (bumpers, molding, trim)

Time required: *0:45*
    30–45 minutes

Materials needed:
    soft cloth
    tar remover
    chrome cleaner/polish (see box)
    toothbrush
    cotton swabs
    steel wool (00 or 000)

A good chrome polish renews and shines most chrome. Once chrome has been cleaned and shined, apply to it the same carnauba wax used on the finish. Waxing a car's chrome is as important as waxing its finish. Wax preserves chrome's brilliance and prevents rusting. Most chrome is cleaned and polished with a dual-purpose chrome cleaner/polish (see box). Where chrome is pitted or rusting, a two-step chemical cleaning treatment often works best (see Chapter 9, "Getting Rid of Rust"). Very fine steel wool (00 or 000; for a thorough discussion of steel wool grades, see "Making Chrome Rust Disappear," in Chapter 9), gently applied, often rids chrome bumpers quickest of "collision" paint (where you've bumpered into something, perhaps a wall or another car). Chrome-plated plastics—as grilles and trim on some late models—are best cleaned and protected by products specially designed for chromed plastics.

Clean and polish body chrome—chromed molding and stripping—before glazing the finish (just after you apply cleaner or polish) to prevent chrome cleaner from streaking the glaze. When you wax the finish, wax body chrome, too. Non-body chromed parts, as bumpers, can be cleaned, polished, and waxed later.

Steps:

1. With a soft cloth, apply chrome cleaner/polish to a small area of chrome. Let it dry, then rub and buff with a clean cloth.

2. Inspect the cleaned area. Remove any road tar with tar remover. If there are pits or scratches in the chrome, soak a toothbrush in cleaner and scour them clean. Rusty places may require two or three applications of cleaner and gentle use of steel wool (00 or 000).

3. Be careful not to get chrome cleaner on the finish, or in the crevices of chromed fittings (for example, headlight and taillight assemblies). Most chrome polish, once dry, is hard to remove from crevices, rubber, and plastic components (such as taillight lenses). Removing the cleaner from unwanted places is time-consuming and tedious, even using a clean toothbrush or cotton swab. Shorten the cleanup time by *not* getting the cleaner where you don't want it.

4. When the chrome is clean and shined, wax it.

Chrome and Metal Cleaners/ Polishes/Protectants

Blue Coral Chrome Brite
Eagle 1 Aluminum Wash & Brightener
Eagle 1 Chrome Guard (protects against winter rust, corrosion, and salt)
Eagle 1 Mag & Chrome Polish
Espree Everbrite Metal Cleaner/Polish
Meguiar's Professional Chrome & Metal Polish
No. 7 Chrome Polish
OxiSolv Aluminum Cleaner
Simoniz Chrome Cleaner
Turtle Wax Chrome Polish
Turtle Wax Silver Chrome Cleaner and Sealant
Westley's Espree Aluminum Cleaner

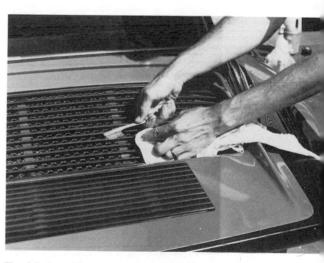

Fig. 4.6 A toothbrush wetted with carwash solution or dishwashing detergent and water gets into the many dirt-hiding places of complex louvers such as these.

Detailing vinyl bumpers and other exterior vinyl parts

Vinyl or plastic bumpers, after washing, are cleaned with a vinyl cleaner/polish, then waxed (for instructions on detailing vinyl tops, see Chapter 11, "Renewing Vinyl and Convertible Tops"). Clean black vinyl or rubber bumpers with any good vinyl cleaner, followed by waxing. There are products available that are specially designed for cleaning and restoring black vinyl and rubber bumpers and trim (see box).

Detailing wheels and tires

Wheels and tires are "show parts." In detailing wheels, especially, consult your owner's manual for any special manufacturer's instructions. Clear-coated or painted wheels can be scratched or permanently damaged by abrasive cleaners or polishes. Wheels made of magnesium ("mag") or aluminum clean and shine best and safest with special products.

It works best to detail one wheel at a time and to detail the tire/whitewall areas first.

Detailing tires

Time required: *0:15*
   15 minutes per tire

Materials needed:
   tire brush
   household steel wool and soap pad
   whitewall cleaner (see box)
   all-purpose cleaner
   protectant (see box)
   touch-up paint (see appendix)

Steps:
1. Clean whitewalls with a whitewall cleaner or with wetted household steel wool and soap pads (or with both). Black curb scuffs are often difficult to erase. First apply a whitewall cleaner; then, if necessary, use the steel wool and soap pads. Rinse, and observe your progress. Repeat the process as needed.
2. If your whitewalls are splotched with scuff-caused intrusions of black or white into adjacent tire areas, touch out the intrusion places with touch-up paint (as described in Chapter 8, "Paint Touch-Up: Erasing Parking Lot Scars").
3. When the touch-up is thoroughly dry, use a tire brush and an all-purpose cleaner to clean the tire to the tread line.
4. Let the tire dry.
5. Apply a protectant to all visible black tire areas. Protectant brings out and renews the tire's deep black color. Most protectants work best when you leave them on for several hours (or, even better, overnight) before wiping off any residue. Never paint a tire's rubber, except for small area "touch outs" (step #2, above).

Detailing wheels

Time required: *0:30*

15–30 minutes per wheel (depends on design and complexity)

Materials needed:

all-purpose cleaner
soft cloths
wheel cleaner (see box)
toothbrush
swabs
garden hose or buckets of water (for rinsing)

Steps:

1. Rewash wheels. Then apply an all-purpose cleaner, as for tires, above. Wheels and their wheel wells are often the dirtiest parts of your car (other than a non-detailed engine compartment). Wheels pick up road tar, grease, and black brake dust.

2. With a soft cloth apply a good wheel cleaner. You can use one of the specialty wheel cleaners designed for the type of wheels you have (as mag, aluminum, or painted), or you can use one of the cleaners that work safely and efficiently on most kinds of wheels.

3. Whatever cleaner you use, use it gently. Wheels are surprisingly scratchable, especially if clear-coated. If your wheels are clear-coated, use only wheel cleaners specified for clearcoat. Work the cleaner into wheel recesses using a toothbrush or cotton swab.

4. Spoked wheels and wheels with intricate designs take some extra doing—generally with a toothbrush, swabs, and a nonabrasive cloth soaked in cleaner or soap suds. And, yes, your fingers, too, which can reach into places many cleaning aids can't. (Many car enthusiasts even detail the *back* of the wheel!) It's a labor-intensive job, but the good news is that once done right, spoked, finned, and other designer wheels are easier to clean the next time around.

5. Rinse with a hose or bucket(s) of water and let dry.

6. Wax with the same wax you used on the finish.

Detailing exterior glass: windows, mirrors, and windshield

Time required: *0:30*

20–30 minutes

Materials needed:

glass cleaner or plastic polish, as appropriate (see boxes)
soft cloth, applicator, squeegee, and squirt bottle
soft cloths (for drying)
very fine steel wool (00 or 000)
toothbrush
cotton swabs

Dirty windows make a detailed car look . . . well, undetailed. Besides, they obscure your vision. Although you washed windows and windshield when you washed the

---

Protectants (for vinyl, rubber, plastics, etc.)

Armor All Protectant
Autoglym Silicone Spray
Autoglym Vinyl and Rubber Care
Car Brite Super Kote
Clear Guard Protectant
Connoisseur's Choice Protectant
CSA Vinyl Protector
Eagle 1 Tire Dressing & Protectant
Mothers Protectant
PRO Clear Rubber Dressing
STP Son of a Gun Vinyl Protectant
3M Natural Gloss Vinyl and Rubber Dressing
Turtle Wax Protectant
Ultra Shine Protectant
ZEP All Around
ZEP Protect All

Wheel Cleaners

Car Brite Wire Wheel Cleaner
CSA Premium Gold
Eagle 1 All Finish Wheel Cleaner
Eagle 1 Wire & Chrome Wheel Cleaner
Eagle 1 Mag Cleaner
Entire Whitewall and Wheel Cleaner
Espree Mag Wheel Cleaner
Espree Mag Wheel Cleaner & Polish
Espree Wheel Magic (for painted, clear-coated, plastic, sculptured mag and wire wheels)
Espree Wire Wheel Cleaner
Mothers Mag & Aluminum Polish
Mothers Wheel Mist
OxiSolv Wire Wheel Cleaner
PRO Aluminum & Mag Polish
PRO Professional Wheel Cleaner
The Treatment Mag and Aluminum Wheel Cleaner
The Treatment Mag and Aluminum Polish
Turtle Wax Wheelbrite (for all wheels/hubcaps)
Turtle Wax Wheelbrite Wire Wheel Cleaner
Turtle Wax Wheelbrite Mag Wheel Cleaner

car, they probably need close-up detailing to rid them of bugs, decals (they're "no-no's" on a well-detailed car), and the last vestige of grime. Many car care product makers make good glass cleaners. Also, household glass-cleaning products work well, as does a simple mix of ammonia and water (8 ounces of household ammonia to 2 gallons of water).

!! CAUTION : Use extreme care in handling and working with inflammable products (as petroleum-based engine cleaners), spray-on products (which can be harmful if sprayed or blown into your face or eyes), and products that are potentially harmful if inhaled (such as ammonia or ammonia-based products).

One caution: If your car's windows and windshield are glass, any glass cleaner is safe to use. However, if they are plastic, you should use a plastic cleaner formulated for plastic convertible windows.

Steps:
1. With a soft cloth, an applicator, a squeegee, or a squirt bottle, wet no more than half the windshield.
2. Rub dry, giving special attention where it's seldom given: windshield (and window) corners and edges.
3. If bugs or road tar remains, remove with gentle use of very fine steel wool (00 or 000).
4. Reapply window cleaner. Again rub dry.
5. Inspect in sunlight. Some streaking will probably remain. Detailing aims to clean glass totally. If that is your aim, too, repeat the cleaning cycle until the glass is spotless.

Detailing's details

Here's a quick checklist of detailing's details:

Antennas. Use a good chrome cleaner. Polish, then wax. If antennas are clear-coated, treat as clearcoat finish.

Gas fill port and cap. They were spotless when you bought the car; detail them to showroom condition.

Chromed tailpipes. Use 00 or 000 steel wool to rid them of rust; then use chrome polish. Tailpipe heat makes waxing a waste of time.

Plastic taillight and headlight lenses. An all-purpose cleaner and soft-bristled toothbrush (an old toothbrush, not a new one) routes grime and road film from crevices without scratching scratch-prone lenses. After cleaning, apply a plastic polish.

Radiator grille. If your car has an exposed one, go over it grille piece by grille piece, topside as well as bottom, with an all-purpose cleaner. If chromed, follow with chrome polish. Finally, apply wax. Leave no recess undetailed.

Windshield/rear window wipers. Choose a cleaner appropriate to the finish or material and give wiper arms a thorough cleaning; then wax. While protectant is used on other car rubber, it should not be used on wiper blades because it will affect their wiping efficiency.

Your car's initial bumper-to-bumper detailing, described here step-by-step, admittedly takes time, effort, and energy. But the upkeep—keeping it detailed—is relatively easy. And, if detailing is done regularly—perhaps three to four times a year—requires relatively little time. Some things get easier once done right; detailing is one of them.

A Master Detailer Discusses Clearcoat Finishes

Clearcoat: new high-tech finish

"Today, on many makes and models of cars, there is a whole new system of finishes, high-tech car paints which differ fundamentally from their predecessors in construction and in the way they must be cared for and detailed.

"In simplest terms, the final, top layer of finish on all cars of the past, and still on some today, is a pigmented paint. Detailing these conventional finishes, you work directly on the car's color—the paint layer that gives a car its color. Using polish or cleaner, color actually comes off on your polishing cloth or buffing pad if the paint, aging, is oxidized. But this does not happen if your car is clear-coated.

"On cars with a clearcoat finish, the paint's color layer lies protected by a clear, colorless, usually urethane or polyurethane final finish. The urethanes are part of a new family of high-tech car finishes.

"The urethanes and polyurethanes—often called the 'clearcoat' because they comprise the clear, see-through final top finish overlying the pigmented paint layers—are more forgiving than conventional finishes, yet, oddly, they need more care.

"Faults in the clearcoat finish can be more easily corrected than in such pigmented finishes as enamel, acrylic, lacquer, or other conventional car paints. Scuffs or scratches in these pigmented paint layers are difficult to correct. For one reason, a scratch or deep scuff actually penetrates, and likely mars or even discolors, the finish's pigmented color layers, since the paint's color layers *are* the finish's top layers.

"In the clearcoat, many scuffs—minor scratches, for example—never reach the paint layers. And while in the clearcoat they may be visible, they are usually

Fig. 4.7 Neglected wiper rubber can permanently scratch windshields. Wash wiper rubber with detergent and water (or with carwash solution) to rid it of abrasive particles or slippery wax. If wipers are worn and frayed, replace them.

Master Detailer Steve Okun, formerly Detailing Editor of *Professional Carwashing & Detailing* magazine, is a knowledgeable authority. He is founder and director of the International Academy of Automotive Detailing in Allentown, Pennsylvania; a frequent consultant to pro-detailers, car restorers, and manufacturers of detailing products; and one of detailing's most insightful analysts. He and his organization have car-tested hundreds of detailing products.

Here, excerpted from an exclusive interview, Okun discusses the critical detailing of what is likely your car's "final finish"—the clear, often urethane-based clearcoat, the high-tech finish that today gives many cars, including imports, their brilliance and luster. If your car is clear-coated, it is the clearcoat you will be washing, polishing, and waxing when you detail the exterior.

not nearly as obvious as would be damage to the finish's color layers.

"Still, the clearcoat is vulnerable not only to casual damage, but to environmental damage and degradation. The clearcoat, to maintain its luster and impregnability, demands more frequent washing: once a week, certainly.

"An example of casual damage is the scuffing and scratching that happens when somebody uses his or her car as a shelf for a shopping bag. Slide the bag off the clearcoat, and you leave a scuff mark. With clearcoating, a scuff mark like that is relatively easier to repair than when the damage is in the top, color layer of conventional paint."

Protecting clearcoat from environmental damage

"Environmental damage is a clear and present danger to the clearcoat. And even more so than for conventional finishes. If you live in an area where there's a lot of traffic or you commute long distances, carbon black from other car exhausts builds up on the clearcoat. Live or drive near an airport and there's fallout from jet fuel. In industrial zones of the eastern and northeastern states, and moving farther south every year, is industrial pollution, including acid rain. Acid fog is common in Southern California. So, in the industrial north, is acid snow. Include, too, early morning's acid mist. Every form of precipitation carries the threat of acid fallout and clearcoat damage.

"What happens is this: If your car isn't frequently washed, it becomes coated with acid fallout. A light rain, a morning mist, fog, or dew mixes with the acid particles, putting them into solution. Now your car's finish is wetted with an acid solution. All that's needed for catalytic activity—an increase in finish-destroying chemical action—is heat. It doesn't take much sunlight to supply it. And you have all the ingredients for acid-burning the finish. It probably won't happen in one day, or two. Or even a week. But the damaging process, unless you frequently wash your car, goes on day after day: more acid fallout, an ever stronger acid solution, more catalytic action spurred, day after day, by the sun's heat and light.

"Only washing the car to rid it of acid fallout breaks this potentially damaging cycle. That's why it's so important, especially with the clearcoats, to wash your car frequently."

Washing your car's clearcoat

"The key to washing a car to rid it of acid buildup is to use the right techniques, the right products, and the right tools.

"Two things are basic: (1) you don't ever want to wash your car in sunlight, and (2) you don't ever want to wash a hot car.

"Before you use a wash product on a sun-warmed

hot car, rinse it with cool, clear water. Rinsing washes away the heaviest concentrations of atmospheric pollutants. And, just as important, pre-rinsing cools the finish.

"Neglect the pre-rinse, and you aid and abet chemical activity. The reason is basic: the chemical activity of many carwash solutions, among them the detergents, is accelerated by a car's body heat. Produced is a chemical reaction which can either streak or burn the finish, especially if it's a clearcoat. Before you use a wash product, rinse the car with a flood of cool water. Rinsing quick-cools a hot car. Also, a clean water pre-rinse also gets rid of possibly abrasive materials."

Basic clearcoat systems

"Understanding your car's clearcoat is a first step toward properly caring for—and detailing—it.

"Currently, there are four basic clearcoat 'systems,' although the technology is changing rapidly. There are urethane, polyurethane, polyester, and fluorine high-tech clearcoat systems. All are pretty much built up, layer by layer, in the same way: you've got a primer coat (the first coat on the car's bare metal skin), then one color coat or several (this is the 'base coat,' which is often surprisingly thin), and lastly, the far thicker final clearcoat.

"The color coat can be quite thin in clearcoat finishes because all it does is introduce the color. When, in conventional finishes, the color is contained in the final paint layer, the color layer is quite thick because it serves both as the color-carrying layer and as the final, protective top coat. Today's clearcoat is probably twice as thick as the combined thicknesses of the primer and colored base coats. It's not unusual for the clearcoat to have three times the thickness of the color (pigment) coat—and sometimes more."

Clearcoat: a see-through solar window

"Consider the clearcoat as a kind of window. As viewed through the clearcoat 'window,' the base coat is dull. What illuminates and lusterizes it are properties in the clearcoat—among them screening agents which screen out ultraviolet rays, which, in conventional car finishes, bleach and fade the color layer. The clearcoat's ultraviolet screening agents also protect the color coat from fading. Conventional finishes have no such protection. So, what you have in the clearcoat is not just a window, but a 'solar window.'

"You've got to keep that solar window clean to maintain, in the color finish, what the industry calls 'DOI,'—*Distinction of Image*. In essence, DOI is the deep gloss you are trying to maintain in your car's finish.

"To test for this reflective depth of image, hold a newspaper over the finish. If you can read it from its reflection in the finish, you have depth and clarity in the finish. The same thing happens when, polishing or waxing the clearcoat, you look into the finish for a re-flection of yourself. Detailing or clearcoat flaws show up when your reflected image is wavy or imperfect.

"In detailing, you aim to achieve a 'slippery wet look' in the finish. One example is the wet look of those faddish cars painted with 'neon' colors. The dazzle colors you see are the result of looking through the finish's clearcoat window. For most cars, however, the wet look achieved by the clearcoat is harder to de-scribe precisely—even though it's one of the beauties you get with a clearcoat finish."

Abrasives: clearcoat's kiss of death

"But you can destroy that look if you use the wrong products in detailing the clearcoat. The clearcoat is not designed to have anything—let me repeat and em-phasize, *anything*—used on it which is abrasive. *Any-thing abrasive used on the clearcoat can scuff and scar its surface.* Abrasives are the kiss of death to a clearcoat finish.

"Now, when I emphasize no abrasives, I'm talking about products used by the do-it-yourself detailer. Paint shops, in repairing clearcoats and when finishing a newly repainted/clear-coated car or repair, do use 'abrasive' products and techniques. Commonly used by pro-detailers is ultra-fine wet sanding paper, with an almost nonabrasive 1500 to 2000 grit rating. Wet-sanding enhances the clearcoat finish by removing sags, dust, and other flaws. Flaws removed, the new clearcoat finish is allowed to dry anywhere from 72 hours to 30 days, and then, when cured and dry, is cleaned with a nonabrasive cleaner and then polished. Finally, the clearcoat is waxed.

"Certainly the skilled weekend detailer can wet sand a clearcoat when virtually everything else has failed to restore its original, 'new car' look. But you need skill and a 'feel' for the clearcoat to do it without further surface damage."

Choosing the right wash product

"Now, in washing the clearcoat—and, in fact any auto-motive paint finish—you should use a wash product specifically formulated for car finishes.

"Elsewhere in this book, I know, dishwashing de-tergents have been discussed and recommended for carwashing. On the basis of overwhelming evidence, I totally disagree. Dishwashing detergent is formulated to wash dishes—specifically, to remove grease. That same formulation is going to remove the wax from the car's finish and also any protective silicones. Silicones are contained in many car polishes and in some car waxes. Use dishwashing detergent and you remove them—which means, at the very least, that every time the car is washed with detergent you have to reapply polish and wax.

"The same de-waxing occurs when you put your

car through some commercial or coin-op washes: the detergents generally used, because these wash places' main goal is to turn out clean cars, are strong enough to remove most of a finish's waxes and silicones.

"Saying this, I have to again concede that some professional detailers use all-purpose cleaners and dishwashing detergents. They do so for the very reason the do-it-yourself detailer should seldom, if ever, use them. The professional detailer *wants* to strip all the wax from the finish. This enables him, starting from scratch, to better polish and wax the car. Eliminated by using those products is one of the chores he'd normally have to do—remove the wax.

"Unless, after washing the car, you intend to polish (glaze) and wax it, you don't want to remove the wax. You don't because the wax's purpose isn't simply to 'shine' a car's finish. Wax forms a protective barrier and also a slipperiness which tends to deflect street debris, such as stones, which might otherwise chip the finish. It also resists scuffing, caused, for example, by somebody rubbing against the car in a parking lot. The wax, being slippery, reduces possible abrasive damage. The analogy is the difference between a waxed kitchen floor and one that's unwaxed. Drag something across an unwaxed floor and you leave scratches. Drag something across your car's unwaxed finish and it scratches.

"If you've waxed the car, you certainly don't want to undo what you've done by washing it with an aggressive, all-purpose cleaner. If a wash solution degreases the finish or body parts, you can be sure it will also 'de-wax' the finish.

"To wash clearcoats, use any of a number of products specially formulated for clearcoat washing. Almost all are liquids, not powders. Powders may not completely dissolve in your washwater. The tiny, undissolved granules have the potential to become abrasives."

Defining the just-right clearcoat wash product

"The proper and ideal slippery, soapy solution for frictionless dirt removal from an automotive finish, including clearcoat, can be defined by a number of characteristics:

- High-foaming—inherent cleaning action
- High lubricity—slipperiness, like a lubricant
- Free-rinsing—a solution which, in itself, leaves no residue
- pH balance—a product with an acid-alkaline balance which is slightly alkaline to counter the acidic nature of a finish's collected fallout pollutants

"What commonly available wash products fit these criteria? There are several available (check labels carefully). The choice comes down to personal preference.

"Clearcoats must also be critically washed in a specific way. The 'tools' you use should be just as critically designed for clearcoat washing. Among these tools are natural fiber body brushes, synthetic-wool washing mitts, sponges, and terry cloth towels."

Washing clearcoat finish

"Whatever washing tools you use, the basic washing techniques for clearcoat are the same. First, you hose and clean-water flush the finish to remove any loose dirt or pollutants. Then you wash the finish with a free-rinsing wash solution.

"The first step—flushing with water—purges the surface of anything loose that can be quickly and easily removed.

"If any dirt remains, it's got to be removed with a minimum of friction. What is likely holding dirt on the clearcoat finish is surface tension. To remove stubborn dirt or other stick-to-surface materials—bird and tree droppings being the most common—you've got to disturb the surface tension without creating friction enough to scratch the clearcoat.

"Ideally, what you want your wash solution—your washwater—to do is 'free-rinse,' that is, to dislodge and rinse all pollutants, including abrasives, from the clearcoat and hold them in frictionless, nonabrasive suspension within the washwater. What does it is a soapy, slippery wash solution that meets the criteria for an ideal clearcoat wash product.

"Keep these same criteria in mind when choosing your washing 'tool.' A sponge is not a free-rinsing tool, because grit and dirt can get caught in the sponge's pores. Even less free-rinsing is a towel, or a diaper, because of the weave of the cloth. You're going to trap dirt and grit in the weave of the towel or the diaper, even if you wash with a soapy solution that has high lubricity and is high-foaming, two of the more important criteria of a clearcoat wash solution.

"The *ideal* tool for washing clearcoat finishes is a *natural fiber body brush*. This usually imported, bleached pig's hair brush is super soft. Commonly, the hair is set into a mahogany block with epoxy cement.

"Natural fiber body brushes (they're designed for car washing) are user-friendly tools for washing clearcoats. Using them, you need exert only minimal pressure. That means less friction on the clearcoat—and less washing effort, too.

"The brush has a nap that's about 3 inches deep. You use only the tips of the brush's super-fine hairs—just the first ½ to ¾ inch of the nap. You use very little pressure. All you want to do is loosen the dirt's surface tension and get the dirt into the carrier solution—your soapy washwater or finish shampoo. If you can't find a body brush, then use the second-choice 'ideal' clearcoat washing tool: a synthetic wool mitt.

"One caution: Not all carwash brushes are the hoghair-China bristle natural fiber kind I'm describing. Some, with coarser hair, may be too aggressive—too abrasive—for clearcoat finishes.

"You may have to settle for something less than

the ideal clearcoat washing tool. A terry cloth towel, perhaps, or even a sponge. If you keep them forever lubricated in your washwater to make sure they are clean, and if you use them carefully and with minimum pressure, they'll generally do a satisfactory job on clearcoat finishes."

Clearcoat polishes and cleaners

"Polish. A lot of detailing pros use the words 'polish' and 'glaze' interchangeably. As if they are the same things. Generally, they are not. A polish is a polish. A glaze is a glaze. And a cleaner is a cleaner. Whatever the product, use the least 'aggressive'—the least abrasive. A more abrasive product generally gets the polishing job done faster. But an overly aggressive polishing/cleaning product also risks scratching, and in fact removing, some of the finish—such as the clearcoat.

"A *polish* is a minimally abrasive cleaner and lusterizer. A *cleaner*, more aggressive than a polish, contains chemical cleaning agents. Even more abrasive—often very abrasive—are *compounding* products. Compounds are sometimes the preferred products for treating heavily oxidized conventional finishes. Using a compound—called 'compounding'—you are apt to remove paint as well as oxidation. Today, the cleaners—far less abrasive than compounds—are usually all you need to work with on even the most oxidized conventional finishes.

"While compounds can be used—and still often are—on conventional paints, their use on clearcoat finishes risks major damage. The minute particles of pumice, which give the compounds their cutting action, cut little holes in the clearcoat. The result: 'swirl' marks which are difficult, and sometimes impossible, to remove from the clearcoat.

"'Swirls' are residual evidences of abrasive polishing. There should, of course, be *no* evidences in a finish that it has been polished—just an even, unbroken, reflective shine. Hand-polish swirls are irregular, non-reflective blotches in the finish's polished surface. Machine-polish swirls—evidence of machine buffing—tend to be circular blotches. Swirl marks are the nemesis of detailers, whether pros or weekenders.

"If you get swirl marks when you buff a finish by hand, it means there are abrasive particles in the product you're using. Or, perhaps, some abrasiveness in whatever you're using to apply the product—a rough towel, for example. Or a foam sponge applicator that's not clean and has some grit or hardened cleaner in its pores. In short, there are *only two ways* that swirls develop when cleaning, polishing or buffing a clearcoat finish: (1) the product you're using, whether hand- or machine-applied, is too abrasive; (2) the polishing tool is abrasive.

"In machine polishing, the problem is often a *wool* buffing pad. Wool buffing pads are, by their very na-

‖ **C A U T I O N :** The use of abrasive compounds on clearcoat can be fatal to the finish.

ture, abrasive. Wool buffing pads are an anachronism in today's era of high-tech car finishes, as clearcoat. They are plainly out of date, although wool buffing pads are still being used on conventional finishes. But not on clearcoats. There's no question about it: in machine buffing, wool buffer pads are the number one swirl-maker.

"Today's preferred and widely used machine polishing pads for clearcoat are made of synthetic foam. They all but eliminate swirl marks, and they can be used on both conventional and clearcoat finishes."

How do you know if it's clear-coated?

"One vexing question: How do you know, in this era of fast-changing technology, whether your car has a conventional or clearcoat finish?

"It isn't always easy to tell. One test is to gently rub an out-of-sight place on the finish with a mild cleaner. If color comes off on your cloth, you can be fairly sure it's conventional finish. If no color comes off, you can be almost as sure it's clear-coated.

"Still, there's only one sure-safe rule-of-thumb: *When in doubt, treat it as a clearcoat finish.* Obviously, if your car is clear-coated, it needs special handling . . . and special care."

Detailing a Scratched or Nicked Windshield

Most windshield scratches or nicks defy do-it-yourself fixing. And, in fact, fixing at all. Pro-detailers and windshield glass specialists have a "rule of thumbnail": if, rubbing a thumbnail across the scratch, you can feel the scratch, it's probably too deep to fix.

A tiny surface scratch can sometimes be rubbed or buffed out with very fine powdered pumice or with jeweler's rouge (both are available from glass shops). Make a heavy paste using water and pumice (or jeweler's rouge). Spread the paste on and around the scratch. If machine buffing, use a nonabrasive foam buffing pad on a low-speed orbital buffer. Use very gentle pressure while buffing. You may have to reapply the paste and rebuff several times to buff out the scratch.

Rubbing out the scratch manually involves the same water and pumice/rouge technique, only you use a very soft, nonabrasive cotton cloth as your rubbing tool.

While deeper scratches can sometimes be removed by machine buffing, the result is seldom satisfactory. Although you may rid the windshield of the scratch, deep buffing causes a concave place where the scratch was. Result: Vision through the former scratch area is distorted. Far better to keep the scratch than to cause windshield—and vision—distortion.

On the market are a number of "fixit" kits for reducing the visibility of windshield nicks, rock pocks, and scratches. Generally, the results are not very satis-factory. The patch places are often as obvious as the windshield damage they "correct." In most cases, it's not detailing that an injured windshield needs, but re-placement.

Cracks, in contrast to scratches, can sometimes be corrected by several new processes. The unique "Clear Fix" technique, the specialty of Globe/U.S. Auto Glass Centers and their affiliated USA-GLAS Network, in-jects a transparent liquid resin into the damaged wind-shield area. When cured with ultraviolet light, the resin has the same index of refraction as the glass. Re-stored, claims Globe, is the windshield's visibility and strength. Repairs come close to being invisible, or as Globe puts it, ". . . almost invisible."

The difference between perfection and "almost" may be $150–$300, the cost of replacing the wind-shield. Globe, however, will not repair a damage spot larger than a quarter or one that is within a driver's primary vision area (the approximate 5½- × 8½-inch area swept by the driver's windshield wiper blade). Generally, too, the technique is not advised if the vinyl lamination between the usual windshield's inside-out-side layers of glass has been penetrated or damaged. For information phone toll free: 1-800-USA-GLAS.

Aside from detailing the windshield for visibility and cleanliness, a number of products are available to (1) help keep it clean and clear; (2) reduce fogging or steaming; and (3) disperse rain, snow, ice and sleet.

Rain-X, originally named Repcon and developed for the U.S. Air Force to keep jet fighter windshields rain-free, is a wipe-on liquid that quick-dries to coat the windshield with an optically clear, transparent polymer (plastic) coating, which disperses rain, snow, ice and sleet. Used on windshields, it largely eliminates the "vision tunnels" produced by wipers. In fact, it is often not necessary to operate wipers on a windshield treated with Rain-X. The film causes an aerodynamic runoff of rainwater and snow, clearing the windshield without any, or only infrequent, wiper assist—thus its claim to being "the invisible windshield wiper."

Applied to rear and side windows, and on rear-view mirrors, Rain-X provides greater visibility in rainy or snowy weather. It is also effective on many convert-ible and off-road vehicle plastic windows. The product is not, however, a defogger. Its useful life varies, de-pending in part on a vehicle's speed and use. If you commute several hours daily at superhighway speeds, Rain-X may have to be reapplied every few weeks.

One of the few new detailing products which largely delivers its promise, Rain-X is available at some automotive stores, or from its maker, Unelko Corp., 7428 East Karen Drive, Scottsdale, AZ 85260; (602) 991-7272.

Snow skiers have long used anti-fog, chemically impregnated cloths to keep their goggles clean. Larger versions of the anti-fog cloths work well on wind-shields. You should be able to find them at local ski shops. There are also interior window defogging formulas available—see box for some possible choices.

While there are many useful glass cleaners available, from household glass cleaners to auto-specialized premoistened towelettes for quick-cleaning windshields, what cleans them about as well as most commercial products is ammonia and water. The mix: 1 part ammonia to 4 parts water. (See appendix for a list of specialized glass cleaners.)

To rid windshields of stubborn grime, stains, and bugs, many pro-detailers use super-fine 0000 (be sure it's 4-0) steel wool. The same super-fine, non-scratch grade of steel wool is also frequently used by pro-detailers to polish windshields, especially those streaked by hard-water residues.

The nemesis of interior glass and, in fact, all interior surfaces is *vinyl vapor residue:* the oily vapor given off by vinyl (upholstery, vinyl dashes, other interior vinyls), especially as vinyl grows older, when exposed to sunlight. The hotter the weather—and the hotter a car's interior—the greater the vaporization of the vinyl. Not all vinyls vaporize as readily as others; nor do all give off equal amounts of vapor.

Most people seeing a vinyl-vapor-smudged windshield or windows assume the driver is a smoker. Maybe, but vinyl vapor leaves a far more bothersome residue on glass—and on the car's entire interior—than any dozen packs of cigarettes. In sunbelt states, especially in summer with the windows shut, vinyl residue can come close to coating interior glass in a single day. Not only is the residue car-disfiguring, it is dangerous, limiting visibility. (See Chapter 5 for more information on combatting vinyl residue.)

To remove vinyl residue, use any good household window cleaner, an ammonia-water solution, or all-purpose cleaner.

TECH TIP:

The Advent of "No-Wax" Clearcoat Finishes

The newest technological advancement in clearcoat finishes is a fluorine-type clearcoat that needs little or no waxing. Currently available on Nissan Motor Corporation's *Infiniti* luxury automobile, "no-wax" clearcoats are likely to be available on other cars and from other manufacturers in the future.

The fluorine-type clearcoat finish requires special detailing, especially to correct damage to the clearcoat, and should be treated exactly per the manufacturer's instructions in the owner's manual. *Polishing and waxing in the usual detailing sense are not appropriate for these high-tech finishes.*

For the *Infiniti*, the manufacturer outlines particular procedures and brand-name products for buffing out fine scratches in the clearcoat finish and for wet-sanding finish damage that remains after buffing. Because no-wax/minimum-wax finishes are so different from conventional finishes and from most other clear-coat finishes that have been available to date, it is likely that each manufacturer that produces such a finish in the future will also include very specific product and procedure recommendations for its individual formulation of no-wax clearcoat.

T E C H   T I P :

Buffers—Which One (If Any) For You?

Some of the finest, most lustrous, most flawless polishing and waxing jobs, on some of the world's most expensive and exotic auto exteriors, are done by pro-detailers who advertise, "All work done by hand."

These pros never use a "buffer"—either an orbital or rotary buffing machine. Nor, in fact, do they go looking for customers or need to. Owners of the exotic cars they detail solely by hand often willingly wait weeks for a detailing appointment. Just as willingly, these car owners pay handsomely for the hours of hand labor, expertise, and skill for which these top-echelon detailers are locally—and sometimes regionally—renowned.

Some other pro-detailers, equally skilled and equally capable of producing show car exteriors, regularly use machine buffers to help speed (and, some claim, make better) their buffing jobs. The difference? The time spent, thus the charge, for equally top-quality exterior detailing.

Where the strictly by hand detailer may spend 4–6 hours, and sometimes more than a day, detailing a car's exterior, the buffer-using detailer may accomplish much the same results in 2–4 hours. The manual detailer may charge $100–$300, and more, for the same job the buffer-wielding detailer turns out for $75–$125.

Nonetheless, some owners of exotic cars absolutely will not permit a buffer anywhere near their paint jobs, no matter how skilled and practiced the buffer operator. They know something many do-it-yourself detailers may not: some types of buffing machines, notably the rotary kind, are unforgiving. A momentary lapse of the operator's attention can allow the buffer, because it is powerful, to cut—"burn"—right through a paint job. And, in the case of clear-coated cars, right through the clearcoat and down to, even through, the color layer of paint. By contrast, other types of buffing machines—orbital buffers—are far less apt to do damage, even in the hands of a weekend detailer.

While pro-detailers may endlessly argue whether or not the weekend detailer should attempt to speed exterior detailing with a buffer, there is only one super-safe decision: if you have never before used a buffer, or lack real buffer skill, don't hone your skill on your car's fragile and expensive paint job. Do exterior detailing by hand. If you want eventually to speed the job with a buffer, learn and practice buffer skills on another paint surface.

Still, knowing about buffers and how to use them are important first steps toward deciding, for yourself, whether you will eventually do some detailing with an assist from a buffer.

First, some facts:

1. Almost all makers of professional detailing polishes and waxes offer three choices of products: those designed to be applied only by hand, those designed to be applied only by machine, and those which can be applied either by hand or by machine. Polishes, glazes, and waxes formulated for machine application are almost universally in liquid form.

2. Some of the top producers of detail products, who make both manual and machine polishes and waxes, recognize at least one type of buffing machine—the orbital buffer—as a relatively safe tool even in unskilled hands. Orbital buffing machines get their name from the fact that their rotation describes an ellipse, or orbit, rather than a circle, as do rotary buffers. (Even so, many experts concede that the orbital is not capable of the same exacting paint-finish work as the rotary buffer.)

One type of orbital buffing/polishing machine is called a "random orbital" buffer. Its random elliptical orbits simulate the eccentric circular motion of hand polishing. Another type of buffing machine, although it's more commonly employed in sanding, is a "dual action" (D.A.) buffer. It can be switched from orbital rotation to straight line operation. Some weekend detailers use an electric drill fitted with a buffing pad, although most experts don't recommend it because it is difficult to control.

3. Although wool, synthetic wool, and terry cloth buffing pads (called "bonnets") have long been used as

Fig. 4.8 The wool polishing/buffing pad is still often favored for polishing conventional finishes. The foam pad is favored by pro-detailers for clearcoat and other high-tech finishes (and can also be used on conventional paint).

the buffer's applicator of polishes and waxes, preferred today by many pro-detailers, and certainly when working on many clearcoat car finishes, is the new foam buffing/polishing pad.

On clearcoat finish, especially, wool buffing pads are notorious for leaving swirl marks—the circular pattern of the buffer's action. Wool is also abrasive. The new foam pads, properly used, are virtually non-abrasive. So are the best of terry cloth buffing pads, although to a lesser degree.

4. Buffer speed is critical to achieving a brilliant finish without finish damage. Do-it-yourself detailers should use low buffer speeds—in the order of 1200 to 1750 rpms. Buffers operated at higher speed (1750–3000 rpm) require professional skill.

There are two buffer types, with basic differences. Their detailing uses are discussed below.

Orbital buffers

Orbital buffers are suited for the application of non-abrasive products to improve gloss without leaving buffer swirl marks. The results are similar to those created by hand buffing, it's just easier. Do not expect to remove paint defects or oxidization with an orbital buffer, but it is ideally suited to an operator with limited skill who might easily burn (damage or cut through) paint with a rotary buffer.

Rotary buffers

The buffing machines used by pros for all types of automotive paint finishes are rotary, available in a range of speeds. The correct buffing speed is determined by the type of vehicle paint being worked on:

- Low-speed buffers (1200–1750 rpm) are most effective on the newer, high-tech paint finishes which are more reactive to excessive heat buildup and static electricity.
- High-speed buffers (1750–3000 rpm) are ideal for use on conventional acrylic lacquer and acrylic enamel auto finishes. High-speed buffers require a greater level of operator skill.

Variable speed machines—which can operate effectively at both high and low rpms—are also available. While high-quality "variables" do an effective job, low-quality "variables" often lose their speed when pressure is put on them.

Buffing machines can often be inexpensively rented for a few hours. Pads cannot be rented; you'll have to buy fresh ones.

How to Use Buffing Machines

Basic rules and techniques:

1. Use only polishes, waxes, and other buffing products specifically designed—and designated—"for

Fig. 4.9 Wax tends to build up on the fibers of a wool pad; foam pads remain virtually free of abrasive wax buildup.

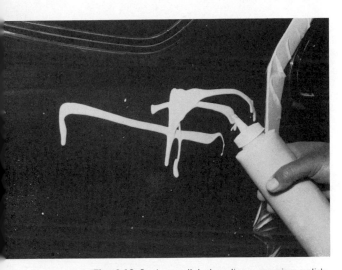

Fig. 4.10 Squirt parallel glaze lines, covering polishing area. Some product labels say "use sparingly"—considerably less glaze than is being used here.

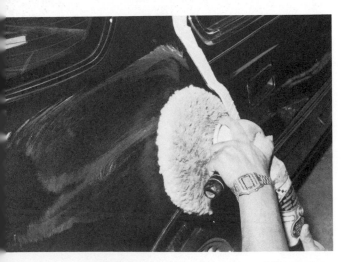

Fig. 4.11 With the buffing machine OFF, use the wool pad to spread liquid glaze over the area you intend to polish. To spread glaze evenly, hold pad flat to surface and move it back and forth.

machine buffing." Almost all are liquids, not pastes or waxes.

2. Use only buffing pads or bonnets recommended for the buffing products you use. There are two types of conventional wool buffing pads: cutting pads, used with slightly abrasive polishes to remove oxidation and scratches, and finishing pads, used with nonabrasive wax, to remove swirl marks left by the cutting pad and to create a final mirror-like finish.

3. If you buff with several different products, use a separate buffing pad for each. Change or clean pads frequently to avoid abrasive buildup of the buffing product (Fig. 4.9).

4. Buff only a small area of the finish at a time— an area about 2 feet × 2 feet.

5. Never buff a car's finish with the buffing pad alone (dry). Always buff using a buffing product.

6. Buffing products are *usually* applied (squirted from a squeeze bottle) directly on the small surface to be buffed, rather than on the pad or bonnet. (However, some buffing products are applied to both the pad and the surface of the finish.) If the label instructs you to apply the product directly on the finish, don't make a puddle. Squirt the product in a continuous line pattern to cover the area.

7. With the machine turned off, use the buffer's pad to manually spread the buffing product evenly over the area you plan to buff.

8. Before you turn the machine on, be sure you have firm and controlling grasp. Most buffing machines are equipped with a side grasp or handle. In effect, the operator's hands are working at right angles to one another for better control. Even so, buffers are not lightweight. (Buffers offered by one maker weigh from 7 to 8¼ pounds.) If the buffer feels too heavy, an indication that you may not have the strength or skill to control it, play it safe—don't attempt the machine buffing. Buff the finish manually instead.

9. Buff only on a clean, cool surface. The friction of buffing causes heat buildup, which must be avoided. If, after a couple of passes, the surface you're buffing feels warm or hot to the touch, stop. Turn off the machine and let the surface cool. Or, in some cases, depending on the product you're using, you can quick-cool the surface with a damp cloth. Usually, two to four passes complete most buffing jobs.

10. Never let your eyes or attention wander from what you're doing. To do so risks "burning" through the finish. Burning can happen in a split second. To avoid distractions, such as the buffer's electric cord hanging up on a car part or scraping over the finish, drape the cord over your shoulder, keeping it away from the car's finish.

11. Hold the buffer so that the pad is flat (parallel) to the surface you're buffing. As you buff, you can tip the pad slightly in the direction you're buffing: tip it to the right when moving the buffer to the right, and tip it left when moving the buffer left. Tipping the

pad slightly gives better buffing control. But never tip it so much that you're buffing with the pad's edge. Edge buffing can easily burn through the finish.

12. *Keep the buffer moving at all times.* Move the buffer in short, straight, even, and overlapping strokes. Exert minimum pressure to achieve the results you want (removal of oxidation on conventionally painted surfaces, if you're using a cleaner/polish; luster and shine, if you're using a final wax).

13. Do not, ever, buff over "ridges"—such "ridge lines" as the edges of fenders, head and taillights, hood "ridges," or the like. Running a buffing pad over ridges, where finish is thinnest, risks instant burning. Instead, spread whatever liquid product you're using up to, but on either side of a ridge. Buff up to the ridge, never over or right on it. Very gently, very carefully, "feather" (tilt, with virtually no pressure) the pad so as merely to brush the ridge. That is buffing enough on such thin-painted, vulnerable ridge areas.

14. Clean buffer pads frequently. Wool pads (used on conventional finishes only) can be rid of wax or other product buildup with a special pad-cleaning tool called a spur. It's available at most auto supply stores. Or you can use a dull screwdriver, although, unlike the spur, it can damage a wool or terry cloth bonnet. To clean a bonnet, grasp the machine firmly, perhaps resting it on your knee. Turn the buffer on and as the pad spins, apply the spur (or screwdriver) to the pad. Buildup will be dislodged. Dislodged, too, whether you're buffing or cleaning the bonnet, will be product splatter. If you buff, expect splatter. Wear old clothes and, as do some pros, protective glasses or goggles. Wool and terry cloth bonnets may also shed. Splatter or bonnet shed—or whatever—that falls on the buffed finish can be removed with a clean, soft, nonabrasive 100% cotton cloth.

15. Static electricity sometimes causes excessive buildup of buffing products on bonnets and pads. Some pros, before starting to buff, ground the vehicle to prevent the buildup of static electricity. A simple grounding wire is clamped to any bare metal chassis member and run to the nearest bare metal water pipe, or to a metal grounding stake.

16. Besides avoiding ridge lines, work carefully around places—and appendages—where the whirling bonnet or pad can get caught. Or, worse, tear off car parts, such as windshield wipers (front and back), antennas, fuel doors, or retractable headlight covers. If possible, remove such vulnerable parts as wipers and antennas before buffing.

17. Frequently evaluate the results of your buffing. Check the surface under full sunlight, and from various angles. If working indoors, use a shop trouble light to reveal swirl marks or flaws. Excellent for in-garage or shop inspection is a 300-watt quartz halogen light, available at hardware and home supply centers. Fluorescent lights generally fail to fully reveal swirl marks and faint scratches. (A foam buffing pad can be

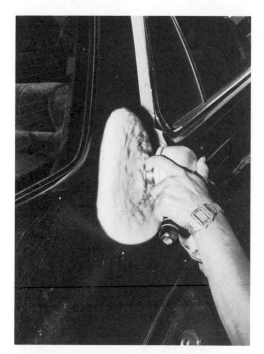

Fig. 4.12 Position machine flat to surface and turn power ON. Use light pressure, keep pad moving, and avoid body ridges. Work systematically and stop frequently to check for overheating (see text).

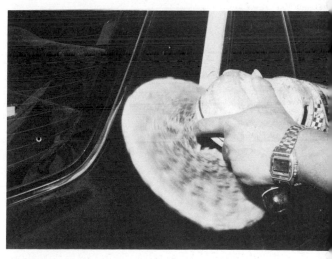

Fig. 4.13 Even where metal is rounded or where it bends, keep pad absolutely flat to the contour you are polishing.

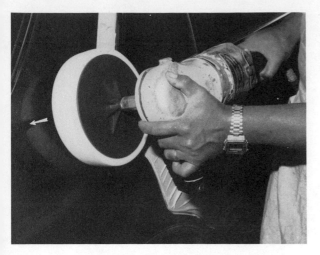

Fig. 4.14 A foam pad polishes wax and also removes any swirls left by a wool pad.

used to remove any swirls a wool pad may leave behind.)

18. You can begin buffing the finish almost anywhere. Some detailers prefer to start with the roof. Since it is usually flat, there's little chance of burn-through. Others begin at one side of the hood, working from windshield to front, then doing the hood's other half. For the right-handed, it's generally easier working to the right, all the way around the car. Lefties usually find it easier to buffer in the opposite direction. "Leading" with one's strongest hand gives most buffer-users more confidence and control.

Both confidence and control increase with practice. The more you buff, the easier—and quicker—the buffing. No doubt about it, buffing shortcuts exterior detailing and often achieves a mirror-finish that's arduous to achieve manually.

3-Hour Detailing: Inside and Out

Automotive purists may spend 20 hours or more over a couple of weekends detailing their cars, inside and out. If you don't have 20 hours or two weekends to spend and are satisfied with a "good," but not "super best," detail job, you can do the required detailing in about 3 hours' time.

To detail your car inside and out and under the hood in so short a time assumes that (1) your car's finish is in average shape, and not excessively oxidized or faded; (2) you don't have a convertible or vinyl top, which adds 30 minutes to the total time; (3) you're willing to skip such niceties as a repainting underhood; (4) you prepare for the quickie detailing by having in hand, before you start, all the products and tools you'll need for the job; (5) you have average car care skills and are willing to apply them efficiently and stick steadfastly to the job once begun; (6) you're willing to take necessary shortcuts—for example, doing the dirty work at a self-service carwash, and applying one-step products rather than the more professional two-step products—to "beat the clock" and finish in the allotted 3 hours.

The basic (minimum) tools and products you'll need are listed below:

Tools:
soft cloths, as diapers prewashed in softener (for drying cars and for applying various detailing products)
steel wool, grade 00 or 000 (for cleaning chrome)
cotton swabs (for getting into crevices)
paper towels (absorbent and nonabrasive, for various finishing touches, such as drying and polishing windows and windshield)
air/hot air dryer (for drying wetted upholstery, carpets, etc.)

Products (see appendix or sidebars in this chapter for
   lists of these products):
   whitewall tire cleaner (if your car has whitewalls)
   one-step cleaner and wax (for cleaning and waxing
      exterior finish)
   one-step chrome cleaner/polish (for cleaning and pol-
      ishing chrome trim, bumpers, etc.)
   all-purpose sudsy cleaning solution (for cleaning vari-
      ous vinyl and plastic materials)
   upholstery cleaner (shampoo for fabric upholstery;
      cleaner/conditioner for leather; cleaner/condi-
      tioner or protectant for vinyl upholstery)
   protectant (for cleaning vinyl upholstery;
      brightening vinyl/plastic dashboard and other
      similar materials; and brightening tires)
   carpet shampoo
   glass cleaner

‖ **C A U T I O N :** Never attempt to detail your car's exterior
finish in sunlight. That's my advice, as well as virtually every detailing product label. The reason is simple: direct sunlight dries
solutions before you have a chance to properly use them,
causing spots and streaking.

Procedures and Time Allotments
for 3-Hour Detailing

Fig. 4.15 Washing your car at a self-service coin-op
saves time.

Detail Step	Allotted Time	Description
Place: Steps 1, 2, and 3 are done at a self-service coin-op carwash.		
1. Exterior:		
Wash and dry, including wheels/tires and wheel wells	30 minutes	Wash the exterior yourself at a self-service wash bay. (A commercial carwash could save you time and energy in this initial step, but a self-service place has added quick-detail advantages, outlined below.)
2. Underhood:		
Degrease and wash	20 minutes	Detail underhood areas at an engine detailing bay of a self-service carwash. (You save time here because most self-service coin-op places have everything on the premises: washing and engine degreasing bays, and vacuum machines for vacuuming the interior.) Products needed for the job (sudsy water, degreasing solutions) are supplied and dispensed by the wash/ degreasing bays (see "Step-by-Step: How to Steam-Degrease the Engine," in Chapter 6).

Fig. 4.16 Drying the car after a quick wash at a
self-service bay is a 5- to 10-minute chore with a
chamois.

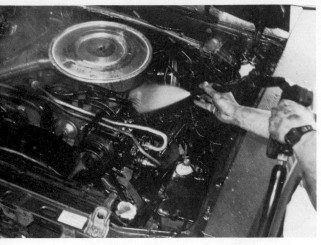

Fig. 4.17 Selective engine degreasing at a self-service bay.

Fig. 4.18 When cleaning a rear window that has an electrical defrost grid, work vertically, between the wires, even though they are within the glass.

Detail Step	Allotted Time	Description
3. Interior:		
Vacuum carpets, upholstery, and floor mats	10 minutes	While you're at the self-service place, vacuum the interior, including carpets, fabric upholstery, and floor mats. If mats are vinyl or rubber, wash them.

Place: Steps 4 through 9 can be done at your home or at any other suitable place.

Detail Step	Allotted Time	Description
4. Exterior Finish:		
Clean, wax, and buff	45 minutes	Now that the car is washed, clean it (to rid paint/clearcoat of oxidation) and wax it with a hand-applied one-step cleaner/wax. Hand-buff to a brilliant shine.
5. Exterior Chrome:		
Clean, wax, and polish trim, bumpers, etc.	15 minutes	Clean and brighten exterior chrome with any good chrome/metal polish; then wax and polish trim and bumpers. If bumpers are painted, or plastic, clean and wax.
6. Upholstery:		
Clean and condition fabric, vinyl, leather, velour, etc.	30 minutes	Shampoo fabric upholstery; clean and condition vinyl or leather. Upholstery vacuuming was done previously, at self-service vacuum bay.
7. Interior Trim:		
Clean and brighten dashboard, instrument panels, door/window/windshield moldings, etc.	10 minutes	Clean; then apply protectant to dashboard, instrument panels, shift console, window/windshield molding, in-car electronics, etc. Most interior trim can be cleaned/renewed with a rub-on/rub-off protectant.
8. Interior Glass:		
Clean windows, windshield, and other interior glass	10 minutes	Clean windows and windshield with any good household glass cleaner or with weak ammonia/water solution.
9. Carpets and Seat Belts:		
Shampoo carpeting; wash seat belting	10 minutes	Shampoo, rinse carpeting; wash seat belting. Use any good carpet shampoo or neutral soap and water.
Total time	**3 hours**	

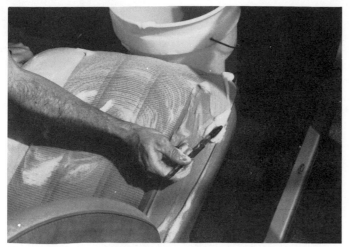

Fig. 4.19 When shampooing fabric upholstery, use a toothbrush to work suds into seat crevices and seams.

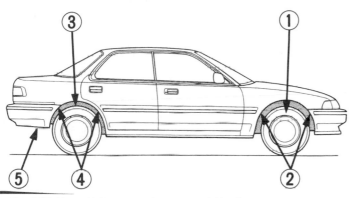

Fig. 4.20 Use a high-pressure hose to wash/detail these undercar areas: (1) above subframe, (2) inside front fender, (3) rear suspension, (4) inside rear wheel housing, and (5) under rear bumper.

Interior detailing is "super housekeeping" applied to your car.

Car carpeting is shampooed much as is your home's carpeting, but more intensively. Car upholstery—whether vinyl, fabric, or leather—is cleaned and rid of stains using methods and products similar to (or the same as) those used on upholstered furniture, but with greater attention to details. What cleans your home's windows cleans your car's, but windows and windshield (as well as sunroofs) need more frequent and more careful cleaning. For example, a car with finely finished wood molding can be detailed with the same polish used to protect and brighten fine furniture, but special attention must be given to crevices and contours.

The major difference between a car's interior and your home's is *use intensity*. Because your car's interior is used intensively and subjected to all the abuses that use intensity implies, its detailing must be intensive, differing significantly from routine "housecleaning."

Consider the facts. Depending on your life-style and how much time you spend at home, you may only occasionally use your living room's sofa or any particular upholstered chair. However, driver seat upholstery may be used and unavoidably abused half the hours—and more—of every day. Car carpeting, unlike most home carpeting, is often continuously "tracked"—with dirt, oil, grease, snow, and slush. Whereas home carpeting is seldom systematically worn in any one small spot, a driver's right heel, forever nudging the accelerator, first dirties and then sometimes wears through a particular place in car carpeting (unless that particular place is protected by a car mat).

In its lifetime, moreover, your car's interior may become a bedroom (for a quick snooze at a highway rest area), a restaurant, an office, a sick bay, a store-room, a moving van—you name it.

And all of this use and abuse occurs literally under glass and within the relatively tiny confines of the average car. Use of a home may be spread over 1200–5000 square feet, or more. A car's interior use takes place in seldom more than 45 square feet. And, in some downsized models, less than half that.

Moreover, unlike your home's carpets and upholstered furniture, or even windows, a car's interior is subjected to extremes of heat, cold, and sunlight. Daily it is exposed to atmospheric pollutants, road grime, and contamination from its own and other engines. Even a tightly closed car interior cannot escape all of these natural and unnatural extremes.

Thus, interior detailing, far from being merely routine "housecleaning," aims to restore, wherever possible, a car's interior to its showroom condition and appearance. Anything less may produce a reasonably clean interior, but not one that is detailed.

"Detailed," when it comes to your car's interior, means simply that: minute, painstaking, time-consuming attention to details. See a smidgeon of dirt or

CHAPTER 5

Good "Housekeeping" Inside Your Car

Fig. 5.1 A pro-detailer brushes dirt from a grille directly into waiting vacuum crevice tool.

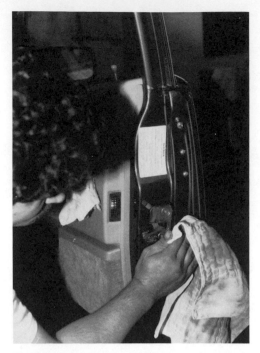

Fig. 5.2 *Remove outdated service stickers; however, when detailing door jambs and underhood, leave informational stickers in place.*

grime? Get rid of it. An upholstery seam crevice not as clean as the area around it? Clean it. The steering wheel's underneath places begrimed by sweaty hands? Degrime them. An outdated service sticker on a door edge or jamb? Remove it. If it didn't come with the car's interior when you took delivery, or if it did but shouldn't have, do away with it. *That's* interior detailing.

1 ▶ 2 ▶ 3

S T E P - B Y - S T E P :

Detailing the Interior

There is no "one right way" to super-detail your car's interior. But a systematic, orderly way is outlined below:

Carpeting and fabric upholstery

- Vacuum
- Shampoo
- Rinse
- Dry
- Protect (optional)

Vinyl upholstery

- Vacuum
- Clean
- Protect

Leather upholstery

- Vacuum
- Clean
- Condition/protect

Dashboard, moldings, trim (plastic, vinyl, or rubber)

- Clean
- Restore
- Protect

Interior metal, including chrome

- Clean
- Polish

Windshield, windows, mirrors

- Clean
- Protect (optional)

You can detail the interior piecemeal—say, do the carpeting and upholstery one day, the rest of the interior another—or get it done with one effort.

Doing it in a single shot usually means you'll need to do all of the interior molding, chrome, the dash, windshield, and windows first, before you do the upholstery, because upholstery that seems to have dried requires several hours, or even overnight, to dry thoroughly. Since you don't want to sit on a wet or damp seat while doing the dash, windows, ceiling (headliner), and other interior detailing, it makes sense to do those jobs first.

Vacuuming

Time required: *0:10*
   5–10 minutes

Materials needed:
   vacuum
   vacuum accessories (crevice tool, drape and blind attachment)
   a whisk broom, clean paintbrush, or toothbrush (for dislodging stubborn dirt ahead of the vacuum)

Any good home vacuum with a plastic (not metal) crevice attachment works well. Portable vacuums, despite their popularity and increased power, generally lack the power to vacuum car carpets as they should be vacuumed. Vacuums at the coin-op places may have power enough, but the clamor of other car owners to use the vacuum you're using, plus the need to keep feeding the meter, often discourage a thorough job.

Fig. 5.3 Coin-op vacuum for vacuuming car's carpets, floor mats, and upholstery.

Steps:
1. Start with the upholstery. Using the attachment usually used for drapes or window blinds, vacuum seat backs and seats. Push seats forward to get behind and beneath them. On rear seats, don't neglect seat fronts, the back edge of seats facing the rear window, and around armrests.
2. Switch to the plastic crevice tool (plastic rather than metal which, if bent or sharp, risks tearing the fabric, vinyl or leather, or cutting stitching). The crevice tool is for getting deep into upholstery seams and pleats. With one hand working ahead of the tool, spread the upholstery's seams; with the other hand, work the crevice tool into the seams (Fig. 5.4). Seams collect a lot of dirt, so you may have to go over them several times.
3. Now vacuum the carpets. Use the drape and blind attachment to vacuum rear carpeting. Unless you have a van, wagon, or motor home, rear carpeting isn't extensive.
4. Move to the front carpeting (under and ahead of seats). Move seats forward, then backward, to their full forward-rear positions to get under them. This is probably the dirtiest carpeting area in any car. The next dirtiest is the carpeting in front of the driver's seat.
5. With the palm of your hand or a brush, beat the carpeting just ahead of your vacuum tool. Carpet beating dislodges deep-down dirt and brings it to the surface for vacuuming.
6. With the crevice tool, get into crevices of the seats' floor tracks; all around the perimeter of the carpeting, front and back; and especially in the driver's foot area

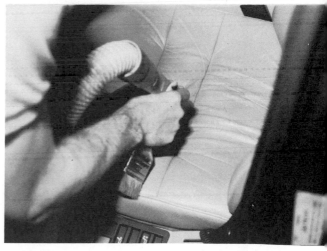

Fig. 5.4 Whether upholstery is leather, vinyl, or fabric, the first step is vacuuming. A soft-bristled brush and the crevice tool of the vacuum work together to rid seams of dirt.

Fig. 5.5 In many areas, a vacuum alone can't dislodge all the dirt. Here, a soft-bristled paintbrush and a vacuum crevice attachment work in unison to clean dashboard nooks and crannies. Note the shortened length of the bristles on the paintbrush; reducing bristle length makes the paintbrush a more effective detailing tool.

Upholstery/Carpet Cleaners/ Protectants

Armor All Multi-Purpose Cleaner
Autoglym Fabric Protector
Auto Wax E-Z Clean
Blue Coral Automotive Rug & Carpet Cleaner
Blue Coral Dri-Clean
Blue Coral Velour & Upholstery Cleaner
Car Brite Blue Max
Car Brite Nu-Look
Eagle 1 Spot Remover/Auto Interior
Mar-Hyde Rug, Upholstery and Vinyl Cleaner
Mothers Upholstery & Carpet Cleaner
PRO Aerosol Fabric Cleaner
PRO Heavy Duty Interior Cleaner
PRO Upholstery and Carpet Cleaner
Rally Upholstery/Carpet Cleaners
Scotchgard Carpet Cleaner and Protector
Scotchgard Upholstery Cleaner and Protector
Turtle Wax Carpet Cleaner & Protector
Turtle Wax Spot Remover
Turtle Wax Vinyl-Fabric Upholstery Cleaner & Protector
Turtle Wax Velour Upholstery Cleaner & Protector
Ultra Shine Upholstery Cleaner
Westley's Clear-Magic

(around the pedals and dimmer switch, if it's located on the floor).

7. Use the crevice tool aided by a paintbrush (see Fig. 5.5) to vacuum the instrument panel, floor console, and around the windows and windshield molding, especially where the windshield meets the dash. If the crevice tool won't squeeze into this often small but particularly dirty area, use a "detail stick": a ⅛- or ¼-inch-diameter length of wood doweling wrapped in a clean piece of cloth or cheesecloth.

8. Finally, using the drape and blind attachment, vacuum the headliner—but gently. Headlining is fragile: exert minimum pressure.

Detailing fabric upholstery

You have several method and product choices (see box), described below. The first two methods are outlined on the following pages.

- *Shampoo fabric upholstery* (including cloth, velour, sheepskin, or combination vinyl/fabric upholstery) *with a good sudsy household wash product.* Some choices: a sudsy solution made with liquid hand soap; any good neutral soap and water; a soap made for hand-washing delicate fabrics; fabric and rug shampoos shelved in supermarkets; car-maker upholstery shampoos available from the dealer from whom you bought your car.
- *Use a spray-on/wipe-off fabric cleaner*
- *Hire others to clean it.* Arrange to bring your car into the shop of any reputable home carpet/upholstery cleaner. For a usually small fee, someone there will use the shop's heavy-duty equipment to clean your car's upholstery and carpet and to extract the rinse water so as to speed the drying process.

Car cloth is the most difficult type of upholstery material to keep clean or to clean after it becomes dirty or stained. That's one reason pro-detailers usually charge more to clean the interior of a fabric-upholstered car.

Shampooing fabric upholstery

Time required: *0:45*
    30–45 minutes

Materials needed:
    soft-bristled brush
    cloth or sponge
    wet-dry vacuum or paper towels and hair dryer
    stain remover (if necessary)
    bucket for mixing/using shampoo
    suds-making product (fabric cleaner or soap)
    toothbrush

If there's any secret to shampooing car upholstery (or, for that matter, car carpeting) it's *rinsing*. Rinse water must be sucked from upholstery and carpets with a home shop wet-dry vacuum, a carpet wet-dry machine rented from a local supermarket, an extractor, or a vacuum available at coin-op carwash places.

Whatever the fabric cleaner—name-brand or no-name generic—test it first. Try it on a small area of the fabric that normally isn't in view. If what's happening doesn't look right (you detect fading, or a tint of fabric color shows on your cloth), stop right there. Let things dry. Then test another fabric cleaner on another spot.

Steps:
1. Remove any spots or stains (see "Tech Tip: Upholstery—Out Damned Spot," in this chapter).
2. With soft-bristled brush, gently but firmly scrub seats and seatbacks with a circular motion (Fig. 5.6). Get into seams and crevices with the same brush and with the assistance of a toothbrush (Fig. 5.7).
3. Wipe away suds with a damp cloth or sponge (Fig. 5.8).
4. Rinse with clean water. Use as little water as necessary to rinse thoroughly.
5. Extract rinse water with a wet-dry vacuum. Or use paper towels and a hair dryer for speed drying. To avoid scorching, be careful not to hold the dryer too close to the fabric.
6. Allow to dry overnight.

Using spray-on/wipe-off fabric cleaner

‼ C A U T I O N : Always read a product label and heed the maker's advice. Some spray-on car carpet protectors warn: "Keep small children and pets off carpet until thoroughly dry."

Time required: *0:45*
    30–45 minutes

Materials needed:
    spray-on/wipe-off fabric cleaner (see box earlier in this chapter)
    cloth or sponge
    vacuum

Note: The steps listed below are for a specific product that is typical of the spray-on/wipe-off cleaners. Follow manufacturer's instructions for the product you select.

Steps:
1. Test for colorfastness by cleaning a small, inconspicuous fabric area. Allow to dry. Do not use if color or texture is adversely affected.
2. Shake can vigorously. Hold the spray nozzle 4–6 inches from the fabric. Spray a thin, even layer of foam over a small area (Fig. 5.9). Use a cloth or sponge to remove overspray from adjacent, nonupholstered areas.

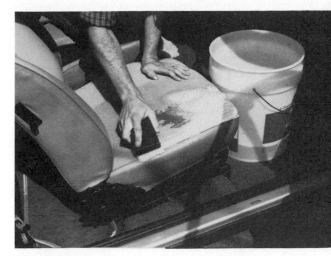

Fig. 5.6 Apply upholstery shampoo with a soft-bristled brush.

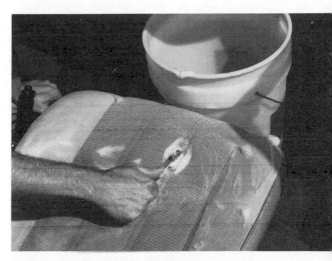

Fig. 5.7 When scrubbing upholstery, work suds into seams and crevices with a toothbrush.

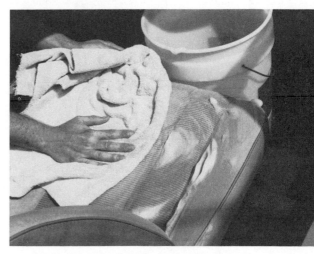

Fig. 5.8 Use an absorbent terry cloth towel to remove sudsy water. Then rinse thoroughly with clean water. Sop up rinse water with a clean absorbent towel or with a wet/dry vacuum or extractor.

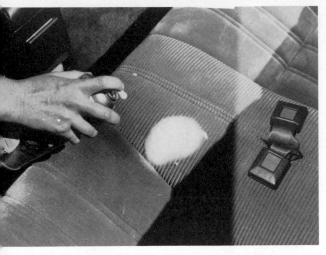

Fig. 5.9 After testing fabric for colorfastness and for the effect of the cleaner on the texture, hold can 4–6 inches from the fabric and spray on a thin, even coat of cleaner.

Fig. 5.10 Using a damp, clean sponge, work foam into fabric with overlapping circular strokes. When fabric is thoroughly dry, vacuum again. (Rinsing is not recommended because it would remove cleaner's residual fabric protection.)

3. With a clean, damp sponge, work foam into the upholstery with overlapping, circular strokes (Fig. 5.10). Rinse sponge clean and squeeze dry frequently.
4. Repeat procedure on a small area at a time until entire upholstery is cleaned and protected. Depending on the product, special stain protection may remain after cleaning. It acts to prevent further soiling and stains and helps to maintain the original repellency of upholstery treated with a stain repellent.
5. When upholstery is thoroughly dry, vacuum.

Detailing vinyl upholstery

Time required: *0:30*
20–30 minutes

Materials needed:
cloth
mild household detergent or cleaning formula (optional)
toothbrush
vinyl cleaner (see box)
protectant (see box)

Vinyl is the easiest car upholstery to clean, but it is not necessarily the easiest to keep clean. Vinyl collects grime faster than other upholsteries do (you can actually feel the grime). And vinyl, despite claims to the contrary, fades noticeably, especially when subjected to intense sun exposure—as the rear seatback, for one example.

There's really no reason to buy a vinyl product that just cleans, when soap and water—or any of many all-purpose household detergents and cleaners—will do just as well. But, unless you're very careful to rinse the vinyl well and then wipe it dry, soap and some other household cleaners can dull or streak vinyl. Special vinyl clean-

---

Vinyl Cleaners/Conditioners
Armor All Multi-Purpose Cleaner
Autoglym Vinyl and Rubber Care
Blue Coral Leather & Vinyl Conditioner
Car Brite Vinyl Beauty (vinyl interior/top)
Connoisseur's Choice Cleaner
CSA Premium Gold
Eagle 1 Spot Remover/Auto Interior
Mar-Hyde Rug, Upholstery and Vinyl Cleaner
Meguiar's Vinyl/Leather/Rubber Cleaner/ Conditioner
Nu-Vinyl
PRO Wipe-On Vinyl Dressing
Turtle Wax Vinyl Top Cleaner
Turtle Wax Vinyl Top Wax
Westley's Clear-Magic
Westley's Leather & Vinyl Cleaner
Westley's Vinyl-Top Lustre

Fig. 5.11 Regular treatment with protectants would probably have prevented the cracks in this vinyl.

ers—and they abound—do more than merely clean: most also impart a sheen to vinyl.

Steps:

1. Optional wash. Using a clean, damp cloth, thoroughly wash vinyl with a mild household detergent or cleaning formula. Some choices: ammonia and water (4–6 tablespoons of ammonia to 1 quart of water); dishwashing detergent and water.
2. Work the solution into seams, seatbacks, along seat, and backrest edges. Use a toothbrush to reach hard-to-reach places.
3. Rinse with clean water. Buff dry with a clean cloth. Allow to dry completely, at least one hour, depending on the weather.
4. Apply a good vinyl cleaner or a combination cleaner/protectant. Let it work for a few minutes, then rub dry with a clean cloth. The object is to bring up vinyl's natural sheen.
5. Finally, if you applied a vinyl cleaner, conclude with a straight protectant. Protectants restore vinyl's original color and sheen. Apply with a clean cloth. Let the formula work a few minutes, then buff dry.

Restoring sun-faded vinyl

Time required: *1:00*
    30–60 minutes

Materials needed:
    protectant
    cloth and/or sponge
    toothbrush

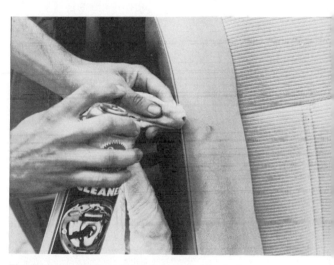

Fig. 5.12 Two passes with a cloth soaked in vinyl cleaner is usually enough to remove a spot like this.

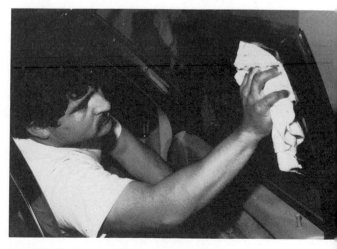

Fig. 5.13 A diaper is a favorite cleaning cloth among pro-detailers. (Diapers used this way should be washed in water softener to reduce abrasiveness.)

A good protectant can sometimes restore nearly original color and sheen to even extremely sun-faded vinyl.

Steps:

1. Apply the protectant with a cloth and a toothbrush and let it work and penetrate overnight. Next morning, rub and buff off any excess.

2. If restoration is not complete, repeat. Three applications and three overnight soak-ins may be necessary—but the results can be amazing.

3. For worst-case sun-faded vinyl upholstery, you may have to repeat the treatment every 3–4 months in summer, less frequently during less sunny seasons.

Detailing leather upholstery

Time required: *1:00*
45–60 minutes (20–30 minutes if leather is coated)

Materials needed:
soft cloth or sponge
leather cleaner (see box)
soft-bristled toothbrush
leather conditioner

Leather is much different from other upholstery materials. If your upholstery is genuine hide, it is perishable. Neglected, it will harden, crack, fade, and, in time, deteriorate into a rash of sandlike granules that sluff off at the mere brush of an arm. Detailing ensures that your costly leather upholstery will retain its resiliency . . . and its life.

There are several products available for cleaning and preserving leather. Saddle soap, once the conventional cleaner for leather, is seldom used today by pro-detailers. And, yes, some Owner's Manuals still advise doing nothing but wiping leather with a damp cloth, then thoroughly drying.

Before applying any product to leather, test it. Many foreign leathers are topically dyed, meaning they aren't dyed completely through the hide. Noncompatible products will "pull dye"—that is, dye comes off on your cleaning cloth.

On the other hand, many late model American car leathers are coated with a protective plastic. The plastic, usually a PVC (polyvinylchloride), prevents penetration of any of the various leather cleaners and conditioners. Treat vinyl-coated leather exactly as you'd treat vinyl upholstery. As for leather cleaners/conditioners so essential for "raw," uncoated leather? Forget them. They can't get through the protective plastic barrier.

To test whether your leather upholstery is "raw" or plastic-coated, apply a few drops of clean water to the leather. If the water is easily and quickly absorbed, the leather is uncoated; if the droplets aren't absorbed, the leather probably has a protective coating.

The steps listed below are for a specific brand of leather cleaner and conditioner. Follow manufacturer's instructions on the product you select.

Leather Cleaners/Protectants

Armor All Leather Care
Autoglym Leather Care Cleaner
Blue Coral Leather & Vinyl Conditioner (cleans, restores, protects)
Connoisseur's Choice Cleaner
Connoisseur's Choice Protectant
Eagle 1 Creme Leather Care & Conditioner
Hide Food
Leather Clean
Leather Lotion
Lexol-pH Balanced Leather Cleaner
Lexol Leather Conditioner and Preservative
Meguiar's Vinyl/Leather/Rubber Cleaner/Conditioner
Scotchgard Leather Protector
Westley's Leather & Vinyl Cleaner

Steps:

1. With a soft cloth, apply the cleaner in overlapping strokes.
2. Use a soft-bristled toothbrush to work it into seams and crevices. Cleaner's foaming action (use cleaner enough for sufficient foaming) loosens embedded dirt, "floats" dirt from crevices, and cleans the leather.
3. Rinse with clean water and a soft cloth or sponge.
4. While the leather is still damp, apply the conditioner evenly over the entire surface and into crevices and seams. Wipe off excess with a soft, clean cloth. The conditioner lubricates and restores leather's suppleness and its rich, natural luster.
5. Allow to dry thoroughly before use.

Detailing car carpeting

What cleans the carpets in your home will clean the carpets in your car. The same spot removers that "de-spot" your home's carpeting will de-spot your car's. Carpet-wash solutions sold for supermarket rental carpet cleaning machines generally do an equally good job on your car's carpeting. Cold-water home fabric wash products are also popular with pro-detailers for cleaning both wool and synthetic car carpeting.

Most common household carpet cleaners tend to be "wet formulas." Even when a wet-dry vac or extractor is used to pull out most of the water, carpets are still pretty wet and may need several days to thoroughly air dry. Spray-on car carpet formulas do a credible cleaning job without undo wetness.

Removing road-salt stains.

Time required: *0:45*
    20–45 minutes

Materials needed:
    vacuum
    saltwater solution
    soft-bristled brush or cloth
    carpet shampoo

After vacuuming but before cleaning and washing carpets, remove any spots or stains (see "Tech Tip: Upholstery—Out Damned Spot," in this chapter, for spot-removal techniques).

Unlike car upholstery, however, carpet is often tracked with road-salted snow and slush, which not only whiten or grey the carpeting but also stain upon melting. A simple procedure and homemade antidote often rids car carpeting of road-salt stains.

Steps:

1. Brush away snow and slush. Vacuum remaining residue.
2. If stain remains, remove with a carefully applied salt-water solution: 1 cup of table salt to 1 quart of water.

3. Use a soft-bristled brush or cloth to work the salt solution into the stain place. Feather outward from stain's center to avoid leaving a ring in the carpeting.
4. With stain removed, shampoo the stain area and adjacent carpeting.

Carpet cleaning with a "wet formula"

Time required: *0:30*
20–30 minutes

Materials needed:
"wet formula" wash solution
soft-bristled brush
dry absorbent cloths or paper towels
wet-dry vacuum, extractor, coin-op vacuum, or paper towels

Steps:
1. Clean the dirtier front-seat carpeting first. If your "wet formula" wash solution becomes dirty, mix new before cleaning backseat carpeting.
2. Apply generous amounts of a "wet formula" with a soft-bristled brush. Use vigorous, circular, overlapping strokes.
3. Work brush and suds deep into the piling.
4. With a dry, absorbent cloth or paper towels, wipe off any excess.
5. Rinse well and deeply with clean cool or cold water.
6. Soak up rinse water with paper towels. Or, far better, remove with an extractor or a wet-dry home shop vacuum. Or drive to a coin-op place and use its wet-dry vacuum.
7. Let dry overnight. When nearly or completely dry, fluff carpet's nap with a dry, soft-bristled brush.

Carpet cleaning with a spray-on formula

Time required: *0:30*
20–30 minutes, depending on degree of soil

Materials needed:
spray-on cleaner
cloth or sponge

Steps:
1. Apply spray-on cleaner as outlined step-by-step, above, for spray-on upholstery cleaning.
2. Although some spray-on carpet cleaners may also help to protect newly cleaned car carpets from quickly resoiling, a product designed specifically as a protector gives double protection.

Applying carpet protectant

Time required: *0:10*
5–10 minutes

Materials needed:
carpet protectant
clean white cloth
vacuum

Fig. 5.14 Spray bottle administers "wet formula" to door trim. Next, trim is scrubbed, rinsed, and allowed to dry.

The steps listed below are for a specific brand of protector. Follow manufacturer's instructions on the protector you select.

Steps:

1. First, test colorfastness. Spray a small amount on a hidden area of carpeting. Wipe with a clean white cloth. If any color shows on the cloth, do not use the product. If no color rub-off shows, proceed.
2. Shake spray can vigorously. Hold can 4–6 inches from the carpet and make circular, overlapping passes. Spray an even, light coating over entire carpet area.
3. Protector will foam. Foam disappears within a few minutes. Wipe any overspray from adjacent, non-carpet areas.
4. Let dry. Protector usually completely drys within about 2 hours.
5. If, after carpet is dry, any whitish residue remains (evidence that in places you applied too much protector), vacuum clean.

Cleaning and sheening dashboard, instrument panel, and most in-car vinyl, plastic, and rubber

The detailing cure-all for restoring the original good looks and sheen of vinyl, rubber, and plastics is a protectant. Protectant is wiped on, allowed to work for anywhere from a few minutes to overnight (in the case of badly sun-faded vinyl upholstery), and then wiped and buffed off.

Many driveway detailers, however, neglect one vital first step: cleaning. A protectant cannot work its considerable restorative wonders unless the surface to which it is applied is clean.

Protectant pre-cleaning

Time required: *1:00*
30–60 minutes

Whether restoring the dashboard, door moldings, shift console, rubber weather stripping, headrests, sun visors or other in-car appendage, clean the surface before applying protectant. You can use an all-purpose cleaner (such as a dishwashing detergent solution, a weak ammonia-water wash, or any of numerous brand name general-purpose cleaners) and soft cloths to thoroughly wash and dry the surface on which you intend to use a protectant. Or you can apply a pre-protectant rub-on/wipe-off cleaner.

Applying protectant

Time required: *0:30*
20–30 minutes

‖ CAUTION : Since protectants tend to make surfaces slick, do not use on foot pedal rubber (as the brake or accelerator pedals) or on the steering wheel.

Fig. 5.15 Between thorough in-car detailing sessions, wipe dash every few weeks with a cloth wetted with protectant. Scratches in plastic dial or gauge lenses can be removed with a plastic cleaner; plastic can then be polished with a plastic polish.

‖ CAUTION : Use extreme care in handling and working with inflammable products (as petroleum-based engine cleaners), spray-on products (which can be harmful if sprayed or blown into your face or eyes), and products that are potentially harmful if inhaled (such as ammonia or ammonia-based products).

The same protectants that restore vinyl upholstery can restore other in-car plastic, rubber and composite materials (see box for list of protectants).

Protectants do more than simply restore original color. They keep rubber moldings flexible and functioning, protect vinyl from scuffing, and reduce sun-fade.

Protectants need periodic reapplication. To apply, spray or wipe protectant on surface; let it work, then wipe off and buff to a sheen. Most protectants perform better when left on a surface for awhile (for anywhere from a few minutes to several hours), rather than being wiped off immediately.

Detailing interior windows, windshield, and mirrors

Time required: *0:20*

For windows, windshield, and mirrors, use any good glass cleaner or a weak solution of ammonia and water. Treat interior convertible windows as you did their exteriors, with a scratch-removing plastic cleaner/polish (see box).

Reaching the hard-to-reach places

Time required: *0:20*

A car's interior hard-to-reach places can be reached with a vacuum's crevice tool, a "detail stick," or a thin, long-handled paint brush. Often dust and dirt can be dislodged with a few zaps of air pressure from an aerosol can of one of the pressurized air products used to rid precision instruments, including camera innards, of dust.

Cleaning and polishing interior chrome

Time required: *0:45*
20–45 minutes

Materials needed:
soft cloth
masking materials, if needed
chrome polish (see appendix)

Any good chrome cleaner/polish used to clean and polish exterior chrome can be used to clean and polish interior chrome, as well. However, the interior application and polishing must be done far more carefully to avoid getting chrome cleaner on upholstery or other interior materials to which chrome trim and strips may be attached. Quick application of masking tape eliminates the risk.

Fig. 5.16 A cellular phone and its cord attachments join the "to do" list when a car's interior is being detailed. Also on the list: stereo speakers, CB radio, and in-car fax machine.

Steps:
1. Mask what you intend to polish, if masking is applicable.
2. Apply chrome polish with a soft cloth.
3. Work polish into chromed crevices and channels.
4. Wipe off and buff with a clean soft cloth.

Care and Detailing of Aftermarket-Tinted Windows

If you had your car's windows tinted *after* you bought the car ("aftermarket-tinted") to reduce glare, reduce ultraviolet fading of upholstery, lessen the work load of air conditioning, or provide privacy, disregard everything this chapter says about the routine way to detail plain glass windows. Yours aren't plain glass. Because their interior sides are coated with a sun-screening film, their detailing may require something more than routine doing.

How much more depends on the kind of film the tinter used. Older-type films are particularly vulnerable to scratching unless you use great care and, most important, a super-soft nonabrasive cleaning cloth. Technology has greatly improved the durability and toughness of the newer tint films. The new films can be safely cleaned much as you would clean your car's untinted glass. If in doubt as to whether your windows are tinted with older- or newer-type film, clean them as though they were the older, more scratch-prone type. If you detail windows tinted with the older-type film as though they were ordinary plain glass, you can destroy the special film with a single cleaning.

Windows tinted after delivery from the factory have a thin layer of tinted plastic film on their in-car surfaces. The film, old or new, is vulnerable to grime (the film's chief enemy), scratches, the mechanical action of a window's mechanism (which can cut, scratch, and groove the tint film), and everyday use.

Detailing window tint films of the older type requires a gentle approach. The number-one rule: *Never use a cleaning solution that contains ammonia*. To clean, use a mild dishwashing detergent solution: 1 ounce of biodegradable, no-color dishwashing detergent mixed with 20 ounces of distilled water. Use a spray bottle to apply the mix. Spraying, which eliminates application or wiping with cloths, reduces abrasive contact with the film. No-color dishwashing detergent won't cloud or discolor the tint; some colored detergents may.

After spraying solution on the tint film, dry the film with an extremely soft and pliable squeegee, or with a soft sponge. If you have neither, use a super-soft cotton cloth. *Avoid using paper towels; no matter how soft they may feel to you, their fibers can scratch the tint films.*

The new tint films can be cleaned much as plain glass windows: with any of the usual window cleaning solutions, with soap and water, or with a solution of dishwashing detergent. Once clean, newer films can be dried with very soft paper towels.

Some car owners protect the tint, whatever its type, with a sheet of clear plastic, carefully cut to fit the window exactly. Protective window plastic is available from window-tinting shops (see box).

Application of the plastic is exacting, but easy. Clean the tint film, as described above, and dry. Mix a

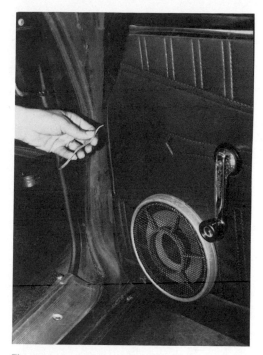

Fig. 5.17 Any visible speaker wires should receive some detailing attention, as well as a quick checkup.

Protective Film
Madico High Performance Window
   Film
Sunpro Sun Protective Tinting Film

solution of dishwashing detergent (3–4 squirts of detergent to a quart of water). Wet the window tint with the soapy solution. Lay the plastic over the tint film. With a squeegee, press the plastic to the tint. Working from the center to the extremities of the plastic, squeegee out any soapy water or air bubbles. In two or three days this protective tint sandwich will be dry, and the tint film will be permanently protected.

Besides normal wear and tear, particular things, such as soft drinks spilled on tinted windows not protected by plastic, can deteriorate some types of tint film. So can cigarette smoke, hairspray, and a buildup of road grime. Also, too-tight window rollers and other parts of the window mechanism can squeeze unprotected tint, damaging the film.

One way to reduce damage caused by a window mechanism is to spray-coat the tint with a silicone vinyl protectant. A number of them, available at some auto supply stores and most window-tint shops, are specially formulated for "lubricating" window tint film. Lubrication makes the tint film slightly slippery, helping to reduce window mechanism damage. Lubrication also makes the film more resistant to scratching.

One additional warning: *If your car's windows are aftermarket-tinted with the older-type film, especially if the tint is not covered with a plastic protector, don't let the carwash people touch them.* Do the tint windows gently (and with the right products) yourself. Carwash window treatment tends to be rough (the cloths they use) and tough (the pressure they use, which is seldom gentle). A single swipe with a rough cloth can leave unprotected older-type tint films permanently disfigured.

In contrast to aftermarket-tinted windows, factory-delivered tinted windows have the tint manufactured in the glass. Factory-tint windows are detailed just like ordinary plain-glass windows.

TECH TIP:

Upholstery—Out Damned Spot

Fabric upholstery falls victim to all kinds of staining agents.

The first rule is *get to work on a stain agent immediately, before it has a chance to set or permanently stain.* The second is, if it stains, *know what to use to remove the stain best, fastest, and safest.*

Upholstery fabrics vary greatly. So do stains. But, generally, there is a right way and a right cleaner to handle each type of stain. While getting rid of stains is part of detailing any car's interior, you should always work on stain-causing materials as soon as possible, before they permanently stain the fabric—because it may be weeks or months before you are able to do a thorough interior detailing.

Upholstery fabrics, including the popular velours,

stain more easily and are harder to rid of stains than either vinyl or leather. Some pro-detailers charge more to clean auto interiors upholstered in fabric because more work is involved.

Still, you may be surprised how easily the majority of staining agents and their stains disappear from fabric upholstery when you use nothing more than warm water—and even how they disappear even more easily when you use a mild "neutral" soap or a dishwashing detergent and water solution.

"Neutral" soap is soap whose pH factor (a measure of acidity or alkalinity on a scale of 0 to 14) is neither acidic nor alkaline. On the pH scale, 7 is neutral. Factor numbers higher than 7 denote increasing alkalinity; numbers lower than 7 denote increasing acidity.

Neutral detailing soaps, as other neutral detailing products, do not harm or remove paint, wax, or other detailing products. Non-neutral detailing products can.

When attacking most fabric stains, try soap and water first. Only when that fails should you progress to fabric cleaners, shampoos, and other stain-removing fabric formulas. Use the mildest, least harsh cleaners first (for one example, a very mild ammonia and water solution: 4 parts water to 1 part ammonia). If that fails, dry excess moisture from the area—using paper towels or a hair dryer—and try a slightly stronger fabric cleaner.

Some stains may defy your best efforts. They never entirely fade away, no matter what techniques and cleaners you use, because the staining ingredients have penetrated and indelibly attached to the fibers of the fabric.

In some cases, what appears at first to be a simple spotting job—perhaps just a little suds or cleaner—becomes more complex. For one thing, the stain may "bleed" into the surrounding fabric. Or a ring may form that is more noticeable than the potential stain itself—and can only be gotten rid of by cleaning the entire area, perhaps a whole seatback or seat cushion.

Still, there are methods which work most often in potential stain situations common to car upholstery. Almost all have a single starting point: remove the foreign material, whether it's fruit drink, chewing gum, or something you can't identify.

The removal methods, usually obvious, depend on the foreign material. Paper towels sop up and remove liquids—as blood, juice, and soft drinks. Adhesive materials—road tar and chewing gum, for example—must be scraped off using a dull knife blade. Or, better and beyond error, a stiff piece of cardboard, perhaps a folded match cover *with the matches removed* (on the chance they might add to the stain).

Assuming you've removed most of the foreign material—at least as much as is visible, the no-longer-visible having soaked or seeped into the fabric—try these specific stain removing methods:

Greasy or oily stains

Lipstick. Lipstick is among the more difficult substances to remove because it contains a variety of dyes and oil-like substances with an affinity for fabrics. Application of a quick-dry cleaning solvent—as dry-cleaning fluid (lighter fluid may also work)—may do the trick. So may various powdered fabric cleaners, available from new car dealerships and recommended for cleaning fabrics used in specific makes and models.

Should the powder-to-suds cleaners fail to eradicate stains as stubborn as lipstick, most car-makers—as well as the makers of fabric-detailing products—have available a variety of solvent-type liquid cleaners.

If the lipstick stain is small, test a tiny quarter-inch place, using a cotton swab gingerly dipped (not soaked) in a solvent cleaner. If the fluid won't work on a quarter inch of the lipstick stain, it won't work on any of it. And, frankly, you're probably stuck with the stain.

If, on the other hand, your quarter-inch solvent test significantly or completely removes the stain, use a little of the solvent cleaner on a clean cloth (a piece of cheesecloth works best). Begin at the outside of the stain and gently, without excessive pressure, work inward to the center.

Working from the outside in minimizes accumulation of fluid at the stain's outer edges and thus reduces the chance of the stain "bleeding." Even if you succeed in removing the lipstick, you may create a ring which only a thorough washing of the entire area (seat cushion or seatback) will wholly remove.

Crayons (wax). Wax-type crayon stains are removed much like lipstick.

Oil, grease, butter, margarine, vegetable oil, cosmetic creams. After you have scraped off or otherwise removed the residue, blot lightly with a clean paper towel, taking up the remaining visible residue. Then use a solvent-type fabric cleaner as in "Lipstick," above, carefully working from the outside in. After each solvent application, blot with a clean paper towel. Continue the removal treatment until the visible stain is gone and no more stain is picked up by the blotter.

Road tar and asphalt. These two are difficult to remove and even harder to prevent from permanently staining fabric. One problem: the solvent-type fabric cleaner, which is used on these substances as for "lipstick," dissolves tar and asphalt, risking "bleeding" into adjacent areas. One way to prevent or minimize bleeding is to blot frequently as you work, blotting up with clean paper towels any tar or asphalt dissolved by the cleaner.

Chewing gum. Generally, removing the gum itself solves the problem, unless it's colorful bubble gum, which can stain unless promptly treated. First, use ice cubes to harden the gum. Then as the gum hardens, scrape it from the fabric with a dull knife. A little solvent-type fabric cleaner makes the process easier and, used ahead of your knife and after it, usually removes all gum remnants.

Shoe polish (wax and paste types; see "Water-soluble inks and polishes," below).   The procedure described above under "Lipstick" usually works for wax and paste shoe polishes.

Coffee (with cream).   The procedure for removing coffee with cream is similar to that described above under "Lipstick"—with some differences. Coffee stains generally cover more fabric area because more substance is usually spilled—say, half a cup of coffee rather than merely a dab of lipstick or a wad of chewing gum. After the solvent/cleaner procedure and a thorough blotting of the last lingering evidence of the cream-laden coffee spill, a ring is often visible. In that case, the entire seat or seatback must be scrubbed with a mild soap solution, blotted, rinsed with clean lukewarm water, and then blotted some more. Finally, the area should be spot-dried with a hair dryer (some plug into the car's cigarette lighter; use an extension cord if yours does not).

When using a hair dryer, hold the nozzle far enough from the fabric to prevent scorching. To test the dryer's heat, lay your hand flat on the fabric and turn on the dryer. Increase the nozzle's distance until you feel heat, but not extreme heat, on your hand. Slower drying is better than permanently disfigured fabric.

Nongreasy stains

Scrape or blot away the nongreasy residue. Sponge the area with cool water, then blot semi-dry with clean paper towels. If the stain disappears without leaving a ring, carefully dry the still-moist area with a hair dryer (as noted above, some plug into the car's cigarette lighter; if yours does not, use an extension cord).

If remnants of the stain (or its odor) remain, one of the two procedures outlined below can probably help, depending on the nongreasy substance (as discussed on the following pages):

Use a foam-type fabric cleaner such as those available at some dealerships. Mixed with water, as directed on the label, the powder cleanser produces a suds-like foam. Using a clean sponge, spread the suds over the stain area. Don't rub vigorously or saturate the fabric.

When the stain disappears, remove surplus suds with the sponge, then rinse with a clean sponge and water. Wipe up and blot any remaining moisture with a slightly damp paper towel. Immediately dry with a moderate heat source: heat lamp, hair dryer, or air hose. Finally, merge the treated place and surrounding fabric by rubbing gently over the entire fabric area with a clean, slightly dampened soft cloth.

Some spray-on upholstery cleaner/protectors formulated for de-staining cloth or velour auto fabric deposit a fabric protector after the stain has been removed.

Use mild neutral soap or dishwashing detergent and water, followed, if necessary, by judicious use of cleaning fluid or a solvent-type cleaner/spot lifter. Blot the stain with paper towels and dry with a hair dryer or other gentle heat or air source.

Although you have removed the stain, an odor may linger (particularly if the stain was from urine or vomit). If so, after blotting up most of the moisture, and before final forced-heat or air drying, apply a deodorizing mix of baking soda and warm (not hot) water (for example, 1 teaspoon of baking soda mixed in 1 cup of lukewarm water). Apply the mix with a sponge and allow it to remain on the affected area for about a minute. Wipe up the residue with a clean sponge moistened slightly with water. Repeat if necessary. Then rinse the area using a sponge and warm water, blot up excess moisture, and apply heat to dry.

Ammonia and water acts as both an odor-destroyer and acid neutralizer, especially on urine stains. The mix: 5 parts water and 1 part household (colorless) ammonia. Avoid lemon-scented ammonia because of its color.

Coffee (black).   Use a foam-type cleaner, as described above, with lukewarm water. Unless coffee is the heavy-residue "Turkish" type, follow directions above. Either procedure should remove black coffee stains.

Catsup.   Gently rub stain with cold water. Use neutral soap or dishwashing detergent, if necessary. Be sure your cloth is clean. Keep switching to a clean place on the cloth rather than wiping over the stain place with a catsup-stained section. When the stain is removed, blot and air or heat dry.

Mustard.   Mustard produces one of the harder stains to get rid of because its usually intense color acts like a dye. First, scrape off the residue; then sponge the stain with warm water. Use neutral soap or dishwashing detergent for the most stubborn mustard stains. Blot dry.

Fruit juice, soft drinks, wine, fruit, egg.   Treatment for all of these nongreasy stains is similar. Remove by following directions for using a foam-type fabric cleaner, above. Do not use soap and water, which may set the stain. If the foam cleaner does not remove all the stain, you may also need to use a solvent-type cleaner. Red wine stains, like those from colored soft drinks and egg yolk, are obviously more troublesome and time-consuming to remove than, say, white wine or colorless soft drink stains. Intensely colored stains in this group may need to be treated with a solvent-type cleaner in order to get them to do a total disappearance act.

Urine. Sponge with a lukewarm suds mix (water and suds), then rinse in cold water. Follow this with an ammonia/water mix, applied with a sponge or clean cloth. Let the ammonia and water (see mix formula directions for using mild neutral soap, above) "work" on the stain place for at least one minute. Finally, rinse with a clean, water-wetted cloth or sponge. Blot and heat dry.

Vomit. Vomit sometimes produces a nasty, hard-to-remove stain. After removing residue, sponge with cold water. Follow with a mild soap and warm water wash. Then apply the deodorizing baking soda/water mix (see mix formula directions, above). Conclude with a cold-water sponge rinse. If any stain remains, use a solvent-type cleaner or cleaning fluid. Finally, use a sponge to rinse with cold water, then blot and air/heat dry.

Blood. Do not use soap or hot water on blood. They will set the stain, perhaps permanently. Use nothing but cold water. Soak and rub the area with a clean cloth or sponge soaked in cold water. Keep turning the cloth to a clean place and use clean cold water each time. When the stain is removed, blot and dry.

Combination stains

Ice cream. As you might suppose, chocolate ice cream stains are harder to remove than vanilla and other less colorful ice creams.

Apply hot water on a clean cloth. If stain persists, wash with a warm neutral soap suds solution, followed by a cold, clean water rinse. Dry or let dry. Any remaining stain can usually be gotten rid of with a few dabs of solvent-type cleaner.

Candy (non-chocolate). Rub gently with a clean cloth soaked in hot water. Let dry. Any remaining stain can be erased with gentle dabs of cleaning fluid, using a clean cloth.

Candy (chocolate). Use the same stain-obliterating technique described for non-chocolate candy. In the final cleaning fluid step, continue applying the fluid and blotting with paper towels or an absorbent dry cloth until all stain remnants are blotted up.

Stains from unknown source. Clean with cool water, blot, and dry. Solvent-type cleaner, applied after stain area dries, will usually remove any remaining stain.

Ballpoint pen ink. Stains produced by a ballpoint pen are among the most difficult to remove from auto upholstery (or any other kind of fabric). Sponge-wet with cool water, then with cool water and detergent; follow with a cool water rinse. Persistent ballpoint marks can sometimes be removed with rubbing alcohol applied with a damp, clean cloth.

If that fails, try a solvent-type cleaning fluid. The risk with ballpoint marks is that the ink, liquefied by the various treatment liquids, will spread to the adjacent fabric. One way to minimize potential spreading is by blotting thoroughly (using super-absorbent paper towels) after each application of water, alcohol, or cleaning fluid.

Sometimes all techniques fail, and the fabric is indelibly ink-stained. Much depends on the type of ink.

Water-soluble inks and polishes. Some inks and a few polishes are water-soluble, and they disappear with only a careful cool water treatment, followed by blotting and air or forced drying.

By contrast, ball pens or markers that use indelible ink may, whatever your treatment, stain indelibly.

Today's auto fabrics are often sprayed at the factory with a water- and oil-repellent protectant. Once a fabric stain area is thoroughly dry (seldom in less than a day's time, longer in humid weather and regardless of apparent surface drying by heat or air), renew its factory protection with a quick spray application of a good fabric protector (see appendix).

Only your garage mechanic will know. Not many others, in the entire life of your car, will ever lift the hood to see whether you maintain a tidy engine compartment. Why, then, the considerable effort to detail underhood to keep it looking factory-new?

For one thing, cleanliness underhood increases your car's value when it's time to trade in. You can bet that the sales lot car buyer will look under the hood—most likely it will be among the first places he or she looks when evaluating your car as a trade-in and future sale.

But long before you trade, a clean engine compartment pays dividends and can save you repair bills. And even your life. With things tidy underhood, problems are easier to spot before they become big problems. You can spot a drip in the radiator before it becomes a gusher. Or the first signs of engine belt wear. Or the telltale oozing of oil leaking from beneath an engine gasket.

In fact, it's not unusual for a mechanic to insist on having an engine steam-cleaned before he or she will attempt to sleuth a problem to its source. Take, for example, a power steering fluid leak. In a grimy engine, the mechanic may not be able to pinpoint the trouble source even when the leak's so persistent that you have to fill the steering unit reservoir every few days or so.

Simply to stay on the road is reason enough—owner pride and detailed good looks aside—to tidy things underhood.

Unmasking dangers underhood

Sometimes hidden leaks (hidden when an engine and its environs are dirty) can go dangerously undetected. Gasoline leaking from the carburetor is an example of such a leak.

If you commute the freeways, you've probably been amazed to hear the traffic monitors on the radio report a car fire almost every time you tune in. As most drivers, you probably never realized that so many cars catch fire during the daily commute. Well, they do. The National Highway Traffic Safety Administration (NHTSA) reports there are three non-collision fires per 1000 cars per year in the United States. With something like 176.5 million cars and light trucks on the road at last count, that's an average of 53,000 non-accident vehicle fires which flare spontaneously each year on our highways and streets. Some result in deaths; almost all cause serious vehicle damage or total destruction.

Cautions an NHTSA spokesman, "A contributing factor (to auto fires) is the higher temperature that exhaust systems now run, which makes gasoline, oil, and antifreeze fires more likely than in the past. People need to realize that antifreeze can burn. But so, of course, can gasoline and oil."

CHAPTER 6

Under the Hood: Making It Look Factory-New

"Total" versus "visual" engine detailing

Underhood detailing involves some decisions and compromises: Should you do a total underhood detailing, which involves virtually every engine compartment part? Or should you settle for a "visual detailing"—a detailing of only those parts readily visible when you lift the hood?

Having made that decision, you have others: Should you have your car's engine steam-cleaned at a local car wash? Rent a steam-cleaning machine (available at most rental lots) and do it yourself? Steam-clean it at a do-it-yourself coin-op wash? You can also opt to skip the steam and instead chemically degrease the engine and its accessories with any of numerous solvents, either with one of the handy spray-on degreasers available at auto supply stores or with kerosene, which is just as effective.

The basic decision—a total engine compartment detailing versus a visual engine compartment detailing—may depend on the model of car you drive. A quick look beneath your car's hood shows why there's any need for a decision at all.

Older cars have relatively few accessories, besides the engine, underhood. Most are relatively easy to reach with solvents or steam. However, if your car is a late model, the engine compartment is most likely jam-packed with accessories—and many of them are layered, hidden beneath yet more accessories.

A *total engine detailing* reaches and cleans—and treats or repaints—most engine parts, including the engine itself, the hoses, the wiring, the firewall (the part of the car body that separates the engine and passenger compartments), and even the sound-absorbing and insulating/fireproofing material on the hood's underside. Jam-packed parts and major assemblies are all but impossible to reach unless most parts are removed for detailing, which is something the most fastidious of detailers do.

For most owners of late-model vehicles, a *visual detailing*—detailing only those parts and engine compartment areas readily visible when you lift the hood—will do.

Steam or chemical cleaning

Should you steam-clean or chemically clean the engine? One shortcut to detailing is to have the engine compartment cleaned commercially (most carwashes have steam-clean facilities). Or you can steam-clean it yourself with a rental steam unit or do it at a handy, low-cost, self-service steam bay. Once the engine has been steam-cleaned, you can set about the job of final-detailing the engine and its various assemblies.

If you steam-clean the engine yourself at a steam-clean place (rather than using a rental steamer at home) you may wind up doing some things twice. Parts of the engine (such as electrical connections, underhood electronics, and, especially, spark plugs) that you mask or protect in some other way from solvents, steam, and water will have to be unmasked to allow you to drive home safely and then remasked and re-protected if, during finish-detailing at home, you decide to repaint the engine and some of its parts. Then, again, you may decide to take your chances and hardly mask at all (see "Is Engine Masking Really Necessary?" later in this chapter).

And there's yet another point worth considering. Commercial or do-it-yourself steam-cleaning has one drawback which may afflict older engines—engines that have been driven, say, 25,000 miles or more. The original engine paint, repeatedly subjected to searing engine heat, often peels off under the twin cleaning attacks of steam and high pressure. Result: like it or not, you have to repaint the engine.

Kerosene, any number of spray-on engine cleaners, all-purpose cleaners, and even plain soap and water all do an excellent job in detailing underhood. They tend to degrease the engine and its components, rather than strip them of paint. When you chemically clean underhood (rather than steam clean), repainting is minimized.

But chemical cleaning, without an assist from steam, also has its disadvantages: (1) more time and work are involved; (2) even spray-on chemical cleaners seldom reach and clean the hidden places with the same thoroughness of high-pressure steam; and (3) it's a dirtier job. After all, if it's been steam-cleaned first, you begin detailing with a degreased engine compartment. With chemicals, you do the degreasing largely by hand. That, in itself, poses an environmental problem. Driveway detailing, involving engine degreasing, is illegal in some areas—unless, of course, you have some way of disposing of grease, solvents, and oily wastewater other than letting them drain to the curb.

Once thoroughly detailed, the engine and its accessories won't likely need a second go-around for a year, at least, and perhaps even longer. One way to stretch out the time between underhood detailing treatments is simply to wipe up any spills—oil, anti-freeze, transmission and power steering fluid, battery acid, and the like—as they occur. If you do that, plus wipe the engine and visible components clean every now and then with a warm detergent and water solution, an all-purpose cleaner/degreaser, or kerosene (if there's a particularly grimy place), you can put "underhood" at the bottom of your "Detailing—things to do" list.

1 ▶ 2 ▶ 3

S T E P - B Y - S T E P :

Detailing Underhood

Time required: *2:00*

    2 hours (includes 30 minutes for masking and wet-proofing)

‼ C A U T I O N : Use extreme care in handling and working with inflammable products (as petroleum-based engine cleaners), spray-on products (which can be harmful if sprayed or blown into your face or eyes), and products that are potentially harmful if inhaled (such as ammonia or ammonia-based products).

Fig. 6.1 *Many self-service engine-cleaning bays have degreasing-solvent dispensers with long nozzles.*

‼ CAUTION : Don't warm the engine if your car has a turbocharged or high-performance engine. The fast-revving turbocharger can become extremely hot even with the engine idling. Wetting or spraying a hot turbocharger can cause serious damage, including warping and cracking.

‼ CAUTION : Never use spray-on paints or degreasers in a closed-in area in which there is any danger of a stove or furnace pilot light—or any flame—igniting the product's fumes or spray. Also, don't smoke or permit anyone else to smoke nearby when you are using such products.

Materials needed:
  towels, drop cloths, rags, or diapers
  spray paint (optional) for most accessories
  high-temperature spray paint for the engine and parts subject to extreme heat (see box)
  masking materials (plastic kitchen bags, masking tape, duct tape, aluminum foil, plastic wrap, towels, etc.)

The first job is to rid the engine and engine compartment of grease and oil—that is, to get down to metal and insulation (on wiring).

Steps:
1. Begin by warming the engine. Let it idle for about five minutes. A warm (not hot) engine cleans easier than a cold one. In addition to the turbocharger (see **CAUTION**), the headers on high-performance engines (which become extremely hot even at normal engine-operating temperatures) can also be damaged by water or solvents. The headers/valve covers on a V-engine are the two long covers, one atop either "V" of the engine, that protect the engine's valves. On most other engines, a brief warmup speeds detailing.
2. Idling concluded, turn off the ignition. With the engine warm and the hood open, protect the surrounding body paint. Towels, drop cloths, rags, or diapers (the latter favored by many pro-detailers), laid all around the engine compartment and covering the fenders and other painted body metal to a width of about a foot, isolate your detailing area from the rest of the car. Water-wetting the toweling helps keep it in place.
3. Remove the air cleaner (which usually hides a lot of the engine) and put it aside. (You can clean it later. It will probably also benefit from a quick-dry spray painting. The spray paint color: invariably, black.)
4. Next, cover and wet-proof all engine parts and compartment accessories that should not be wetted: the distributor and its cap, the alternator, spark plugs and their wire harness connections, electronic boxes, the carburetor intake (now that the air cleaner has been removed), electrical junction boxes, headlight connections (if they protrude into the engine compartment), and anything else that looks as if it shouldn't be wetted.

If you don't care to do much wet-proofing, at the very least wet-proof the distributor cap and the carburetor inlet pipe (which was exposed when you removed the air cleaner).

Handy for wet-proofing are those little plastic bags commonly used for sandwiches. They slip easily over the open throat of the carburetor, around the alternator and electronic boxes. Use their own plastic or metal ties to seal and hold them in place. Or doubly seal out wetness with masking or, better, duct tape. Some engine components can be adequately wet-proofed with aluminum foil, kitchen plastic wrap, or even towels.

Actually, the hardest components to wet-proof are the spark plugs, which is one reason even some pro-detailers nix wet-proofing them (see "Prepping It: Detailing's All-Important First Steps," in Chapter 2).

One way to make quick work of wet-proofing spark plugs is to shape an aluminum foil barrier around each plug, then overlay the foil with two or three layers of towels or diapers. Or you can disconnect the electrical harness wire to each plug, and fit (and tape) a little plastic bag around each plug. But be absolutely sure you number each harness wire and the corresponding spark plug to which it belongs. To do this, wrap a piece of masking tape around the end of each harness wire and, using a waterproof, indelible marker, number it to correspond with the number you've marked (with the same marker) on its particular spark plug watershield. If there's one big "no-no" in engine detailing it's pulling all the spark plug wires (4, 5, 6, 8, 12, or even 16 of them, depending on the number of cylinders the engine has), and not knowing, when you're ready to reconnect them, to which plugs they belong.

1▶2▶3

STEP-BY-STEP:

Chemical Cleaning (A "Visual" Engine Cleaning)

Time required: *1:00*
> 20–60 minutes (done manually, not at a coin-op place)

Materials needed:
> detergent and water or any spray-on engine degreaser solvents (see box), kerosene, or a general-purpose degreasing cleaner (if you're degreasing the engine at a coin-op steam bay, solvents, soapy water, steam, and final rinse water, dispensed by a nozzle-like "wand," are yours at the flip of a selector switch)
> chrome cleaner for polishing chrome engine parts
> cleaning mitt to keep your hands clean, but which also serves as a cleaning tool; lots of rags
> hard-bristled brush (or special engine-cleaning brush, if your engine is very grimy)
> scouring pads and/or household steel wool and soap pads, or double-0 (00) or triple-0 (000) steel wool
> hair dryer or vacuum cleaner (set to exhaust an airstream, not ingest air and particles), for final engine and component drying
> toothbrush, for working cleaning agent into crevices and hard-to-reach places
> spray bottle, for spraying nonaerosol cleaning solutions, as detergent and water

Depending on how dirty the engine is, you can start "strong" (with an aerosol-sprayed degreasing solvent or with kerosene) or "mild" (with a detergent and water mix

---

Engine Cleaners/Degreasers
Auto Wax Motor Degreaser
Berryman B-33 Engine Cleaner
Car Brite All-Purp (water based engine cleaner)
Car Brite 10,10,10-The Perfect One
CSA Biodegradable Engine Cleaner
Cyclo Engine Clean
Gunk
KleanStroke All Purpose Cleaner
McKay Clear Magic
McKay Motor Shine
Mechanics Engine Degreaser
Mechanics Heavy Duty Degreaser and Cleaner
OxiSolv Degreaser & Rust Remover
PRO Engine Degreaser
PRO Red Devil Degreaser
Simple Green
3M Engine Degreaser
Turtle Wax Engine Cleaner
Ultra Shine Tar Remover & Motor Degreaser
Varsol Engine Cleaner

or with a nontoxic, nonabrasive, nonflammable general-purpose degreasing and cleaning product).

Use specific cleaners for specific components. A number of engine compartment components are best and easiest cleaned with specific cleaners and cleaning tools:

- Engine and particularly grimy parts should be treated with a degreasing solvent, then scrubbed with steel wool or a scouring pad. For grimiest places, use a stiff-bristled engine-cleaning brush or a long-handled scrub brush.
- Plastic parts, such as windshield washer or radiator reservoirs, come clean with mild cleaner and a scrubbing pad, even if the parts are stained.
- Hoses, wiring, and vent pipes can often be most effectively cleaned with household cleaner/degreasers.

Work systematically. Whatever cleaner you use, work systematically:

Steps:

1. Clean the underside of the hood first—but with caution. This area is usually cleaned first, if at all, because any removed dirt and grime will drip onto the engine and its components. Some detailers choose to clean the hood's underside last—so *they* won't be dripped on during engine cleaning. To avoid drips, once you've cleaned the underside, let things stand awhile. This will give the underside area time to dry, eliminating the drip problem.

    You should clean the underside of your car's hood only if its insulation/fire-retardant material is cleanable (see "Prepping It: Detailing's All-Important First Steps," in Chapter 2). Some underhood linings should not be cleaned and don't clean well. If in doubt, test a small area of the material. If it cleans easily and the cleaning does not affect the material's bond to the underhood, it is safe to clean.

2. With the same engine degreasing solvents or all-purpose cleaner, clean the removed air cleaner housing, readying it for replacement once the engine and its accessories have been detailed. Once clean and thoroughly dry, the housing often benefits from a quick, spray-on painting. For this step-by-step how-to of painting the engine and its components, see "Repainting Underhood," in Chapter 12.

3. If necessary, remove other engine compartment accessories—the fewer the better.

Some detailers remove the battery, not to prevent its wetting (batteries generally love water), but to (1) clean the casing and clamps and (2) clean and possibly repaint the battery box or whatever it is that holds the battery.

To remove the battery, loosen the battery cable clamp bolts with a wrench and remove the clamps. Lift out the battery and set it aside. Neutralize any corrosion around the battery posts and clamps with a slurry of 50% baking soda and 50% water. Use a steel-bristled brush to remove

> **! ! C A U T I O N :** Follow all the directions on a product's label carefully. Product manufacturers want their products to work for you and your car because they want you to become a repeat buyer. Label directions aim to make the product perform as well as it can for you, so it pays to follow the manufacturer's step-by-step instructions.

what corrosion remains. Any good all-purpose cleaner cleans the battery's case.

The battery box, which usually remains in the engine compartment, gets the same degreasing/soaping/rinse treatment as the engine and other accessories. It, too, often deserves a spray-on repainting.

Total Engine Compartment Detailing

Start at the radiator and work entirely around the engine compartment. Many detailers leave the engine, itself, to do last.

Spray the degreasing solvent or a detergent and water mix (1 part dishwashing detergent to 1 part warm water) or full-strength mild cleaner successively on engine parts, then rinse with a controlled spray from a garden hose. Do a little at a time: spray with cleaner; scrub the part with a cloth, triple-0 (000) steel wool, a scouring pad, synthetic scuff pad, or your cleaning mitt; then rinse with water.

Clean and rinse one small section at a time. You'll do a more thorough job and will be better able to control and limit the amount of rinse water you need. To avoid wetting parts and connections you've sealed in plastic, use as little rinse water as possible.

Wires, hoses, and hard-to-reach places

As you go, clean wires, cables, linkages, and hoses, and work the solvent (kerosene works fine) or cleaner into the dirtiest places—for example, brackets which support various engine parts, areas near the engine oil and transmission fluid fill pipes, and parts and accessories installed deep within the engine compartment.

Wires and hoses are cleaned by grasping them lightly with a cleaner-wetted rag and running the rag their entire length. Some hoses—the radiator's lower hose, for one—are admittedly hard to reach. To clean the radiator's lower hose, spray it with cleaner, then scrub it top, underside, and all around with a long-handled brush (a toilet brush is used by some detailers). Where grime has collected in recesses and where parts bolt to the engine or compartment, use a stiff-bristled brush and toothbrush, wetted with cleaner, to remove the grime.

Pay attention to details. Clean all engine attachments, including their bolts, and the front of the engine (belting, thermostat well, pulleys and their hubs, the fan's blades, and, of course, the radiator and its grille).

Cleaning some areas will stretch your ingenuity. For example, a baby bottle brush, dipped in solvent or cleaner, gets into the individual cells of the radiator grille. To clean around bolts, wrap a dull knife or screwdriver in a solvent-wetted cloth and work it all around a bolt. A toothbrush and solvent gets into crevices and "wells" on the front of the engine.

Another handy tool, used wet (solvent-soaked) or dry (for getting at dirt before you apply solvent or detergent-cleaner), is a 2-inch-wide nylon-bristled paintbrush trimmed so that the bristles are only 1 to 1½ inches long. Trim them with a sharp knife or scissors.

The same cleaning routine applies to the engine itself. Spray on a controlled amount of solvent or detergent/cleaner. Scrub dirtiest areas with a cloth, your cleaning mitt, or a soft-bristled brush. Where parts—including the engine, headers, engine bolts, and spark plug harness guide—are *unpainted*, use the cleaner and triple-0 (000) steel wool. Also effective on unpainted underhood parts are household steel wool and soap pads, but *do not use these pads on chromed engines or their parts.* Their steel wool is too aggressive (abrasive). Instead, use a chrome cleaner/polish (the same as you use for exterior chrome). Or, use very fine steel wool, as 00 or 000, and a detergent/cleaner. Whatever the cleaner, use a toothbrush to work into crevices the larger brush can't reach.

Special detailing for super-dirty engines

Extremely dirty engines—as those which have never or seldom been detailed—may need a final cleaning with kerosene or any of the spray-on engine solvent/cleaners (see box). Makers of most of these cleaners recommend that the cleaner be applied to a warm, but not hot, engine.

On dirtiest engines, you may have to do two complete degreasings, followed by rinsing.

Using the engine to dry itself

With the engine and its compartment components clean, you can now unseal the carburetor inlet, spark plugs (if you protected them), and the distributor cap, and replace the air cleaner and spark plug wires. Sop up any puddled water with a terry towel or absorbent cloths. A household vacuum cleaner used as a blower can reach, and blow out, puddles not reachable by towels. Then start the engine. Let it idle 10–15 minutes, or until the engine and engine compartment are thoroughly dry. Figure 20 minutes, tops, for engine heat, circulated by the engine's fan, to dry the engine compartment.

Finish-detailing underhood

Shut off the engine and let it cool. With things underhood cool, consider spray-painting what obviously needs repainting (see "Repainting Underhood," in Chapter 12).

The finish-detailing—polishing parts, including chromed parts, that can be shined; getting at the last bit of dirt; brightening wiring with fine steel wool, followed by a treatment with a vinyl/rubber protectant (see appendix)—is time-consuming but simple. The good looks of many engine parts can be restored using merely metal or chrome cleaner or any of the extremely fine steel wools (double-0 [00] to quadruple-0 [0000]).

Alternator. Clean the alternator with an all-purpose cleaner. Use the cleaner sparingly so as not to drip cleaner into the alternator's electrical works. Then polish with 00 or 000 grade steel wool. Finish-detail with a polishing wax (the same one you used on the car's finish) or, if the alternator is unpainted, with a chrome/metal polish (see appendix).

Wiring, hoses, and linkages (which are the metal rods that operate various components, such as the carburetor). Clean with all-purpose cleaner or solvent or with a specialized cleaner. Polish with 00 or 000 steel wool; finish-detail with a coating of protectant (see appendix).

Belting. Degrease the belts and finish-detail with steel wool.

Radiator and its grille. Finish-detailing prescribes a spray-repainting—unless the radiator is chromed—for most radiators and their grilles. The painting involves just a few spray-can passes with high-temperature engine paint (usually black, and usually flat black rather than gloss).

‖ CAUTION: Never use spray-on paints or degreasers in a closed-in area in which there is any danger of a stove or furnace pilot light—or any flame—igniting the product's fumes or spray. Also, don't smoke or permit anyone else to smoke nearby when you are using such products.

Far more time-consuming is the preparation: the radiator is, so to speak, out in the open, not confined to the engine compartment as are most other parts. Moreover, it is usually the largest repainting job (in terms of area) done in detailing, which generally confines painting to small-area touch-ups.

The entire hood and fender areas around the radiator must be scrupulously masked (newspaper and masking tape work well). Anything less risks disastrous overspray. And with the radiator and its grille, in particular, don't spray if there's so much as a whiff of breeze. Any breeze at all risks overspraying.

Firewall and tops of wheel wells. While some detailers spray-repaint the firewall and the tops of wheel wells where they protrude into the engine compartment, both areas usually look almost as good if they are simply polished and waxed—assuming, of course, they were degreased during the cleaning phase of engine-compartment detailing. Use the same polish and wax you used on the car's exterior finish.

Should you decide to paint them, the masking,

‖ CAUTION: Don't use protectants on belts or pulleys: it tends to make them slippery.

which should be done scrupulously, can be tedious, especially for the hard-to-reach, component-packed firewall. But to simply spray paint over a galaxy of wall-mounted components is a "no-no" in detailing. To detail the firewall properly, if you've decided to paint it, *every* component must be masked, so that you paint only the firewall itself.

!! CAUTION: Never, never spray the engine compartment or any of its components with a clear lacquer, as some do-it-yourself (and even a few pro) detailers have done. Lacquer or similar finishes may look great, but drive a few miles and (1) the gleam melts with heat, as may the lacquer; (2) the once-clear lacquer begins to yellow; (3) your risk of having an underhood fire is greatly increased.

Hood underside. Depending on the sound insulation/fire-retardant material on the hood's underside, finish-detailing can be as simple as doing nothing to it or polishing/waxing it. Generally, the hood's underside should not be painted. Painting can reduce, if not defeat, the material's reason for being there. It is there to deaden engine noise, and sometimes also to help fireproof. Painting negates both purposes. If the material is cleanable without debonding it from the hood, do the finish-detailing with an all-purpose cleaner.

With the underhood detailed and its factory-new look restored, you'll smile with satisfaction every time you lift the hood. Probably you'll even convince yourself—and who's to say it's not true—that a clean engine has more guts and go.

1 ▶ 2 ▶ 3

STEP-BY-STEP:

How to Steam-Degrease the Engine

Time required: *0:10*
  10 minutes, using coin-op equipment

Materials needed:
  solvents, sudsy water, steam, rinse water (dispensed by coin-op "wand")
  cloths, towels
  engine brush
  toothbrush

Steam/engine-degreasing bays at many coin-op self-service wash places give you about 5 minutes for your money ($1.50–$2.00, a bargain considering that commercial steam-cleaners charge $35–$75 for the job). In your allotted time you degrease the engine compartment with spray-on solvent, rinse with sudsy water or steam, or both, and do a final rinse with clear, usually warm, water.

Don't expect to thoroughly steam-degrease the engine and its accessories in just 5 minutes. At minimum, figure on feeding the coin slot twice, giving you 10 minutes for the entire job, from start to clear-rinse finish. Or, you can take a shortcut by letting the steam be the final rinse. Either way, you've got to work fast to get your money's worth and end up with a clean engine compartment.

Here is one scenario for using steam/engine-degreasing bay time—10 minutes in all. Note that most of the time is allotted to degreasing with the solvent. In most

Fig. 6.2 Degrease an engine compartment that's as jam-packed and high-tech as this one? You can—and a self-service engine-cleaning bay makes the job easier, quicker, and cleaner. Here, a car owner meticulously searches out deep-down grime and directs the nozzle of the solvent gun where it's needed.

coin-op steam bays, there is one "wand" (a long-handled spray nozzle) and a control panel that lets you select what the nozzle delivers—the choices usually are solvent, soapy water, steam, and clear rinse water. The scenario begins with the assumption that you've masked those parts of the engine and its accessories that require protection against solvent, steam, and water.

Coin-Op Bay Steam Degreasing

Cleaner	Minutes	Procedure
1. Solvent	2	Spray solvent over the engine, engine components, and the entire engine compartment. Don't use solvent on the underhood insulation/fire-retardant material unless you have tested it and know it can withstand solvent.
2. Solvent	2	Apply solvent specifically to those parts and deep recesses still caked with oil/grease/grime. You may have to work up close to see and reach these persistently grimy places.
3. Soaking	2	Let engine stand while solvent "works."
4. Soap	1	Spray the engine, engine compartment, and underhood insulation/fire-retardant material with sudsy soap solution.
5. Steam	2	Steam-clean the engine compartment, including engine and accessories. Do not steam-clean underhood insulation unless you are sure it can withstand steam.
6. Rinse	1	Rinse with clear-water spray, if available. If not, continue steam treatment until coin-clock shuts off system.
	10 minutes	

Remove protective covers and plastic from engine parts. Replace the air cleaner assembly. Start the engine and let it idle 5 minutes to dry the engine and compartment. Where water remains puddled, sop up with rags or paper towels; or extract with wet-dry vacuum or extractor; or blow dry with a hair dryer or a household vacuum operated in blower mode.

Next, polish chrome or painted parts. If they appear to need it, consider spray-painting most visible painted parts, such as the engine, the air cleaner, and the battery box. Remember, any paint used underhood should be the high-temperature type, capable of withstanding at least 1000°F. This is especially true for paint used for the engine and its on-engine accessories (such as the air cleaner assembly). (See "Repainting Underhood," in Chapter 12, for details.)

Fig. 6.3 After routing out grime and dirt with spray-on solvent, give engine and compartment a restrained suds-and-water dousing.

Fig. 6.4 Hit especially dirty places with well-aimed sudsy water, trying to avoid electrical components that might be vulnerable to wetting. Your best bet is to protect electrical parts before you begin washing the engine.

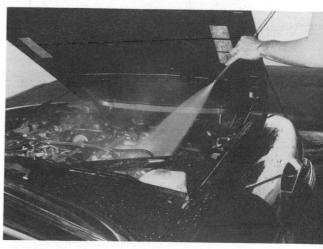

Fig. 6.5 Finally, rinse with clear water.

Engine Cleaners/Degreasers
Auto Wax Motor Degreaser
Berryman B-33 Engine Cleaner
Car Brite All-Purp (water based engine
    cleaner)
Car Brite 10,10,10-The Perfect One
CSA Biodegradable Engine Cleaner
Cyclo Engine Clean
Gunk
KleanStroke All Purpose Cleaner
McKay Clear Magic
McKay Motor Shine
Mechanics Engine Degreaser
Mechanics Heavy Duty Degreaser and
    Cleaner
OxiSolv Degreaser & Rust Remover
PRO Engine Degreaser
PRO Red Devil Degreaser
Simple Green
3M Engine Degreaser
Turtle Wax Engine Cleaner
Ultra Shine Tar Remover & Motor De-
    greaser
Varsol Engine Cleaner

STEP-BY-STEP:

How to Use Spray-On Engine Degreasers

Time required: *0:45*

Materials needed:
    spray-on engine degreaser (see box)
    plastic film or metal foil (for masking)
    hard-bristled engine brush
    coin-op steam bay or sponge, all-purpose cleaner, and
      hose
    towels, rags

Degreasing is the first step in engine detailing. Engine-degreasing solvents now come in handy spray-on aerosol cans. There are many brands to choose from at auto supply stores (see box). Spray cans usually contain 16–18 ounces of solvent. While one can may get the job done on a relatively new, relatively clean engine, especially one that is regularly degreased, a grimy engine usually requires two cans.

Following is the spray-on degreasing procedure, step-by-step:

Steps:
1. Warm up the engine for 5 minutes. Then shut it off. Warm (not hot) engines are the easiest to clean.
2. Remove the air cleaner. With plastic film or metal foil, cover the carburetor's throat, the distributor, electronic "boxes," and, if possible, the spark plugs, to keep them dry.
3. Spray the solvent generously on the warm, dry engine. If the engine is particularly grimy and requires two aerosol cans of degreaser, spray the entire engine with the first can. With the second, spray particularly grime-caked or hard-to-reach areas.
4. Let the solvent "work" for 10 to 15 minutes. During this time, use a hard-bristled engine-degreasing brush

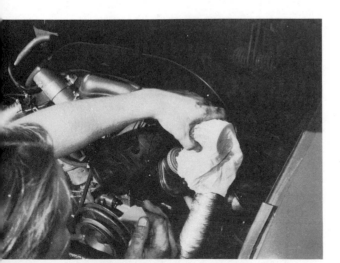

Fig. 6.6 Among vulnerable parts to mask on a small engine: air inlet, oil inlet, distributor, coil, voltage regulator, and spark plugs. With air cleaner removed, wrap plastic around the air inlet pipe.

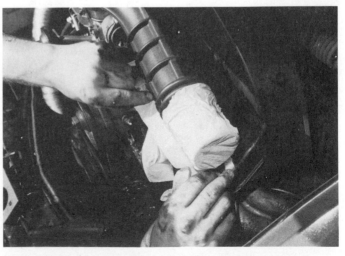

Fig. 6.7 Next, secure the plastic with masking tape to form a watertight cocoon.

Fig. 6.8 This photo shows an engine with the waterproofing nearly complete. The masking protects the air inlet, coil, and oil filler pipe.

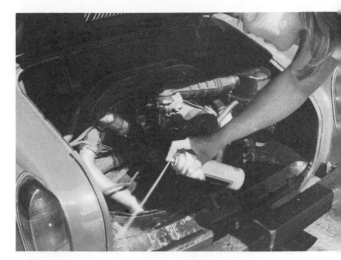

Fig. 6.10 Two cans of degreasing solvent are usually needed to detail even a small engine. Say veteran detailers: "One can wets it; two cans clean it."

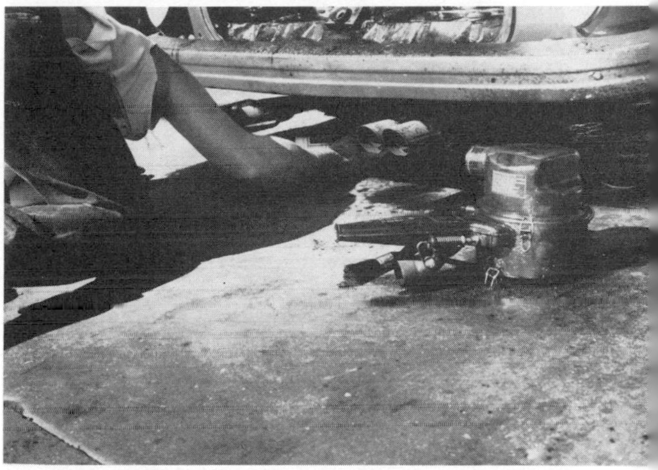

Fig. 6.9 Spray degreasing solvent liberally onto warm (not hot) engine and its grimy components.

Fig. 6.11 While waiting for solvent to work, start on some other degreasing chores, such as spraying solvent beneath the engine compartment.

to help get solvent to—and to help dislodge—the heaviest grease deposits. Don't hurry the job. The solvent needs time to soften and remove the grime.

5. If degreasing at a coin-op bay: Rinse engine, engine compartment, and removed components with a strong stream of water or steam. Steam is available at most self-service coin-op engine-degreasing bays. If soapy water is also pressure-dispensed at the coin-op bay you use, after degreasing the engine, thoroughly clean it with a strong stream of soapy water, then switch to clean rinse water or steam, or both.

Alternate 5. *If degreasing at home:* To remove the solvent and grime, rinse the engine with a sponge soaked in all-purpose cleaner, used full-strength. If the spray-on degreasing solvent has done an extremely effective grime-removal job, high-strength cleaners may be diluted: 1 ounce of cleaner to 8 ounces of water. If you have one of those garden hose attachments that

Fig. 6.12 Degreasing the air cleaner housing.

Fig. 6.13 If needed, give the engine a second sudsy water workover—and do some sudsing under-chassis, as well.

Fig. 6.14 Your deserved rewards: an engine compartment that practically sparkles. A pretty sight, but it is doubtful that a spanking clean engine runs cooler and better, as some pro-detailers claim.

penses garden chemicals you have an even better system at hand. Fill the dispenser with full-strength all-purpose cleaner. Rinse, using a medium spray. Hose water will automatically mix with, and dilute, the cleaner.

Finally, using the garden hose without its spray attachment, rinse thoroughly with cold water.

6. When the degreased engine has been thoroughly rinsed, remove the protective coverings from the carburetor, distributor, and other engine accessories. Replace the air cleaner. Immediately start the engine and let it idle for 15 minutes, or until the engine is dry. A warm engine dries itself best and quickest.

Immediately rinse any solvent overspray from body paint or chrome. If you use degreasing solvent at home, avoid parking the car on any surface affected by petroleum-based solvents (the basis for all of the degreasing aerosols). Do not degrease the engine if parked on asphalt, blacktop, or asphalt-painted surfaces; rubber or plastic tile; or other materials vulnerable to damage (often extensive) by petroleum-based solvents.

Is Engine Masking Really Necessary?

This chapter and most pro-detailers advise you to carefully wet-proof vulnerable engine parts before degreasing the engine compartment with steam or chemicals. But is such careful pre-cleaning protection *really* necessary?

Visits to a dozen coin-op engine cleaning places where car owners were steam-cleaning their engine compartments found that only one in ten bothered even to remove the engine's air cleaner, much less protect spark plugs or electrical-electronic parts against water and steam damage. Most, working against the clock (approximately 5 minutes for the entire engine cleanup, with a deposit of $1.50–$2.00 worth of coins), simply shut off the engine, lifted the hood, and began dousing the engine compartment first with a degreasing solvent, then with sudsy wash-water, and finally with a full-force steam or warm-water rinse. And all but one of the engines thus cleaned restarted on the first crank (and even that one got going after less than a minute of drying).

Do such everyday engine cleanup demonstrations debunk the recommendation of experts to protect vulnerable engine parts from water or chemical wetting?

No, they do not. Perhaps some of the sampled car owners were simply lucky. And maybe some of their cars' electricals sustained damage that, for the moment, went unnoticed—but which could severely shorten the useful lives of those components.

Pro-detailers are well aware that many do-it-yourselfers shortcut engine-component protection and masking. Comments one pro-detailer:

"The whole quick-cleaning process at the coin-op places is hurry up and wait. You wait in line, often, for an engine cleaning bay to open. When it does, there are a couple of other drivers behind you wanting you to hurry up and get done so they can do their cars. A lot of people faced with that kind of detailing pressure haven't the time, nor do most even remember, to protect chemical- and water-vulnerable engine parts. You can hardly blame them, considering the hurry to get with it. But you've got to ask yourself a question: did dousing it, unprotected, do any lasting damage?

"That's hard to say," he continues. "It's like failing to change engine oil frequently. Or using poor grade, cheap oil in a high-priced engine. Sure, engine life is shortened, maybe by thousands of miles. But the damage done seldom shows up for miles or years. By then, it's too late to repair the damage or really fix the blame."

Concludes another veteran pro-detailer, "Sometimes, of course, a neglected engine or neglect in protecting it when steam-cleaning or wetting shows up pretty quickly. If car owners don't do lasting damage by leaving critical parts exposed to steam and water, they're plain lucky . . . at least, for the moment. From my experience, not everybody is that lucky, for sure."

Some car underbellies are more street-visible than others. But even when the under-chassis isn't, it deserves periodic detailing to check for problems (as leaks, and muffler or tailpipe pinholes); prevent and correct rusting; get rid of accumulating grease, mud, dirt, and snow that can splatter and disfigure the car's exterior extremities; quiet road noise (perhaps with spray-on undercoat sealer and sound deadener); and paint what visibly needs repainting, as the often all-too-visible wheelwells (fenderwells).

Sunbelt cars may not need under-chassis detailing more often than once a year. But if you live in colder areas where road salt can corrode even chassis parts corrosion-proofed at the factory, some owner's manuals recommend far more frequent under-chassis snow and salt removal.

CHAPTER 7

Beneath the Chassis: Under-Car Cleanup

1 ▶ 2 ▶ 3

STEP-BY-STEP:

Detailing the Underbody

Time required: *1:00*
20–60 minutes
For this aspect of detailing, there is a dress code: the oldest clothes you have.

Materials needed:
  garden hose with a strong-stream nozzle
  degreasing solvent
  all-purpose cleaner
  putty knife (for scraping off grease and dirt)
  stiff-bristled brush
  spray-on paints:
    rust-proofing base coat
    rust-protective final coat
    high-temperature paint
    undercoat/sealer
  masking tape and masking paper (newspapers)
  steel wool (00 and 000)
  steel wool soap pads (household variety)
  car wax (100% carnauba)
  rags (many)

Getting beneath the chassis

Whether you merely hose beneath the chassis or steam-clean it, you are likely to encounter the problem of accessibility.

Although this option is seldom available to home detailers, ideally, you should raise the car on a lift and work beneath it, standing up. Some neighborhood gas stations rent "under-chassis accessibility time"—the use of their stationary (floor) or portable hydraulic lifts. Heavy-duty, 2-ton-capacity hydraulic jacks are also available, at rather modest cost, from some discount home centers. Having one or two in your home shop simplifies under-chassis detailing. When you're not detailing, you'll find other good uses for these handy lift-and-support tools.

‖ CAUTION: Protect your head and face. Wriggling under-chassis risks head bruises and bumps. And eye splatter, too. Protect your head with a stiff cap, your eyes with goggles or minimum-tint sunglasses.

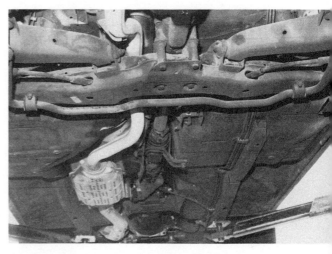

Fig. 7.1 Ideally, a car should be hoisted for under-chassis detailing.

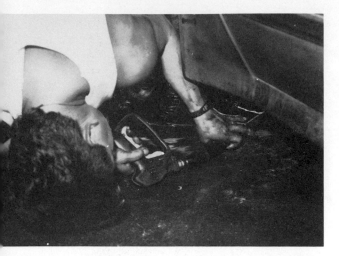

Fig. 7.2 One (dirty) way to detail the under-chassis. This do-it-yourselfer is using a self-service engine bay's steam gun.

‼ CAUTION : When cleaning under the chassis, do not rely on bumper jacks or any jack designed merely to raise a wheel while you change a flat.

Fig. 7.3 The jetstream at a self-service engine bay can wash a wheel well in a matter of seconds, ridding it of accumulated road dirt and debris.

Most home detailers settle for something considerably less, usually one of the following: (1) jack stands, one supporting each axle (you jack the car up, slip the stands beneath first one axle and then the other, and lower the car on them); (2) the curb as a kind of jack, first for the front wheels, later for the rears; (3) a "creeper," the 4-wheeled platform used by mechanics to work, prone, beneath a car ($12–$20 at auto supply stores); or (4) the classic wriggle underneath the car (a difficult and sometimes impossible maneuver if yours is a low-riding sports model).

Cleaning under the chassis

Although a garden hose is better than nothing, no amount of spraying with a garden hose, strong as the water stream may be, really equals steam-cleaning beneath the chassis. For steam-cleaning details, see "Step-by-Step: How to Steam-Degrease the Engine," in Chapter 6. The fastest, most efficient place to degrease, de-dirt, and de-salt under-chassis is at a coin-op degreasing bay. For your money ($1.50 and up), a steam bay usually dispenses, at your progressive selection and usually from the same nozzle ("wand"), (1) degreasing solvent, (2) high-pressure steam, (3) soapy warm water, and (4) clean, final-rinse water.

Steps:
1. Start degreasing the dirtiest places of the under-chassis: beneath engine and transmission, gearing, and all four wheelwells. Then give attention to shocks, the inside of bumpers, springs, frame members, and especially the inside of all four wheels.
2. Let the degreasing chemical work for a few minutes; then, with a putty knife and stiff-bristled brush, dislodge stubborn buildups of grease and dirt.
3. If you have soapy water at your disposal, douse the degreased area.
4. With the most obvious buildup removed, steam-clean or hose the entire under-chassis area. Doing it without wetting yourself (from spray splashback or drips) can be quite a trick. Let things dry, or dry and wipe clean with rags.
5. Inspect your handiwork. If any dirt or grease remains, go over the places with a rag soaked in all-purpose cleaner. At this point, most painted under-chassis surfaces should be whistle-clean.
6. Check the muffler, tailpipe, tailpipe tip, and catalytic converter, and other parts with surfaces subjected to extreme engine heat. They are likely to be rusted or otherwise corroded. De-rust them with steel wool: first with a wetted, soapy, household steel wool pad, and then with dry 00 or 000 steel wool.

With the cleaning done, you face a decision: whether to (1) simply wax and shine all exposed under-chassis surfaces, except those (as muffler and tailpipe) subjected to high engine heat, or (2) paint, rustproof, and/or sound-proof underbelly areas that obviously need it. Waxing, alone, is essential to thwarting future buildup of grime, dirt, and snow. A slick, waxed surface gives these under-car intruders nothing to cling to. Besides, as purists will tell you, a shiny underside—even though few if any but its owner will ever see it—gives owners the feeling of detailing completeness.

Painting under the chassis

Happily, everything you need to paint, corrosion-proof, or soundproof under-chassis comes in handy spray-on cans: high-temperature (able to withstand 1000°F) paint for the muffler and tailpipe; anti-corrosion auto primer and final coat for rust-prone surfaces; auto enamel for frame members and the like; and sound-deadening undercoating for the inside of wheelwells, the oil pan, and chassis sheet metal subjected to ricocheting rocks and similar road debris.

‖ C A U T I O N : Never use spray-on paints or degreasers in a closed-in area in which there is any danger of a stove or furnace pilot light—or any flame—igniting the product's fumes or spray. Also, don't smoke or permit anyone else to smoke nearby when you are using such products.

Fig. 7.4 View of a hoisted wheel well, an especially visible part of the under-chassis.

The color choice for under-chassis painting is black, in gloss, semi-gloss, or flat finish. Usual exceptions are silver for the muffler, tailpipe, and catalytic converter, and possibly a color that matches the car for wheelwells especially visible from outside the car.

Painting under-chassis is far less demanding than doing exterior paint touch-up. A little overspray can be quickly corrected. Besides, you aren't treating highly visible surfaces, as on the exterior. However, one masking job is essential: masking all around the outer edges of the chassis to prevent overspray from reaching the exterior body and tires. The simplest way to do the masking is to hang sheets of newspaper, held in place with masking tape, from the body's exterior—and all around the car. Once that is done, and you have a shop light illuminating the under-chassis and some sheets of heavy paper (as 8½- × 11-inch or 11- × 17-inch 24-pound copy paper) for spot masking as you spray, you are ready to paint or spray sound-deadening undercoating on what needs either or both.

Assuming that you've thoroughly cleaned the under-chassis, here are step-by-step procedures for the most common under-chassis painting/sound-deadening jobs:

Primer coat. Use any of several rust preventives available at auto supply stores. Below are sample instructions for a specific rust preventive; follow manufacturer's instructions on the product you select.

After grease, oil, rust scale, and salt have been removed, and with air/room temperature above 65°F:

Steps:
1. Shake can for 1 minute after agitator is heard.
2. Hold spray can 12–16 inches from surface.

3. Apply two to three light coats of primer, allowing 3–5 minutes drying time between each.

4. Allow 24 hours to dry completely.

Finish coat.   Below are sample instructions for a specific finish coat; follow manufacturer's instructions on the product you select.

(Apply at temperatures above 50°F and when humidity is below 85%)

Steps:

1. Shake can for 1 minute after agitator is heard.

2. Hold spray can 12–16 inches from surface.

3. Apply several light coats a few minutes apart to assure adequate coverage and thickness.

4. Recoat, if necessary, after 1 hour.

A number of primers can be used as the rust-inhibiting base coat for most brands of spray-on automotive enamels and lacquers.

Other anti-rust primers serve both as primer and as a flat, final finish when two or more coats are applied. Drying time between coats: generally 12 to 24 hours (the longer drying period is used if humidity is high).

Body paint used under-chassis.   Any spray-on paint formulated for the car's exterior works just as well under-chassis, so long as you follow label directions. Most, but not all, suggest—and may require—a primer coat. Some that are resin- or urethane-based (see their labels) advise the use of a like-brand primer, which is especially formulated to be compatible with the finish coat.

Undercoating for sound deadening.   Undercoat sealers and sound-deadeners act as both an under-chassis finish and a sound-absorbing medium. Factory-applied sound-deadening undercoating tends to form a thick, sometimes spongy coating, not unlike the sound-absorbing material sprayed onto home ceilings.

Undercoating reduces road noise in chassis areas especially prone to pelting by road debris: the wheelwells, obviously, but also the entire sheet metal underfloor.

Most of the easily applied and readily available do-it-yourself spray-on sound-deadening coatings are generally less thick and able to absorb less sound than the factory's original. But many do a credible job of hushing road noise and rock ricochet. What most apply-it-yourself sound-deadeners have in common is splatter. Any overspray must be immediately wiped off. Masking is a must. Also, undercoating should not be applied to heat-prone surfaces, as the tailpipe, muffler, or catalytic converter.

There are several spray-on undercoatings available at auto supply stores, formulated with various bases (for example: asphalt, rubber). See box for list of appropriate brands.

❗❗ C A U T I O N : When working under-chassis, use a mechanic's shop light—the kind that encloses the bulb in a protective metal shield. Using a bare bulb in the close quarters of the under-chassis risks bulb breakage and possible electric shock.

Undercoatings
CSA Rubberized Undercoating
Cyclo Under Coating
Mar-Hyde Undercoating
McKay Under Kote Spray
3M Underseal Rubberized Undercoating
Turtle Wax Super Seal
Westley's Rubberized Spray Undercoating
Westley's Spray Undercoating

Is this scenario familiar? As you prepare to get behind the wheel in a parking lot, you give your car's finish a quick, sweeping glance. Looking huge to you, but actually scarcely larger than a pinhead, a *new* nick specks the car's shiny door finish. Perhaps the damage was caused by the driver next to you, carelessly swinging open his car door—or by somebody's umbrella or grocery cart. The "who" or "what" isn't important, but that tiny new nick *is*.

While detailing can't prevent those aggravating nicks, it can erase them from the finish, one by one, as they occur.

Touch-up of finish nicks is usually well within the skill of do-it-yourself detailers. Some nicks can be erased with a mere dab of touch-up paint. Others take considerably more effort. Still, there are some touch-up tips worth knowing (some of them previously discussed, see "Tips from the Pros," in Chapter 2), and some touch-up limitations.

Black finish is the easiest of all to retouch, followed closely by white. If your car has a metallic finish (tiny flakes of metal seem to float in the finish), be aware that retouching may accentuate, rather than hide, a nick in the paint.

While it is human nature to put things off, nicks and dings in your paint job should be corrected as they occur, and not allowed to accumulate. The more nicks there are, the more tedious they are to detail. A collection of nicks can be overwhelming. They can cause a car owner either to shrug and let them go, or dash through the doing, detailing none of them well.

Can a quick touch-up, even with paint that matches exactly, *really* hide the nicks, stone chips, and scratches that most cars are bound to collect?

The answer is yes . . . and no. Very small "surface" nicks can often be erased by touch-up detailing. Deeper nicks—what most car owners call "dings"— probably can't. Because dings are deeper, and may actually have dented the metal, they create a shadow effect which usually defies quick correction or even paint-matching. The correction of dings, which may necessitate the complete refinishing of a door or body panel, requires the skill and know-how of a body or refinishing shop.

Here are some pointers worth knowing:

1. If you know your finish's factory paint code (see "Locating Factory Paint Codes," later in this chapter), you can obtain an exact color-match at your dealership, or have an exact match mixed at stores specialized to automotive paints. If yours is a late model car, it may be possible to find a color match at an auto supply store.

2. Always test the paint you intend to use. Dab a little of the paint on some obscure place on the finish. Let the test dab dry. Carefully compare the match.

3. When touching up, use an artist's or modeler's brush, not the far thicker brush or applicator that comes with most bottles of touch-up paint. A #2 art-

CHAPTER 8

Paint Touch-Up: Erasing Parking Lot Scars

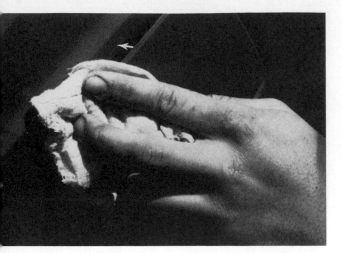

Fig. 8.1 Glazing can discover a nick that needs to be retouched.

ist's brush is ideal for touching up nicks and stone chips. Art stores stock the brushes.

4. Don't attempt a touch-up in cold or even moderately cold weather if you're doing the job outdoors. For best results, the car's surface temperature should be above 60°F.

5. The place to be retouched must be scrupulously clean and absolutely free of all detailing products (as wax, polish, and glaze), as well as dirt, oil, and grime.

6. Recognize that detailing has limitations. Detailing is appropriate for small scratches, nicks, chips, and the like—but not for large trouble areas.

1 ▶ 2 ▶ 3

S T E P - B Y - S T E P :

Retouching Nicks, Chips, and Scratches

Basic touch-up technique

Apply enough thin layers (coats) of color-matching paint so that the surface of the touch-up is level with, or slightly higher than, the surface of the surrounding finish. If higher, level the touch-up, when absolutely dry, to finish height using extremely fine wet-sanding paper (at least 600 grit), followed by a polishing compound (only experienced nick-fixers should use rubbing compound, which is more abrasive). Then detail the repaired nick place and a small finish area surrounding it as you would ordinarily detail the finish: apply glaze or polish; then wax and buff.

Quick fix for very small, nonrusted nicks

Time required: *0:20*
  5–20 minutes (per nick)

Materials needed:
  all-purpose cleaner or carwash solution
  color-match paint
  artist's brush
  extremely fine wet-sanding paper (at least 600 grit)
  masking tape (optional, depending on scratch size and
    location)
  cotton swab
  glaze (see appendix)
  wax (see appendix)

Steps:
  1. Thoroughly clean the nick area, using a cotton swab wetted with all-purpose cleaner or carwash solution.
  2. When dry, apply a dab of color-match paint to the nick using a modeler's or artist's brush. (Some detailers use the tear-off end of a match from a matchbook.)
  3. Let dry. If the surface of the touch-up is not even with, or slightly above the surface of the surrounding finish, repeat the dab-and-dry cycle until it is.
  4. Wait a day or more, even a week, to let the touch-up thoroughly dry. Car paint takes far longer to dry completely than most car owners believe.

5. When you are sure the touch-up is dry, very carefully level it (if it is not already level) with the surface of the surrounding finish. Rub the spot gently and only enough to bring it level, using a very small piece of 600 grit (or finer) wet-sanding paper.

6. Apply glaze to fill in any scratches left by the sandpaper. Then wax and buff the touch-up and a small area surrounding it.

Touching up larger nicks and scratches

Time required: *1:00*
   30–60 minutes (per touch-up)

Materials needed:
   all-purpose cleaner or carwash solution
   masking tape (1½ or 2 inches wide)
   cotton swab
   artist's brush
   fine steel wool (000 or 0000)
   color-match paint; primer, if needed
   extremely fine wet-sanding paper (600 grit or higher)
   polishing compound
   glaze
   wax

This procedure is similar to that given above for the quick fix, but there are some important differences:

Steps:
   1. Mask closely and completely around the nick to protect the surrounding finish. The width of the masking should be at least 1½ inches; 2 inches wide is better.
   2. If the nick is rusted, very gently remove visible rust with fine steel wool (000 or 0000) or with extremely fine wet-sanding paper (600 grit or finer).
   3. If the nick or chip has penetrated to bare metal, apply a base coat (primer) as the first few coats in the paint buildup. When primer coats are thoroughly dry, begin applying thin coats of the color-matching finish paint (Fig. 8.3). If the finish is clearcoat, the final coats must be a clearcoat finish compatible with the original.

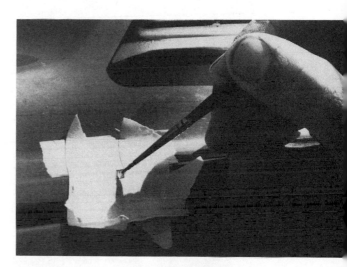

Fig. 8.3 Dab nick with successive thin coats of color-matching finish paint; or, if the nick is in clearcoat, with clear finish that matches your car's clearcoat type.

Fig. 8.4 After paint has dried for a full week, you must prepare the repainted nicked spot to blend with the rest of the finish and also prepare it for rewaxing. The first step in post-touch-up is to gently wet-sand the new paint with 600–1200 grit wet-sanding paper.

Fig. 8.2 Masking establishes the retouch work area.

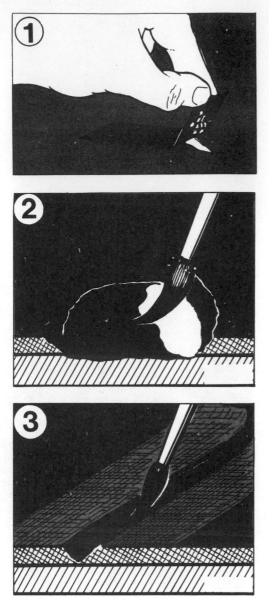

Fig. 8.5 Hints for quick stone chip and scratch repair if chipping has penetrated finish to metal: (1) Remove dirt and loose flakes of paint with masking tape; (2) Apply primer coat with artist's brush, and, when primer is dry, apply finish-matching final coat the same way; (3) For a scratch, mask both sides before applying primer or finish coat.

4. After leveling the touch-up paint with sandpaper (if necessary), very carefully use a polishing compound to remove any scratches left by the sanding operation.

5. Conclude, as above, by glazing, waxing, and buffing.

Retouching whitewall tires

Time required: *0:20*
> 10–20 minutes (working time; does not include drying time)

Materials needed:
> whitewall and tire cleaners (see appendix) or all-purpose household cleaner
> household steel wool soap pad
> model airplane enamel, white and black
> artist's or modeler's brush (very thin)

As white sidewall tires age and become curb-scuffed, some of the black and white areas may be abraded, so that the whitewall's white shows in the black areas and the tire's black shows in the whitewall area. This unsightly intrusion can be corrected by retouching:

Steps:
1. Carefully clean the intrusion places. Use usual whitewall and tire detailing cleaners, such as an all-purpose household cleaner or a special tire cleaner. Pay special attention to intruding whitewall areas. If necessary, clean with a soapy household steel wool cleaning pad or with a whitewall cleaner.

2. Thoroughly rinse and dry the intrusion areas.

3. Let the tire air dry for an hour, just to make sure the intrusion areas are absolutely dry.

4. Using model airplane enamel and an artist's or modeler's brush that is quite thin, touch out the intrusion places. With black model airplane enamel, touch out the intruding whitewall; with white, touch out the places where the tire's black rubber intrudes into the whitewall area.

5. Allow the enamel to dry before driving the car.

TECH TIP:
_____

Masking It Right

Here are some tips on the proper use of masking tape in auto detailing, including small area repainting:

1. Begin by removing from the car, if practical, all parts that will not be painted. Make sure all areas to be taped are clean.

2. For the initial taping of edges and curves, use narrow tape. Wider tape is used for flat, straight areas. Where possible, apply tape in long, one-piece sections. All masking paper must be securely and *tightly* taped down at the seams.

3. To prevent the tape's end from sticking to the

tape roll and having to hunt for it, hook the tape over your forefinger as you remove it from the roll, and tear off the desired amount.

4. Avoid wetting or heating tape. This may damage or destroy the adhesive, and when the tape is removed from the vehicle, it may damage the finish.

5. Masking paper (other than newspaper, commonly used by home detailers) is available in 3-inch to 56-inch widths. Masking paper is available in various bond weights. Keep in mind that the ability of the paper to fold easily around and on the car is its most important characteristic.

6. Most commonly used in auto detailing are masking tapes from ¾ inch to 2 inches wide. Fine-line tapes, used to edge and tape along pinstriping, are available in widths down to ¹⁄₁₆ inch.

7. Make sure the tape you use has good adhesion to both the vehicle and itself. Avoid laying a tape roll on dirty rags or other greasy or dirty surfaces. The tape's adhesive may pick up dirt and transfer it to the finish. Minimize dirt collection by storing tape rolls with a sheet of wax paper between them.

Keeping these simple tips in mind will make any masking job easier—and the finished painting or detailing as professional as proper masking can make it.

TECH TIP:

Locating Factory Paint Codes

When it comes to touching up nicks, dings, scrapes, scratches, and larger problems in your car's finish—outside as well as inside—finding out what paint will give you an exact color match is easy . . . if you know where to look. Every carmaker specifies, by color code, the precise color of a car on a label (usually it's metal or plastic) fixed somewhere on the car. The same label usually also carries the car's Vehicle Identification Number (VIN), also sometimes called the ID (identification) number. This is the factory's coded number that identifies a particular vehicle.

Your car's color code in hand, you can obtain an exact color match at a local dealership. And, occasionally, at an auto supply store's touch-up paint rack. In larger cities, stores specialized to auto paint can also mix and match the color specified by the color code.

The illustration and chart show you where, for most models of cars, the paint color code is located. While locations may vary, year to year, most manufacturers rather consistently locate their paint codes at or near the same place in the cars they make. Find your make of car on the chart and its color code locator number. Then consult the illustration for the code's probable location on your car (Fig. 8.6). Multiple locator numbers indicate placement in various car models produced by a manufacturer.

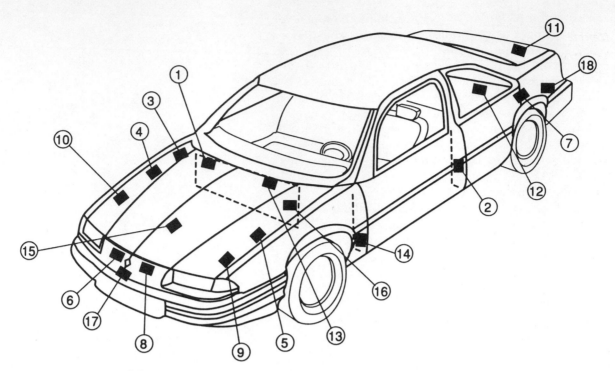

Fig. 8.6 Locating your car's factory paint code.

Factory Paint Codes

Make	Code Location
Alfa Romeo	11
Alfa Sud	11
Austin	1-4-5
Autobianchi	4-5
Auto Union	7-11
BMW	4-5-10
Chrysler	2-9-8
Chrysler (USA)	12-14
Citroën-GS GL, U, B	10
Citroën-GS, GX, 2 CV.	1
Citroën-LN	6
Citroën-VISA	3
DAF	1-13
Datsun/Nissan	1-9-15
Ferrari	4-9-11-18
Fiat	1-3-4-6-11
Ford (USA)	2
Ford	6
General Motors (USA)	1-13-14
Honda	2-13
Hyundai	1
Innocenti	2
Jaguar	4-14
Lada	4-7
Maserati	15
Mazda	6-13

Mercedes	6
Mitsubishi	6-13
Morris	4
Opel	3-4-6-8-9-10
Peugeot	6-8
Porsche	2-13-14
Renault	1-4-5-9-10-12
Rolls Royce	15
Rover	1-9-10
Saab	5-13
Seat	11-13
Simca	3-5-9-10
Skoda	13
Subaru	6
Suzuki	6-10
Toyota	1-10-16
Triumph	1-14
Vauxhall	5-10-13
Volkswagen	4-7-9-12-17-18
Volvo	1-3-6-13
Wartburg	1

Restoring Plastic or Painted Bumpers

Time was when most, if not all, bumpers—front and rear—were chromed. Detailing them (discussed in Chapter 4, "Exterior: Restoring Its Good Looks") was similar to detailing other exterior chrome hardware: wash, allow to dry, use very fine (000 to 0000) steel wool to remove surface mars (as paint), clean and shine with a good chrome cleaner/polish, and, finally, wax (preferably with a 100% carnauba car wax).

Nowadays, however, chances are that your new car's bumpers either are molded from some kind of plastic or are colored, probably matching the body paint.

Handsome? Yes. But plastic or painted bumpers show scratches and bruises more readily than chrome. In addition, while the best of multilayered chrome retained its good looks for years, even decades in some cases, plastic or painted bumpers need to be cared for and detailed on a regular basis. When plastic or painted bumpers are new and all but unmarred, you detail them like other painted or plastic exterior surfaces. However, when they begin to show age and wear they need to be reconditioned.

Some "flexible" bumper reconditioners are urethane-based and are available in a variety of colors formulated to match the original factory bumper color and gloss. Some colors are formulated to match the bumper colors of specific makes and models of cars.

!! C A U T I O N : Follow all directions on a product's label carefully. This is doubly true with touch-up products, especially paint. The tendency of many home detailers is to rush the job and fail to abide by the drying time specified. If it says "permit to dry overnight," or "thoroughly dries in 24 hours," don't shortcut the maker's recommended drying time.

(See box for a list of bumper reconditioners.) With some bumper reconditioners, bumpers must be treated with a prepping product to assure proper adhesion. *Follow the manufacturer's instructions on the reconditioning product you select.*

The good news is that a number of new chemical agents can chemically convert car body (sheet metal) rust to a new inorganic material whose surface is rustproof, usable, and paintable.

The bad news is that, although the detailing of non-sheet-metal car parts—from chrome bumpers and door handles to antennas—can remove rust, conceal it, and prevent its quick return, no amount of detailing can absolutely cure rust nor prevent its eventual reappearance. But there is much the do-it-yourselfer can do to delay for years the inevitable. Read on.

CHAPTER 9

Getting Rid of Rust

1 ▶ 2 ▶ 3

S T E P - B Y - S T E P :

Handling Common Rust Problems

Time required: *3:30*
Varies widely, depending on condition of car

Materials needed:
For minor to moderate rust:
cloth
chrome polish/cleaner with de-rusting agent
soft-bristled toothbrush; 00 or 000 steel wool, if necessary
car wax
For heavy rust:
two-step acid de-rusting system
car wax
For disfiguring rust:
steel wool or sandpaper
rust-preventive base coat
chrome-like silver paint

Minor to moderate rust

Minor to moderate rust on chrome and most metal parts is easily dealt with during routine detailing.

Steps:
1. Make sure the part is clean.
2. Remove as much rust as you can with a good chrome polish/cleaner which also contains de-rusting agents.
3. Follow manufacturer's directions for the polish you select. Most chrome polish/cleaners should be applied liberally with a cleaner-dampened cloth. Let the cleaner work for a few minutes, then wipe off the residue.
4. If rust is still visible below the metal surface, give it another polish treatment. This time, use a polish-soaked soft-bristled toothbrush to work the polish into the subsurface rusted areas. Let it work and wipe clean.
5. Still a hint of residual rust? Try 00 or 000 steel wool. Gently rub rusted areas with this fine abrasive. Wipe away steel wool residue.
6. Give it a final "shine" treatment, using the same polish/cleaner. The aim is to restore the metal's origi-

Fig. 9.1 Chrome and under-bumper frame, pocked by rust, can be cleaned and made to look better by detailing. Steel wool, then a strong chrome/metal cleaner will help but cannot restore body parts or chrome as rust-damaged as shown here.

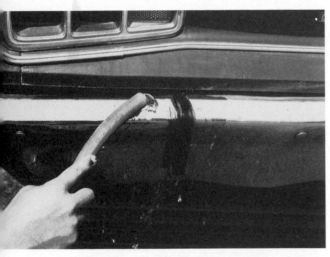

Fig. 9.2 Any two-step rust-removal system first applies acidic cleaner, then neutralizer, with plenty of water used between each step. To begin, thoroughly wet rusted area,

Fig. 9.3 Allow acid/cleaner to set for about a minute. Meanwhile, use a toothbrush to work cleaner into crevices.

nal shine. If cleaner remains in some subsurface spots, rout it out with a dry, soft-bristled toothbrush.

7. Last, apply a good car wax (see Appendix).

Heavy rust

Heavy rust, particularly rust-pocked chrome, calls for sterner methods—which probably means acid-detailing.

!! CAUTION : Although most acid de-rusting products contain only weak acid, the acid can harm a car's paint and plastic parts. When applying any acid product use equal caution to protect your skin, especially hands and eyes. Wear protective gloves. Latex or rubber gloves, commonly used around the home, usually give protection enough. When using acid spray-on products, be especially careful when aiming the spray. Be doubly cautious not to misdirect even weak acid spray at your face or eyes.

Some products use a two-step system, providing separate spray cans. The first contains a weak acid, the second neutralizes the first. Finally, the residue is rinsed off. Heed the label's directions. Any two-step formula should not be sprayed on plastic, nor should it be allowed to dry on metal or chrome. Follow product directions and safety procedures.

After application of the two-part system, rinse thoroughly. When dry, wax with a good car wax.

Disfiguring rust

When a metal or chromed part is beyond recovery, you can (1) buy a new part; (2) have the old one rechromed; or (3) spray-paint it with something that resembles its original color, such as chrome-like silver paint. Rust-disfigured parts are generally found in older cars or in those exposed to humid, salty air (as near an ocean).

Disfigured parts are prepared for painting, not for detailing. Whenever possible, the part should be removed from the car for the cleanup and paint treatment. Parts are cleaned, their badly rusted places smoothed with steel wool, even with sandpaper; they are then sprayed with a rust-preventive base coat. The finishing step is to spray paint with a chrome-like (silver) or other color finish coat.

Do not reinstall the newly restored parts for 24 hours, or until the paint is completely dry.

"Rust Conversion" Systems for Sheet Metal

Body metal has long suffered from the disfiguring cancer of rust. Before carmakers treated body metal against corrosion, "rusted out" cars were visible everywhere in areas where salt and other road chemicals were used to thaw ice and snow.

This book on do-it-yourself detailing cannot ad-

Fig. 9.4 It is doubtful that your best efforts can cover up or even stop the spread of body rust as severe as this.

dress restoring large areas of body rust (that's a job for a body shop), but you can easily learn to tackle small spots and patches of badly rusted body metal.

New chemical agents can now convert rust—which they use as a kind of catalyst—into a rust-free, hard inorganic surface which can be sanded and painted. The conversion process takes time, especially in sanding the newly created surface, but it can make your car "detailable" and forestall an early trip to the junkyard.

The Tech Tip at the end of this chapter, "Using 3M's Rust Avenger Kit," shows you step-by-step how to use this particular rust-conversion product. There are other rust-conversion formulas on the market (see box), some of which react with rust, although in different ways. Many such products produce a hard, sandable and paintable surface and, with careful attention to directions, are well within the abilities of a weekend detailer.

Rust Removers/Converters
Mar-Hyde Rust Dissolver
Mar-Hyde One-Step Rust Converter
    Primer Sealer
OxiSolv Degreaser/Rust Remover
Plasti-kote Neutra Rust
SEM Rust-Mort
SEM Rust-Seal
3M Rust Avenger Rust Converter

Making Chrome Rust Disappear

Some suggested rust removal detailing aids:

    grease remover
    steel wool (grades 00, very fine; 0000, super fine,
        and 000, mid range fine)
    steel wool soap pads
    wet sandpaper, 600–1200 grit
    chrome cleaner/polish (one-step cleaner/rust re-
        mover and polish; two-step acid-neutralizer
        chrome cleaner; or both)
    artist's knife
    artist's paint brush
    aluminum paint
    automotive quick-dry spray-on clear lacquer or
        urethane (gloss or flat finish)

Chrome rust on small areas, such as luggage racks, mirror fixtures, wire wheel spokes, door handles, or molding, calls for a decision: (1) Have it rechromed; or (2) detail it back to good looks and renewed life by removing the rust, repairing (if possible) the rusted area, then preserving its restored good looks with a coat, or several, of clear, spray-on lacquer or urethane, a liquid plastic.

The easy way is to have it rechromed. You merely remove the rusted parts and have a chrome shop rechrome them. However, rechroming can be expensive as well as vexing. To rechrome even an average small car's luggage rack can cost $100, often more. And unless the chrome shop is reputable, you stand an odds-even chance of having to rechrome again 5 years or so down the road.

Also, just as with car repainting, it is probably true that not even the best rechrome job can match the quality or life expectancy of original factory chrome.

Even if you find a reputable chrome shop (look under "Plating" in the Yellow Pages), it may not handle small jobs, whatever the price. Many plating companies replate only jewelry, silverware . . . and, yes, plumbing fixtures! Even those which make it their business to rechrome bumpers often don't handle automotive bric-a-brac, such as luggage carriers.

The logical, inexpensive choice is to detail it yourself. Detailing can often restore rusted chrome to a reasonable—and usable—semblance of its original, gleaming self. Whether or not a rust-corroded small part can be returned to its former glitter depends, obviously, on the extent of the rust. First, do as pro-detailers do: carefully inspect the rust-affected chrome surface, including weld areas, if any. If whole areas of chrome are missing, literally peeled away, no amount of detailing will restore what's no longer there. You have no choice: either have it rechromed or buy new.

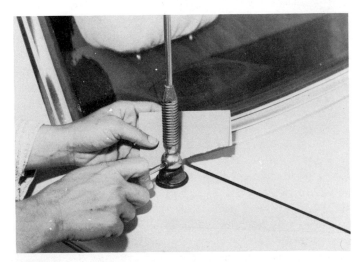

Fig. 9.5 From hidden recesses, rust can spread with surprising speed. Sometimes removing rust-prone accessories is the only way to get at—and stop—rusting.

If your careful inspection seems to indicate surface rust—rust which coats, rather than digs deep into, the chrome—try a simple experiment. Find a small area where rust seems heaviest, and work over the area very lightly with fine steel wool. You may get an unexpected surprise: just a few light strokes with steel wool may clear the surface of rust. Beneath lies gleaming chrome. You've discovered a rusted part that *can* be restored to near-new, usable condition.

Pro-detailers prefer three extremely fine grades of steel wool when working with chrome rust. None, with *proper use,* will scratch, mar, or remove chrome. *Proper use* almost always means *light* use. You exert the absolute minimum pressure necessary to clean and clear—and polish—the chrome surface, no more. All three of these pro-detailer preferred grades of steel wool *polish* chrome as they clean and remove rust. And all have myriad other uses in detailing; for example, cleaning and restoring the white wall areas of tires.

The finest, least abrasive steel wool is "quadruple-0," so called because its numerical grade designation is 0000. It is also often called *super fine* or 4-0 steel wool.

Only slightly more abrasive but widely used by pro-detailers because it gets the job done faster without risk of chrome-surface damage is "double-0" steel wool, whose grade designation is 00 (or 2-0). It is often called *very fine* steel wool.

Mid-range between these two is "triple-0" (3-0) steel wool, whose grade designation is 000. Many pro-detailers prefer the "triple-0" because it "works" faster than the super fine 0000 but is less abrasive than the 00.

The more 0s in a steel wool's grade designation, the less abrasive it is.

All three grades are inexpensive, usually come in ready-to-use pads, and are available in hardware, home center, and auto supply stores.

You can test the detailability of most surface-rusted automotive parts and accessories—that luggage rack, for one—without rushing out to buy steel wool. You probably already have steel wool soap pads in the kitchen. One of these will do an effective job of surface-testing rusted automotive chrome. But the steel wool is coarser (typically 01), so you have to use a *super-light touch.*

Some pro-detailers rid chrome of rust using 600 to 1200 grit wet "sandpaper." These useful papers actually contain no sand, but rather waterproof silicon carbide. This is the same type of "sandpaper" that gives fine furniture and fine cars their final, super-smooth, mirror-like finish.

True to its name, wet sandpaper is used wet. Soak the sandpaper in water. Keep it and the corroded surface wet as you sand away the rust; 600 to 1200 papers are only mildly abrasive (the higher the grade number, the less abrasive). Still, they must be used judiciously, with only light application of pressure. You want to rid the chrome of rust, *not* remove or thin the chrome itself.

Among the least abrasive wet "sandpapers" available are 1200 to 2000 grit wet sandpaper, often used by pro-detailers to achieve a mirror finish on newly repainted cars, including those with a clearcoat finish. Judiciously worked with water-wetted 1200 to 2000 grit paper, then waxed, a car's finish coat achieves a depth of luster and sheen that often looks fresh from the factory.

All abrasive rust-removers are used by pro-detailers with a single purpose: to quickly remove the worst surface rust. Rust that is below the chrome surface must be gotten rid of by other, nonabrasive means, as detailed in the next section.

1 ▶ 2 ▶ 3

STEP-BY-STEP:

Restoring Automotive Chrome

Time required: *4:00*

> 45–60 minutes for usual exterior chrome; 3–4 hours for large chrome accessories (such as luggage racks)

Materials needed:
> dropcloths
> newspaper
> masking tape
> spray-on lacquer or urethane (see box)
> household steel wool soap pad
> 00 steel wool; 000 or 0000 steel wool
> household scouring cleanser and soft-bristled toothbrush or spray-on acid-neutralizer chrome cleaner (for removing weld-seam rust)
> aluminum paint and an artist's brush (to cover weld-seam rust that resists removal)
> chrome cleaner (see box)
> wax (see appendix)

Let's detail a typical chromed car accessory—a luggage rack.

First, remove the rack from the car. All readily detachable chrome bric-a-brac should be removed for detailing, since you risk damaging the car's finish with rust-removal agents. There are exceptions: bumpers can be detailed in place; so, with care, can door handles.

Once you have removed the rack (or other part), if the rust is heavy, you might begin—as do some pro-detailers—with a very light going over with a household steel wool soap pad, soaked in water to release suds. The pad's relatively coarse steel wool should only be used in the initial rust removal step. Switch to slightly abrasive 00 steel wool. Use dry. Then, as most of the rust is removed—and you begin working on the original chrome surface—switch to less abrasive 000 or least abrasive 0000 steel wool. Remove as much of the rust as possible, including

---

Spray-on Lacquers/Urethanes/Acrylics

Autoglym Engine Lacquer (acrylic lacquer designed for engine compartment components, such as wiring, plastic parts, and hoses)
Car Brite Clear Acrylic Engine Paint
Krylon Acrylic Spray Coating
Mar-Hyde Supreme Lacquer
Plasti-kote Classic Lacquer
Plasti-kote Clear Acrylic Spray
Plasti-kote Super Urethane
Zynolyte Spray Lacquer (clear)

Chrome and Metal Cleaners/Polishes/Protectants

Blue Coral Chrome Brite
Eagle 1 Aluminum Wash & Brightener
Eagle 1 Chrome Guard (protects against winter rust, corrosion and salt)
Eagle 1 Mag & Chrome Polish
Espree Everbrite Metal Cleaner/Polish
Meguiar's Professional Chrome & Metal Polish
No. 7 Chrome Polish
OxiSolv Aluminum Cleaner
Simoniz Chrome Cleaner
Turtle Wax Chrome Polish
Turtle Wax Silver Chrome Cleaner and Sealant
Westley's Espree Aluminum Cleaner

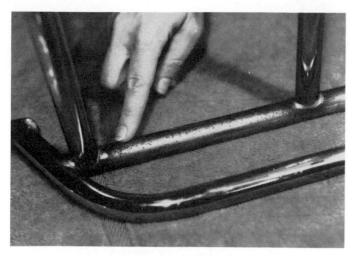

Fig. 9.6 Rust pocks this chromed luggage rack. Can it be detailed back to good looks? Answer: Yes.

tiny pinhole deposits, without marring or removing any of the chrome.

Chrome on some newer cars—and especially on "aftermarket" bric-a-brac—is often thin. It doesn't take much rubbing to rub right through it. The first indication that you have done so is often a dulling of the now-clean chrome surface. That, or the chrome seems off-color because you have reached, or at least are approaching, the underlying plating layers, the top one often being copper.

Happily, on such bric-a-brac as luggage carriers, which are bolted to a car's skin, the heaviest rust is often virtually out of sight—on the underside of the rack's crossmembers. This is because underside areas collect more moisture (rain, dew, snow), are in the shade (not in direct, drying sunlight), and are areas most often neglected in routine cleaning and waxing.

Welds on some car bric-a-brac—luggage racks being one of them—present a special problem. Weld seams (where two frame members are joined by welding) collect rust, too. But with one difference: rust in weld joints is almost impossible to reach or remove with steel wool alone.

How do you get at, and remove, weld seam rust? Sometimes you can work a household scouring cleanser into the weld seam with a toothbrush. Simply moisten a soft-bristled toothbrush with water, dip the wetted bristles into the scouring powder, and go to work on the rusted weld seams.

Or you might try any of several spray-on acid-neutralizer chrome cleaners. These products were developed primarily for cleaning chromed wire wheels (and their spokes) and for chromed bumpers, but may work on weld seam rust as well.

If you use one of the chrome cleaners listed, follow the directions carefully. If, after all this, weld seam rust is still visible, there's an effective last resort. To obliterate the last visible rust from a chromed weld, carefully paint the seams with aluminum paint. The painted joint will not exactly match the tone or color of the chrome, but if you do

Fig. 9.7 Wet chrome surface is successively sprayed with two-step cleaner. First step: Spray on acid rust remover and allow it to work. Second step: Spray on neutralizing solution and allow it to work. Then flood the entire area with water.

Fig. 9.8 After acid and neutralizer treatment, wash with soapy water, then clear water. Finally, brighten using chrome cleaner/polish. Optional additional treatment: Spray chrome-restored rack with protective coating of clear polyurethene or lacquer.

the job right, the aluminum-painted seam will scarcely be noticeable. And, in fact, the slight difference in tone and brilliance is often attractive, lending a distinctly professional appearance.

To conceal tiny rusted weld seams with aluminum paint, you need: (1) quick-drying aluminum paint; (2) an artist's brush—a #2 fine-bristled brush works best; and (3) a steady eye and equally steady hand. The object is to paint just the rusted seams, which may be scarcely $1/16$ inch wide, and not the surrounding chrome.

Some detailers paint seams before polishing, before a final spray-on coat of clear lacquer or urethane. Other detailers polish the chrome first because some chrome cleaner-polishes remove the paint, even when it's thoroughly dry.

With seams painted and rust removed, give the chrome parts a final cleaning and polish before lacquer spraying. Be careful to avoid leaving finger or hand prints on the polished chrome. Grasp the workpiece with a clean rag or paper towel.

Any number of good chrome cleaner/polishes are available at auto supply stores (see box). There are roughly two types of readily available chrome cleaners: those applied and then almost immediately rubbed off with a soft, clean rag; and those which are allowed to dry before polishing. The best products of both types will brighten even once-rusted chrome to almost-new appearance. The let-it-dry/rub-it-off chrome polishes may do a slightly better job than the wipe-off-wet type, but dried residue, while easy to rub off, has a habit of lingering in cracks, seams and crevices. Cleaning every last vestige of dried cleaner/polish from such hard-to-reach places adds considerable time and work to the detailing job.

No polishing product, whatever its claim, seals in the shine of refurbished chrome with the permanence of a spray-on coat of clear lacquer or urethane, available in handy spray cans at most auto and paint stores (see box for list of some possible choices).

For chrome auto bric-a-brac, especially if you've used aluminum paint, choose gloss, not flat, lacquer or urethane. Both are clear final coats, meaning they are see-through, no-color finishes. But the gloss adds luster to the painted seam areas, making them blend in with the rest of the chrome.

You don't have to be a spray-paint artist to do a credible job. But you need patience. Rush the spraying, and you'll botch this final, critical step in chrome refurbishing.

On complex parts, such as a luggage carrier, with its crossmembers and front/back/side surfaces, the spraying—done a little at a time—can well spread over several hours, even several days. Why? Because you spray on a very thin coat of clear finish, then let it dry. Next, apply a second coat. Then turn the rack over and repeat the process until every surface and crevice is overcoated with a clear final finish.

For each of the several critical steps in spray-coating refurbished auto chrome, there's a right way—and a wrong way—to do it.

Steps:

1. Start right. Provide protection against overspraying, even when the detailed part has been removed from your car. Low-cost dropcloths are extremely thin sheets of plastic, some less than 1/10th of a mil thick. Position the dropcloth behind, under, and all around the part you're spray painting. If the part you're spraying is attached to the car, mask all around it with newspaper. Then cover a wide area, 6 to 10 feet all around, with a dropcloth, held in place with masking tape. If there's even a whisper of a breeze (don't spray-paint in anything heftier), extend your masking even more. Breeze-carried overspray can reach distant areas you never dreamed it could reach.

2. Thoroughly mix (shake) the spray can contents. Most directions tell you to shake at least one full minute before using, and shorter periods while you're spraying. Many users don't. The result is something less than a satisfactory job. Most spray cans contain a little ball that mixes the paint; when the ball begins to do its mixing job, you can hear it rattling. Keep shaking the can a full minute (better, two minutes) after the ball begins to rattle.

3. Spray it right. For professional results, spray in quick, thin coats. It's easy to spray too much clear lacquer or urethane because it is colorless and all but invisible. Hold the can 12 inches—or better, 16 to 18 inches—from what you're painting. Make quick, smooth passes, applying a very thin coating. Then stop. Let the thin layer thoroughly dry before you apply another thin layer. Let that dry thoroughly and repeat the process until the entire bric-a-brac is sealed in a crystal clear, glossy cocoon of lacquer or urethane.

4. Wax it. When the protective see-through coating is absolutely dry, wax it with a high-grade auto wax, such as 100% carnauba. Waxing is essential protection for the lacquer or urethane, just as wax is the essential protector of your car's body finish.

Rushing to apply successive coats almost always gives poor results. Sure, the chrome may look and feel dry, but insufficient time between coats results in a rough, splotched finish, not the desired glossy smoothness. A rough lacquer finish can't be repainted unless you want to wet sand and start all over again at square one.

Another helpful tip: Spray cans, for all their convenience, have the nasty habit of clogging. Once the nozzle is clogged, it's next to impossible to unclog. But it won't clog if you follow the simple directions on the label (something a lot of users don't heed). When finished with a spray pass, hold the can upside down, nozzle down, and depress the plunger for about 3 seconds so that the propellant cleans and clears the nozzle.

Restoring Striping and Trim

A car without striping is like a businessman without a tie—in other words, not really dressed up.

If your car is not already dressed up, you may want to add striping. Or, if your car is striped, you may want to repair or replace the stripes because they are worn.

Most pro-detailers agree that "accent" striping, although more routinely done by paint shops and car striping specialists than by detailers, distinguishes a well-detailed car. If striping is worn or if sections are missing or need repair, even a car that has been detailed well doesn't look *well*-detailed.

Striping is within the skill of most driveway detailers, providing you use the type of striping that is easiest to apply—the self-adhesive vinyl type—and go about it the right way.

Basically there are three ways to stripe a car:

1. Freehand pinstriping with an artist's brush. Required, besides a steady hand, is skill possessed only by a few professional freehand striping artists. Their clients are generally owners of expensive, exotic cars who can afford the pro-striper's fee. Free-hand striping is far beyond the skill of most do-it-yourself detailers.

2. Paint-between-the-lines striping. This method also requires paint and a fine brush (although it can be done with spray-on paint), but rather than striping free-hand, the painter paints between tape guidelines.

Of note is the unique guideline tape produced by 3M. Visualize a piece of masking tape. Its full length is precut with narrow ($\frac{1}{16}$- to $\frac{3}{32}$-inch wide) "pull-out" strips. When the tape is in place on your car's finish, you select the number of stripes you want and their widths. You then remove the corresponding pull-out pieces, and the car's paintable finish is exposed between die-straight tape guidelines.

Next, lightly sand or scuff the exposed strip areas for better paint adhesion and paint between the lines. Retouch paint, available at auto supply stores, hands you a palette of striping colors. Some bottles of retouch paint even include a cap-installed brush that's sized just right for guideline striping.

While within the skill of most driveway detailers, guideline striping can involve considerable preparation (such as extensive body masking, if you elect to spray paint between the lines). And once stripes are painted, removal of the tape without fuzzing the edges of the stripes becomes a critical operation.

3. Pre-"painted" self-adhesive vinyl striping. By far the easiest striping to install is the pre-striped, clear plastic (usually vinyl), self-adhesive tape widely used for accent striping today's cars. Various brands are available in a wide range of pre-printed stripe colors and widths.

Installation is basic: simply stretch and taut the tape lightly in place, and when you are sure it's where you want it, run a finger down the tape's length, permanently firming and bonding it to the finish. The adhesive often holds the stripe in place for years—in fact, often for the life of the car—if you properly prepare the car's finish for maximum adhesion and bonding.

Generally, you should work with a partner, especially if you plan to install car-length striping. Two accomplish the job better than one. But even if you work alone, the highly flexible tape is easily handled and manipulated. With the judicious placement of a forefinger you can create curves, corners, and all manner of attractive accent stripe designs. For one example, you can create stripe lines on either side of the hood which, making nearly 90-degree turns, converge at the hood's front and center.

Small lengths of the tape, matched to the stripes already decorating your car, can be pieced onto existing tape to replace missing or worn places. You can piece new tape over the old, or, better, remove worn sections of the old with a tape removal agent and start fresh. With the old tape removed and the finish beneath scrupulously cleaned for maximum bonding, you can fill in the stripe void with new striping. The best of the pre-striped tapes fade relatively little over the years. The replacement tape usually comes close to color-matching the old.

Here are some vinyl stripe installation tips:

Car preparation.   Thoroughly wash and dry the car. Give special attention to the areas you intend to stripe. The finish must be absolutely free of dirt, wax, grease, and anything else that might affect the tape's firm bonding. Easily removed add-ons such as luggage racks should be removed prior to striping (and reinstalled over the striping once it has been fixed in place).

Materials.   Besides tape, you'll probably need a sharp razor blade (to finish-cut the tape's ends); a small bottle of clear lacquer with applicator brush to "glue" any tape junctures, if you plan a design where lengths of tape meet; and some masking tape, to hold one end of the tape to the finish while, tape roll in hand, you unroll the tape, stretch and align it, and tentatively firm it in place.

Car-length striping.   To do a car-length stripe, taut and stretch the tape over the entire length of the car and snap the tape lightly in place (Fig. 10.3). Tape right over doors and other openings to ensure the straight-line continuity of the stripe (Fig. 10.4). Later, when you've firmed and bonded the tape in place, you can cut the tape at door openings and other body breaks with the razor blade.

Turning corners.   To "turn a corner with the tape"—create a 90-degree turn—requires practice. Basically,

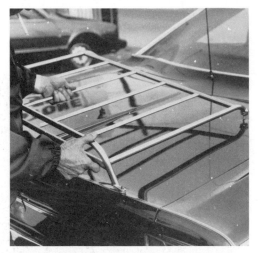

Fig. 10.1 Where removal is quick and easy, strip car of add-ons and other accessories which interfere with striping.

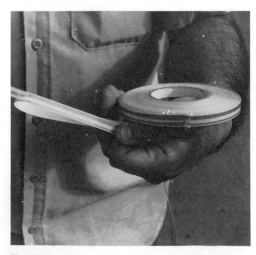

Fig. 10.2 A roll of vinyl striping tape. Resting roll on your wrist allows tape to unroll evenly.

Fig. 10.3 For long striping runs, tape is secured at one end and then pulled taut and straight before being laid against the finish.

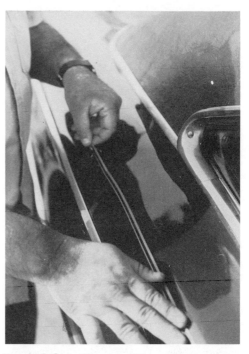

Fig. 10.5 Once it has been laid straight, the vinyl striping is pressed into place.

Fig. 10.4 To ensure straightness, uncut tape is run across door opening. Tape is later cut and firmed into place on either side of the door opening.

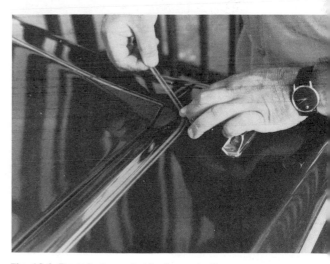

Fig. 10.6 Dexterity is needed for "cornering"— rounding a corner with the tape. Note how a finger is used to "work" the tape around the turn.

use one finger to firm the tape lightly in place while you guide the tape around the "corner" you're turning (Fig. 10.6). As the turn is made, your finger follows the tape, firming it in place. Don't get too worried about messing it up. If you don't make a perfect corner the first time or are unsatisfied with any run of the striping, you can always strip the tape off and try again—as long as it is only lightly firmed to the finish.

Bonding stripes that meet. If, in your design, two lengths of tape meet, with the end of one on top of the other, cement the bond with a dab of clear lacquer.

Tough-Up/Striping/Repaint Aids

3M Imperial Wetordry Color Sanding Paper (micro fine grades, 1200–2000 grit)

3M Wetordry Sponge Pad (for hand sanding with Wetordry Color Sanding Paper)

3M Scotch Fine Line Paint Striping Tape

3M Scotch Fine Line Tape

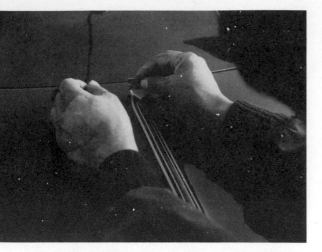

Fig. 10.7 Real artistry is required to shape a stripe's terminal point with a razor blade.

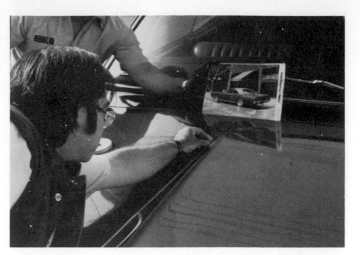

Fig. 10.9 If the car had been striped previously and you liked the way it looked, restripe it by working from a photograph. In this picture, the center hood stripe is being pulled tight before being pressed to the finish.

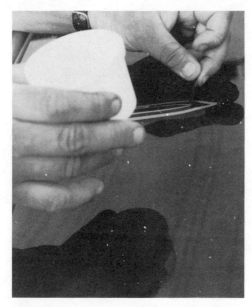

Fig. 10.8 The tape's terminal point is "glued" with a touch of clear lacquer. (Some detailers apply clear lacquer the entire length of the stripe to ensure its bond to the finish, but most pro-detailers say that the tape bonds well enough without the coating.)

Trim

Exterior trim (chrome, plastic, or rubber) is detailed with—and like—the rest of the exterior.

Replacement of trim and scuff strips where they have become worn, damaged, or loose—or installation of trim and scuff strips where they didn't exist before—is another matter. Installation of new trim is best left to a body shop; it isn't something pro-detailers generally do. The exception is often the replacement or installation of protective body molding (scuff stripping), discussed below.

Repair, straightening, or replacement of trim or protective molding may be necessary during detailing. Depending on how it was originally installed at the factory, and its type, some trim can be quickly repaired by the home detailer.

Replacing loose trim. Trim, including common chrome trim, is often held to the car's body with little plastic peglike "inserts." They can pop out of the holes, drilled in the car's body, into which they fit. If a piece of trim is loose (usually at one end), look behind it, align the pulled-out plastic inserts with their body holes, and then simply push them and the trim back into place. The insert fasteners usually run in tracks on the backside of the trim, making alignment easy.

Replacement inserts are available from body shops or new car dealers. New inserts are installed in the trim track, run down the track until they align with their body holes, and are pressed into place.

Replacing missing or badly damaged trim. While trim replacement is usually a body shop assignment, missing trim can sometimes be replaced by home de-

Fig. 10.10 This car has rubber protective trim. You can insert a new protective rubber strip in an old grooved molding channel. If the channel is bent, follow these steps: (1) Remove the channel screws around the channel that is bent.

Fig. 10.12 Most protective strip channel can be straightened by hand. (3) Simply rest hands on finish to guard against scratching the paint. Grasp the channel and apply pressure to straighten. Then replace screws and rubber trim.

Fig. 10.11 Next, (2) remove as much rubber molding as necessary to expose the place in the channel that needs to be straightened.

tailers. You simply order a replacement trim piece from your dealership. Replacement trim that is to be installed with plastic inserts usually comes complete with the inserts. Aligning the inserts with the body holes and pressing the new trim into place with a flat hand (to prevent denting) is no trick. What can be tricky is removing the old trim, especially those inserts which remain in their body holes. Use a wide, dull screwdriver to pry the inserts out of the holes. The danger here is marring the finish as you pry. Use extreme care. Do not use any of the surrounding body, or its finish, as a prying aid. Pry against thick folds of terry cloth towels so as to protect the finish.

Replacing vinyl scuff strips. These protective strips, often called side molding, are available in colors that match common finishes. They are inserted, and run,

Fig. 10.13 Position track sections and use masking tape to hold them in place. Molding tracks come in various lengths. They are usually aluminum and can be cut easily with a hacksaw. Allowance must be made for the decorative tips which butt to track ends.

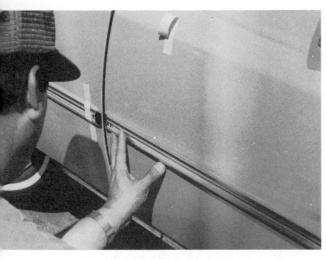

Fig. 10.14 Align track sections on car body. If necessary, level using a small carpenter's level.

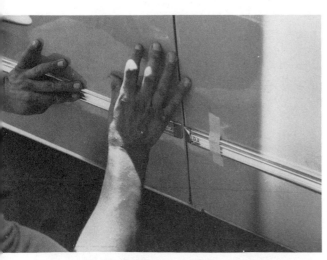

Fig. 10.15 Note the decorative chrome tips and the space left for the door opening.

in narrow (usually ½-inch-wide) aluminum channels that are riveted or screwed to the body. Because scuff strips are designed to be scuffed in place of the finish they protect, they are often abraded, frayed, or disfigured.

The replacement of scuff strips entails little more than buying new vinyl stripping matched to the color of the old, removing the old stripping from the channel, and installing the new. The stripping is available at some auto supply stores and from dealerships. If the channel has an end piece (usually a small, decorative tip), it can often be removed to expose one end of the old stripping. Begin at that end and simply pull the old stripping out of its channel. If there isn't an end piece on the channel, one end of the old stripping can be pried from the channel and the length of the old stripping pulled free. Before inserting the new strip, lubricate the channel so that the stripping slips in easily. Almost any silicone lubricant will do.

Don't precut the stripping. Run it the full length of the channel and then allow an extra 1½ to 2 inches before you cut it with a razor or snippers. Vinyl stripping has a habit of shrinking. Although the extra length may mean you have to force the end of the overlong stripping into the channel, you have thus provided for future shrinkage.

Scuff molding channels. See Figs. 10.13 through 10.23 for illustrated step-by-step instructions on the installation of protective scuff molding, channeling, and protective stripping.

Restoring armrest molding. See Figs. 10.24 through 10.28 for illustrated step-by-step instructions on restoring armrest molding.

Replacing door-edge molding. See Figs. 10.29 through 10.32 for illustrated step-by-step instructions on replacing door-edge molding.

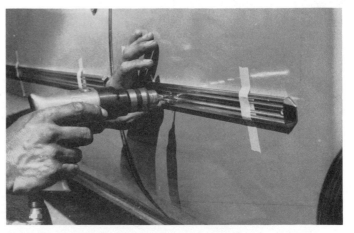

Fig. 10.16 With track taped firmly in place, drill ⅛-inch-diameter holes every 2 to 2½ feet (closer if necessary). Track is attached to body with pop rivets or sheet-metal screws.

Fig. 10.17 A simple rivet tool and some ⅛-inch-diameter rivets do a quick job of fastening the track to the body. (Metal screws work just as well.)

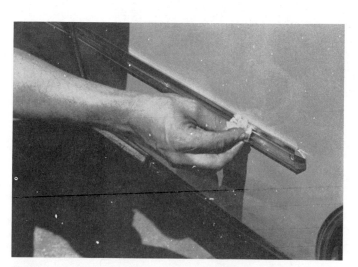

Fig. 10.19 Before inserting the molding strip, lubricate the track with a silicone product or other lubricant to make insertion easier.

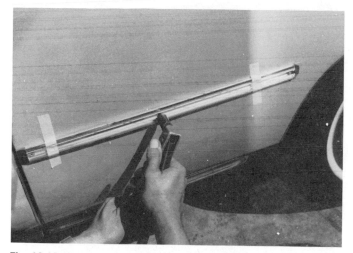

Fig. 10.18 If you are using rivets, attach track by inserting rivet in drilled hole and pressing the riveting tool's handle.

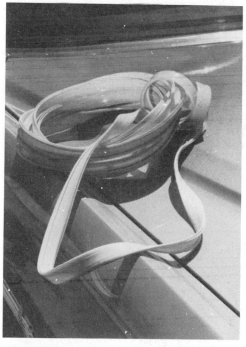

Fig. 10.20 Shown in a roll of ¾-inch-wide vinyl molding. Molding comes in a variety of car colors.

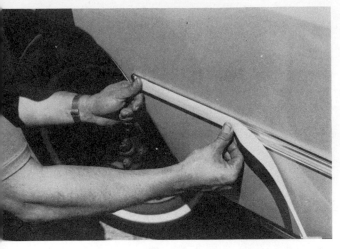

Fig. 10.21 Begin installation at one end of a track section. Press the molding firmly into the track.

Fig. 10.24 Chromed plastic interior molding (as on this armrest) can be restored to good looks, but restoration can seldom achieve the original shine.

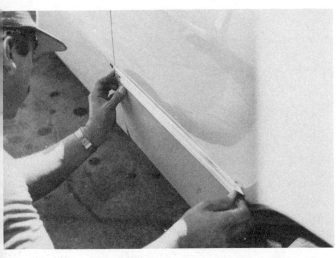

Fig. 10.22 Continue pressing and pulling molding into place until you reach the end of the track section.

Fig. 10.25 Molding should be rubbed smooth with steel wool before and after application of spray-on primer.

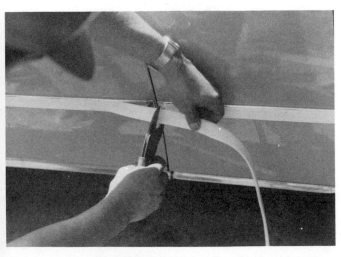

Fig. 10.23 Allow 1–2 inches of excess when you cut the molding because it has a tendency to shrink. The extra length can be pressed into the track.

Fig. 10.26 Spray primer coat. Once primer is thoroughly dry, spray on finish coat of silver or aluminum chrome paint.

Fig. 10.27 *Restored armrest molding, reinstalled.*

Fig. 10.28 *Installation of restored armrest is complete.*

Fig. 10.29 *Beginning at the top of the door, fit door-edge vinyl chrome molding to the edge and firm it in place with the flat of your hand. Don't use a hammer or other tools, as they will permanently dent the molding.*

Fig. 10.30 *With the top portion of the vinyl edging in place, move lower and lower to complete the installation.*

Fig. 10.31 Cut the edging after it has been fitted to the door.

Fig. 10.32 The end result. The edge molding helps to protect the finish.

Everybody knows that convertible tops don't last forever. Neither do vinyl tops. If your car has a vinyl or convertible top, you probably already know the majority of the problems. Vinyl tops dry out, crack, fade, streak, turn brittle, flake, and peel. Convertible tops mildew, fade, streak, discolor, and may be spotted from tree sap, bird droppings, and other fallout. The longevity of both, however, can be significantly extended by *routine detailing* and by more *specialized renewal* (refinishing).

In detailing, you routinely maintain or restore the top's *original* good looks with any of various top-detailing products, not the least of them some common household ones. All are easy to use. Most are rub-on/wipe-off products.

Renewal, on the other hand, involves considerably more: the *refinishing* of the top, whether vinyl, canvas, or another material. Rather than simply restoring its original appearance, you create—using top "paints"—a whole new appearance. And, if you like, even a new top color.

Detailing

Your vinyl or convertible top should be detailed whenever you detail the car, and sometimes more frequently (if your car has a convertible top, be sure to mask the lower few inches of the top when you detail the finish on your car). Intense sunlight, pollutants, and the weather tend to deteriorate a top's vinyl or fabric far faster than a car's "hard parts," its painted and chromed metal and plastics. The evidence of this—usually due to top neglect—is the many cars with vinyl or convertible tops that are cracked and peeling while their finishes, despite equal neglect, are not visibly all that bad.

Even more vulnerable to everyday use—and detailing neglect—are convertible and utility top plastic windows. They require detailing with specialized products formulated to remove scratches and to maintain the plastic's see-through clarity (see box).

Renewal

When, because of neglect or ungraceful aging, the original appearance of a vinyl or convertible top can no longer be restored by routine detailing, it can often be resuscitated by any of several renewal processes and products.

In renewing vinyl tops, you have two basic resuscitating choices, restoration or refinishing.

Restoring the vinyl's original color. For this process use vinyl restorative "dressings" (see box) and follow manufacturer's instructions.

Refinishing the vinyl (or convertible) top. In refinishing, you "repaint" the top, either with its original

Renewing Vinyl and Convertible Tops

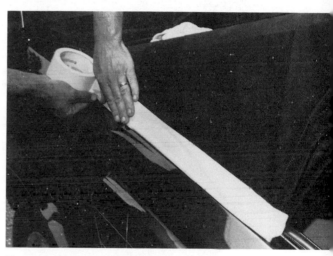

Fig. 11.1 Masking the lower few inches of a convertible top before waxing the car's finish prevents hard-to-remove wax from staining the top material.

Plastics Cleaners/Protectants
Eagle 1 Plastic Polish & Protectant
Meguiar's Professional Plastic Cleaner (for plastic windows, windshields, etc.)
Meguiar's Professional Plastic Polish

Top Cleaners, Treatments, and Dressings
Auto Wax Magic Dressing
Auto Wax Top Coat (for vinyl tops)
Car Brite Blue Magic (top/tire dressing; not recommended for interiors)
Car Brite Top Notch (vinyl top dressing)
PRO All Purpose Cleaner
PRO Wipe-On Vinyl Dressing
PRO Do-All Dressing
Westley's Convertible Top Cleaner
Westley's Vinyl-Top Lustre

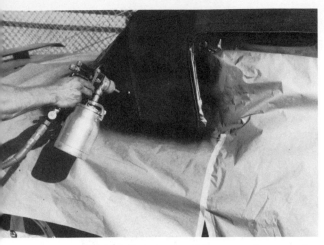

Fig. 11.2 Faded convertible tops can be restored with solvent-based spray-on "paint" (shown here), or with a similar hand-applied water-based product. Before application, thoroughly wash the top and allow it to dry.

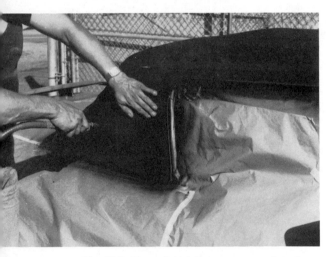

Fig. 11.3 After a light initial spray pass, allow the paint to dry. Use an air hose to blow off any dust or dirt, or wipe them off with a lint-free cloth.

Fig. 11.4 A heavier spray pass completes the restoration. (Note the masking, which protects from overspray.)

color or with virtually any color of your choice. If you now have a black top, but have always wished it were white, here's your chance to make it white.

Refinish products are usually either solvent-based or water-based. The water-based ones clean up with soap and water and can usually be applied with a brush. Generally, they're easier to use than are the solvent-based products. Solvent-based top-refinishing products can be purchased in spray cans, or they may be applied with a spray gun, as shown in Figs. 11.2 through 11.4. They tend to be longer lasting than the water-based products, but their overspray is harder to clean up.

Using either type requires extensive masking to isolate the top you're repainting/dyeing from the car's finish. This is particularly true when using the solvent-based products, whose overspray can do serious damage to a car's finish. But properly applied over a properly prepared top, the best of the refinish products restore vinyl and convertible tops to showroom-new looks.

! ! CAUTION: If you decide to repaint convertible top exterior fabric with a different color, spray on very thin, light initial coats of the new color. This prevents bleed-through of the new color to the underside (vehicle interior) of the fabric—a problem which would necessitate repainting the interior side of the fabric, too.

While there are some other ways to go in restoring tops, these two—routine detailing or refinishing—go a long way toward solving common top problems.

1 ▶ 2 ▶ 3

S T E P - B Y - S T E P :

Detailing Vinyl Tops

Time required: *1:00*
40–60 minutes

Materials needed:
    carwash supplies
    soft-bristled brush
    toothbrush
    all-purpose cleaner or special vinyl top cleaner
    household steel wool and soap pad
    masking materials (masking tape; mailing paper or
        drop cloths)
    garden hose
    color-restorative protectant
    car wax or specialized top wax

There is no "one way" to detail vinyl tops (see also "Prepping It: Detailing's All-Important First Steps," in Chapter 2). Pro-detailers even debate whether a vinyl top should be detailed before or after a routine car wash. Still, their detailing aims are the same: to maintain or restore the top's original appearance.

Steps:

1. Wash the top by hand (if also washing the finish, use the same wash solution); or run the car through a carwash.
2. Dry the top or let it air dry. Start with a dry top to prevent diluting succeeding detailing products.
3. Clean the top. Vinyl, which is often rough-textured, requires more than routine washing. Use a soft-bristled brush, a toothbrush, and an all-purpose cleaner or one of the several specialized vinyl cleaners. Some extra-strength cleaners may have to be diluted (for example, 1 ounce of cleaner to 8 ounces of water). With a circular brush motion, work the cleaner into the crevices. Use the toothbrush along the top's edge molding. To remove tree sap or other persistent fallout, rub gently with a household steel wool and soap pad.

   Masking to protect the car's adjacent finish from drips may be necessary. With masking tape, tape mailing paper all around the top. Or use inexpensive painter's plastic drop cloths, available at home centers and paint stores. Taped into place, the gossamer-thin plastic becomes a quick-to-install finish protector.
4. Rinse with a garden hose and dry.
5. Apply a color-restorative protectant. Let the product "work" for a few minutes. Then wipe dry with a clean cloth.
6. Wax the top. A good car wax, or a specialized top wax, protects the vinyl from fading, drying, and cracking and restores its original luster. Waxing also acts as a rainproof seal over the protectants, some of which have rather short lives when exposed to the weather.

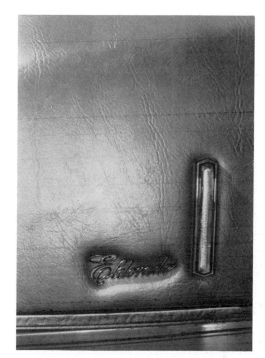

Fig. 11.5 Auto pedigrees imbedded in vinyl roofs are tedious and time-consuming to detail. Cotton swabs and toothpicks can help.

1 ▶ 2 ▶ 3

S T E P - B Y - S T E P :

Detailing Convertible Tops

Time required: *1:00*
    45–60 minutes

Materials needed:
    garden hose
    spot lifter, spot remover, or upholstery cleaner
    powdered household cleanser
    scrub brush
    all-purpose cleaner
    household steel wool soap pad
    toothbrush
    wax-type convertible top dressing (see box earlier in chapter)

Detailing convertible tops is mostly a matter of scrubbing with soap and water or all-purpose cleaner—perhaps with the addition of a bleach if your car's top is white.

Masking to prevent finish damage or streaking is a must. Use the masking procedure described in "Step-by-Step: Detailing Vinyl Tops." However, be aware of two problems peculiar to convertible tops: (1) their plastic windows can be easily scratched by even a soft-bristled scrub brush, and (2) if excessively wetted, water can leak through their side panels into the car's interior.

Steps:

1. Wet the fabric. Use a gentle stream from a garden hose. Avoid directly spraying side panel or other openings.
2. Inspect the wetted top carefully for tree sap, bird stains, and other fallout. Remove with spot lifter or remover or with upholstery cleaner, following manufacturer's instructions. Particularly persistent spotting can be scrubbed off the fabric using a slurry of water and powdered household cleanser.
3. With fallout removed and most of the stains erased, scrub the entire top with all-purpose cleaner, soap and water, or a slurry of water and powdered household cleanser. If any oil or grime spots remain, go over them gently with a household steel wool soap pad. With a stiff-bristled toothbrush, work the cleanser or suds into top seams and around the trim, which is common to many convertible tops. When using either brush, be extremely careful near and around the plastic windows. One brush stroke can permanently scratch them.
4. Rinse thoroughly with a medium hose spray.
5. Let the top air dry.
6. When thoroughly dry, certainly no sooner than the next day, apply a top dressing. Some pro-detailers rub a protectant into the top fabric with a soft-bristled brush, let it work half an hour (or even overnight), wipe off any excess, and buff with a clean cloth. Protectants can restore a top's original color and sheen (if it had a sheen). But protectants weather and dissipate in a short time and must be frequently reapplied. Wax-type convertible top dressings are longer-lasting and help waterproof the fabric.

!! WARNING : Force drying with a hair dryer or other hot air source can shrink the fabric.

Can a badly faded, badly oxidized, even streaked or thin-spotted paint job be saved?

If your car's paint is *this* bad, you face a detailing emergency. And, also, some hard choices. Your car's paint is not simply dull and in need of a shine. It needs something much more than "exterior detailing," as discussed step-by-step in Chapter 4. Your paint job requires "restoration."

First, inspect your paint job. Its "flat-to-the-weather" areas (the hood, top, and trunk deck), which feel the full brunt of sunlight, pollutants, and the weather may be faded, streaked, and heavily oxidized; or, worse, there may be patches, especially on the hood and top, where the paint is obviously thin; or, far worse, besides all the finish deterioration obvious in the previous cases, there are some places, although small, where there is either (1) no paint at all or (2) the primer color, probably grey or beige, shows through the primary color.

Can paint jobs as badly deteriorated as these be rescued? That depends. But one thing is certain: while all three of these bad-to-worse car finishes may be improved by restoration-detailing, there is no way to restore them to showroom-new appearance. Some or much of their former glitter and good looks may, with hard work and some luck, be regained. But some of the damage will undoubtedly linger.

In attempting a rescue, you are trying to avoid, for the time being, a costly repainting. You are hoping by some detailing miracle to restore enough of your paint job's former looks to carry you over the next months and possibly a year or two—before you must either have it repainted or trade in the car.

You face, frankly, a "what have I got to lose" situation. Right now the car needs repainting. If your rescue efforts fail, you have no choice but to have it repainted. If your rescue efforts succeed, you have gambled some time and money (for remedial products) and have pushed the inevitable—a repainting—into the future.

But not all rescue efforts are either possible or worthwhile. Described below are two cases in which a rescue effort is likely to fail—and one case that is worth a shot.

1. If your car is clear-coated (a top layer of the new, high-tech clear finish covers the finish's color layer), and if the color layer that the clearcoat is designed to protect is faded and streaked, a rescue effort will likely fail—and should not even be attempted.

The mere fact that the color layer, which lies below the clearcoat, is streaked and faded, tells you that the protective clearcoat top coat has deteriorated and been breached. If the clearcoat has deteriorated to this degree, you face the need for a restoration of not only the color coat but also the protective clearcoat.

Restoring the clearcoat is beyond the skill and means of the driveway detailer. It is a job for a skilled paint shop. Verdict: Your clear-coated paint job cannot be rescued without professional skill and help. (*Note:* High-tech clearcoat restoration systems, discussed elsewhere in this book, are designed to restore the clearcoat's original see-through clarity and shine. The clearcoat they are meant to restore is intact, not breached or worn through to the color coat they protect).

2. If your car is conventionally finished (is not clear-coated), but some primer shows through the finish—meaning in patches or spots the original color is missing—you may be able to restore much of the paint job, but only to a degree: you can't restore what's not there. Those down-to-primer patches where the original finish color is missing are beyond your help.

In some cases there is a solution. Since most deterioration occurs on the areas most exposed to sun, pollutants, and weather (hood, roof, trunk deck), while side, rear, front, and door finish may be in relatively good shape, you might have the most affected areas—notably the hood—professionally repainted. "Rescue detailing" might then restore the rest of the finish to acceptable good looks.

3. If your car is conventionally finished (again, not clear-coated) and has some spots where the paint is thin, but not missing, it can possibly be rescued. At any rate, it's worth the try.

Usually involved in the rescuing is some hard, tedious, and careful work. And some extended hours. Generally, you can't pull off rescues as these on a car's finish in an hour's time. For one thing, most, if not all, of the rescue effort should be done by hand, without resorting to machine buffers. The exceptions are restorative systems which use and recommend specific kinds of buffer pads, as those made of synthetic foam. For, while machine buffing is often the way to go on merely faded or oxidized car finish, whether conventional or clearcoat, we are speaking here of automotive "basket cases." Color layers are already thin or, in places, missing. Even if you are super-skilled with a buffer, you risk burning through the already-thin paint.

1 ▶ 2 ▶ 3

STEP-BY-STEP:

Rescuing Deteriorated Exterior Finish

In "basket case" detailing there is the quickie rescue and the more conventional approach.

Quickie rescue

Time required: *3:00*
  1–3 hours (depending on condition of finish)

Materials needed:
  carwash supplies

clean cloths
restoration product (see box)
wax

There are a number of restoration products available at auto supply stores or home centers. Below is a sample procedure based on a specific one-step restoration product. Follow the manufacturer's instructions for the product you select.

Steps:
1. Thoroughly wash, rinse, and dry the car.
2. With a soft, damp, nonabrasive cloth, apply the product to a small area of the finish. Apply with circular, overlapping strokes, gently rubbing the product into the finish.
3. Let dry for a few minutes. The restorer drys to a haze.
4. When dry, use a clean cloth to wipe away the formula's residue.
5. Finally, with another clean cloth, gently buff the surface.
6. Do one small section (say, 2 square feet) at a time. Finally, apply wax and hand buff to a shine.

Depending on the condition of the paint on their cars, many users of quickie restoration products report satisfaction.

Conventional rescue

Time required: *4:00*
   2–4 hours (depending on condition of finish)

Materials needed (see appendix for product lists):
   carwash supplies
   clean, nonabrasive 100% cotton cloth
   mildly abrasive and somewhat more abrasive cleaners
   polishing compound
   glaze
   100% carnauba wax

The aim here, on conventional finishes, is to remove the deteriorated top layer of paint, exposing the good paint which lies just underneath. Once this good, new layer has been exposed, it can be glazed and waxed as other conventional finishes.

Depending on the condition of your finish, use either a step-by-step and product-by-product restoration system (Meguiar or 3M) or the following procedure:

Steps:
1. Wash and thoroughly dry the car.
2. Begin with a minimally abrasive cleaner (see appendix). Follow the label's instructions. Apply to a small test area with a clean, nonabrasive 100% cotton cloth. Inspect the results.
3. If results are not satisfactory, use a slightly more abrasive cleaner. Again, apply with a clean, nonabrasive cloth and observe the results.
4. If, with careful application and gentle rubbing, you are

still not able to remove the oxidized top layer of "bad" paint, try a still more abrasive—but not overly abrasive—polishing compound. What you have tested are three cleaning formulas, each slightly more abrasive than its predecessor. "Rubbing compounds," more abrasive than your three test cleaners, should be used, if at all, only as a last resort. With the finish already thin in places, an abrasive rubbing compound might well do more damage than good.

5. When you have found a cleaner that works, very carefully and gently apply it, with clean, nonabrasive cloths, to the entire finish. Work carefully to avoid removing too much paint. Do only a small area at a time, and stop often to inspect results. When you come to thin or missing places in the color coat, feather your strokes. Work up to, not over, these places with mangy-looking paint.

    With careful, unhurried application, stopping frequently to judge results, you may very well have (1) exposed a fresh, deep-toned layer of paint over all or most of the car, and (2) carried the restoration to an acceptably satisfactory conclusion.

6. Conclude the job by applying first glaze, then a 100% carnauba wax (as described in Chapter 4). Hand-buff the wax to a high gloss with a clean, nonabrasive cloth.

With luck, persistence, and considerable skill you may be able to rescue your car's finish—and put off repainting for a while, at least.

TECH TIP:

Paint-Restoring Systems

Faced with restoring your car's paint job to some semblance of its factory-new look, you can pick and choose from scores of products designed to restore its finish. That, or you can follow the step-by-step recommendations of any of several major makers of detailing products.

Through laboratory and day-to-day testing, these makers have devised specific "restorative systems." Each maker-recommended restorative system specifies which of the maker's products should be used—and in what order and what way—to correct various car finish problems.

One considerable caution: Do not overestimate your skill. Most step-by-step systems require that you know how to use paint-cutting compounds (and when to stop using them) and how, skillfully, to use a machine buffer. If you are not skilled in either of these detailing procedures, or in others, do not attempt to use the systems. A misstep anywhere along the way could seriously damage your car's already "problem" paint job.

Make certain, if you use any of the systems, that

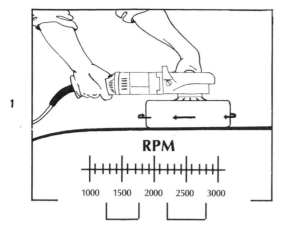

1

RPM

|—|—|—|—|—|—|—|—|—|—|—|—|—|—|—|—|—|—|—|—|—|—|—|

1000   1500   2000   2500   3000

HI-TECH CONVENTIONAL

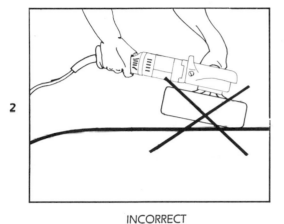

2

INCORRECT

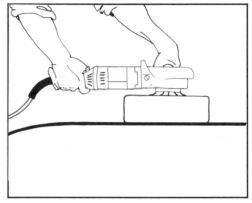

CORRECT

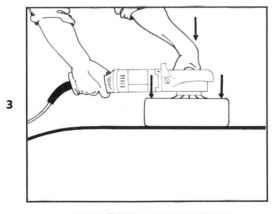

3

APPLY DOWNWARD PRESSURE

Fig. 12.1 For machine buffing/polishing with a foam pad, drawings show: (1) correct polishing speed; (2) correct angle of the pad to the surface; (3) correct way to apply pressure on the surface. Correct machine handling technique is critical to achieving uniform results.

you use the system recommended for your car's type of paint. Make equally sure that you apply the products specifically recommended for the particular finish problem you are seeking to correct and that you follow carefully the procedures outlined. If the system you choose calls for wet-sanding, use the technique shown in Fig. 12.2.

Manufacturer-recommended step-by-step corrective steps and products eliminate the guesswork in finish restoration and in product selection. The systems are proven ways of getting the job done right—backed

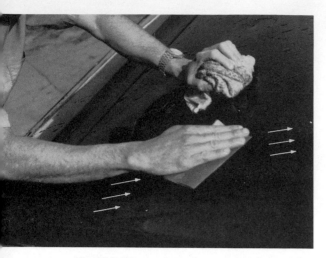

Fig. 12.2 When wet-sanding, one hand constantly squeezes water from a towel onto the finish while the other hand, held flat, gently wet-sands with a forward-backward (not circular) motion.

by their maker's years of detailing and paint correction experience.

Repainting Underhood

Except for touching up nicks and chips in the finish, detailing generally does not involve repainting. Leave that, as do even pro-detailers, to body shop paint specialists.

There are, however, several exceptions. One of them is repainting underhood. Even so, underhood repainting is usually limited to the engine, the air filter assembly, the battery box, the radiator, and possibly the firewall and various engine accessory brackets.

Armed with a few cans of aerosol-spray paint—the high-temperature type—you can do a credible job underhood, if you go about things systematically:

‼ C A U T I O N : Never use spray-on paints or degreasers in a closed-in area in which there is any danger of a stove or furnace pilot light—or any flame—igniting the product's fumes or spray. Also, don't smoke or permit anyone else to smoke nearby when you are using such products.

- Make sure what you intend painting is super-clean, without a smidgeon of oil, dirt, grease or rust. If possible, remove all the old paint.
- Mask sufficiently so that you paint only what you intend to paint, without getting paint or overspray where you don't want it. Most underhood components are spray-painted in place. Only a few, as the air filter, are removed for painting.
- Don't rush the repainting. Allow plenty of time, as specified on the spray can's label, for drying between coats.

1 ▶ 2 ▶ 3

S T E P - B Y - S T E P :

Repainting the Engine

Time required: *3:00*
　　1–3 hours

Materials needed:
　　paint scraper
　　coarse steel wool or sandpaper
　　masking materials (masking tape and newspaper)
　　high-temperature engine paint (see box)

Easiest to use are the self-priming, high-temperature aerosol-spray paints designed for engines. They are used straight from the spray can. No primer coat is required or recommended. The high-temp engine paints, available at auto supply and home centers, as well as at many paint

---

High-Temperature Engine Paints
Mar-Hyde 1375-degree F High Heat Paint
Mar-Hyde Supreme 1500-degree F High Heat Paint
Plasti-kote Engine Enamel (500 degrees F)
Zynolyte 1000F Hi-Temp Paint
Zynolyte VHT Engine Enamel

stores, come in a variety of colors, from black to flaming red.

For a typical engine, a 12-ounce spray can of high-temp paint is usually enough to paint the engine and most or all of the underhood accessories which detailers usually paint. Most paints are designed to withstand a *minimum* underhood or engine temperature of 1000°F.

Before starting, heed a time-tested auto painter's adage: "Ninety-nine percent of the job is preparation."

Steps:

1. After the engine and engine accessories you intend to paint have been degreased during engine prepping (see, "Prepping It: Detailing's All Important First Steps," in Chapter 2), remove flaky old paint and rust from the metal's surface (as much as you can). To remove old paint and rust use a paint scraper and coarse steel wool or sandpaper. If you can get down to bare metal, so much the better.

2. Mask all around what you intend to paint. With newspapers and masking tape, totally isolate what you want to paint from the rest of the engine compartment and its accessories. This may mean either removing some parts (as the engine's air cleaner assembly, if you're painting the engine) or totally masking them so they won't be sprayed during painting. Mask any wiring, brackets, control rods, and the like which are in spray's way.

3. If you plan to paint the engine compartment with the car out-of-doors, wait for a day that is warm (over 70°F) and not at all breezy.

‖ C A U T I O N : If you plan to do the painting in a garage, be sure the paint area is well-ventilated. Spray-paint fumes can be dangerous if inhaled. They are also flammable.

---

4. When the engine and/or its accessories are clean and dry, and other accessories are isolated by masking, you're ready to repaint. Shake the can vigorously. Don't shortcut the shaking, since shaking mixes the paint. Most spray cans have a little mixing ball inside. Shake the can for at least 1 minute after you hear the ball bouncing. Besides initially shaking the can, shake it frequently between sprayings.

5. Hold the can 12–16 inches from what you're painting and make a first spray pass. Initial passes are merely "tint passes": they'll tint the metal with the color you're using, but won't cover the metal.

Spray thin, even coats. Make a spray pass, then rest while that coat quick-dries. "Resting time" between coats may be as short as 30–60 seconds, or up to 10–15 minutes, depending on the paint. Follow the label's instructions. A half dozen passes spread over as few as 15 minutes or as long as an hour or more may be necessary for a thorough engine repainting. Remember to shake the can after each spray pass.

6. When the engine is completely painted, give the paint time to harden—say, a half hour or so—before attempting to remove the masking.

7. Start the engine and let it idle for 15–20 minutes. Let engine heat (which is in the range of 850 to 1000°F) cure and dry the paint.

8. As mentioned in other step-by-step lists, to clear a spray can's nozzle and prevent its becoming inoperatively clogged with paint, turn the spray can upside down and point the nozzle at a newspaper or drop cloth. Depress the spray nozzle for 3 seconds or so, or until the paint stream disappears and only the propellant gas sprays from the nozzle. The gas stream clears and cleans the nozzle.

Acura Bug & Tar Remover
Acura Car Wash
Acura Car Wax
Acura Fabric Car Care Kit
Acura Fabric Dirt Repellent
Acura Glass Cleaner
Acura Leather Car Care Kit
Acura Leather Cleaner
Acura Leather Conditioner
Acura Vinyl/Rubber Conditioner
Acura Vinyl and Rubber Protectant
Acura Wheel Cleaner

Ford Buffing & Polishing Pads
Ford Custom Cream Wax
Ford Custom Paste Wax
Ford Custom Silicone Gloss Polish
Ford Custom Vinyl Protectant
Ford Deluxe Leather & Vinyl Cleaner
Ford Engine Shampoo
Ford Extra Strength Spot & Stain Remover
Ford Extra Strength Tar & Road Oil Remover
Ford Extra Strength Upholstery Cleaner
Ford Extra Strength Whitewall Tire Cleaner
Ford Multi-Purpose Cleaner Concentrate
Ford One-Step Wash & Wax
Ford Soil & Spot Lifter
Ford Ultra-Clear Spray Glass Cleaner
Ford Used Car Reconditioning Polish
Ford Vinyl Hardtop Cleaner & Reconditioner

> *Note:* General Motors Corp. products, available at GM dealerships, are offered under several names, including "GM" and "GM Goodwrench."

GM Buffing Pad
GM Capture Cleaner Spot Remover
GM Chrome Cleaner & Polish
GM Engine Degreaser
GM Engine Shampoo
GM Fabric Cleaner
GM Glass Cleaner
GM Liquid Wax
GM Magic Mirror Cleaner & Polish
GM Multi-Purpose Interior Cleaner
GM Optikleen Windshield Washer Solvent
GM Preservatone Vinyl Top Dressing
GM Spot Lifter
GM Tar & Road Oil Remover
GM Touch Up Paint
GM Trunk Spatter Paint
GM Vinyl Cleaner
GM Washwax Concentrate
GM Wheel Cleaner
GM White Sidewall Cleaner
GM Goodwrench Armor All Protectant
GM Goodwrench Engine Enamel

A P P E N D I X

Detailing Products

GM Goodwrench Fabric Protector
GM Goodwrench Pick Up Bed Coating
GM Goodwrench Reconditioning Paint
GM Goodwrench Silicone Tire Shine

Honda Hondabrite Multi Surface Cleaner
Honda Vinyl Protectant

Mercedes-Benz Autoshampoo
Mercedes-Benz Chrome Preserver
Mercedes-Benz Cleaner for Light Alloy Wheels
Mercedes-Benz Gloss Preserver
Mercedes-Benz Insect Remover
Mercedes-Benz Leather Cleaner
Mercedes-Benz Paint Cleaner
Mercedes-Benz Paint Polish
Mercedes-Benz Plastic Cleaner
Mercedes-Benz Polishing Cloth
Mercedes-Benz Polishing Wool
Mercedes-Benz Priming Stick
Mercedes-Benz Spot Remover
Mercedes-Benz Tar Remover
Mercedes-Benz Touch-Up Paint Stick

Note: Mopar is Chrysler's tradename for products for Chrysler cars, trucks and other vehicles

Mopar Belt Dressing
Mopar Bright Metal Cleaner
Mopar Car Wash (powder and liquid)
Mopar Clean N' Bright (for car rubber, including whitewall tires)
Mopar Clear Top Coat (for body paint durability)
Mopar Convertible/Vinyl Top Cleaner
Mopar Engine Cleaner
Mopar Engine Paints (match OEM colors)
Mopar Fabric Cleaner
Mopar Foam Spray Color Restorer (restores paint, removes tar, tree sap, bird/insect residue)
Mopar Glass Cleaner
Mopar Leather and Vinyl Protector
Mopar Polish & Cleaner
Mopar Polishing Cloth
Mopar Rust Penetrant
Mopar Rustproofing
Mopar Scratch Filler Primer (primes nicks, chips, scratches)
Mopar Silicone Gloss Polish
Mopar Silicone Spray Lube
Mopar Super Kleen (removes tar, spots/stains from upholstery, wax, lipstick, oil, grease, etc.)
Mopar Tar/Road Oil Remover
Mopar Touch-Up Paints (match original colors)
Mopar Total Kleen (cleans velour, corduroy fabric upholstery, carpets, vinyl, leather)

Nissan Liquid Wax
Nissan Spray Wax

Note: Other products for Nissan and Infiniti cars available from dealers:

Bug and Tar Remover
Bumper Black
Glass Cleaner
Suede Leather Seat Care
Vinyl & Leather Cleaner
Vinyl & Rubber Protectant

Porsche
Alloy Wheel Cleaner
Cabrio Top Cleaner
Cabrio Top Preservative
Car Shampoo
Car Wash Preservative
Cockpit Cleaner
Cotton Polishing Pad
Insect Remover
Leather Care
Paint Polish
Paint Protector & Sealer
Polishing Cloth
Silicon Remover
Stain Remover
Summer Windshield Cleaner
Tar Remover
Window Cleaner
Winter Windshield Cleaner

Volvo Car Wash
Volvo Paste Wax (carnauba wax and silicone)
Volvo Polish (pre-wax, water-based, cleaning/polishing formula)
Volvo Wheel Cleaner (for Volvo alloy wheels)

Detailing Products by Specific Job

The following product groups appear in the sequence mentioned in the text.

Washing/Cleaning Chemicals and Soaps

Armor All Car Wash
Blue Coral Car Wash Gel
Blue Coral Car Wash (powder)
Blue Coral Blue Poly Wash
Blue Coral Carnauba Wash Wax
Car Brite Industrial Fallout Remover (pre-wash concentrate)
Car Brite OK Car Soap (liquid)
Eagle 1 Car Wash & Wax Conditioner
Finish 2001 Car Wash
Liquid Crystal Ultimate Car Wash
Liquid Glass Wash Concentrate
Meguiar's Car Wash & Conditioner
Meguiar's Deep Crystal Soft Wash Gel
Meguiar's Hi-Tech Wash

Mothers California Gold Pre-Wax Cleaner
No. 7 Car Wash (powder concentrate)
Nu Finish Car Wash
PRO Super Car Wash
Rain Dance
The Treatment Spray N' Glow
Turtle Wax Minute Wax Silicone Car Wash
Turtle Wax Pro Grade Condition #1 Professional Car
    Wash
Westley's Acid Rain & Water Spot Remover
Westley's Car Wash
Zip Wax Car Wash

Washing Aids/Accessories

Clear Wash
Rally Car Washer Sponge
Rally Big Sport Sponge

Glazes/Sealers

Auto Wax New Car Glaze
Auto Wax Sealer Glaze
Car Brite Super Seal
Car Brite Crystal Shine (clearcoat/basecoat glaze)
Eagle 1 Ultra Glaze & Sealer
Meguiar's New Car Glaze
Meguiar's Sealer & Reseal Glaze
Mothers California Gold Sealer and Glaze
3M Final Glaze
3M Imperial Hand Glaze
3M Imperial Machine Glaze
3M Prep-Team Light Duty Compound and Glaze
TR-3 Resin Glaze
Turtle Wax Pro Grade Condition #3 Professional
    Sealer Glaze
ZEP Auto Glaze

Waxes/Pastes/Pre-Waxing Cleaners

Armor All Car Wax (paste and liquid)
Autoglym Liquid Hardwax
Auto Wax Auto Magic E-Z Wax Paste
Blue Coral Carnauba Premium Paste Wax
Car Brite Butter Wax
Car Brite Crystal Finish (clearcoat/basecoat wax)
Car Brite Easi-Off (carnauba paste wax)
Car Brite Ultimate (carnauba creme wax)
Eagle 1 Cleaner/Wax (pre-wax cleaner/wax restorer)
Eagle 1 Carnauba Paste Wax with Cleaner
Eagle 1 Non-Abrasive Carnauba Paste Wax
Harly Carnauba Wax
Liquid Glass Pre-Cleaner
Meguiar's Deep Crystal Carnauba Wax
Meguiar's Hi-Tech Yellow Wax (liquid)
Meguiar's Yellow Paste Wax
Mothers California Gold Carnauba Paste Wax
    w/Cleaner
Mothers California Gold Carnauba Cleaner Wax

Mothers California Gold Pre-Wax Cleaner
Mothers California Gold Pure Carnauba Wax
PRO Carnauba Cream Wax
PRO Fallout Remover
PRO Yellow Wax
Rain Dance (paste and liquid)
Rain Dance Wash + Wax
Rally Car Wax (liquid and cream)
The Treatment Pre-Softened Carnauba Wax
The Treatment Pre-Wax Cleaner and Conditioner
Turtle Wax Car Wax
Turtle Wax Carnauba Wax
Turtle Wax Plus with Teflon
Turtle Wax Pro Grade Condition #2 Professional
    Cleaner
Turtle Wax Pro Grade Condition #4 Professional
    Yellow Wax
Turtle Wax Super Hard Shell Car Wax
Turtle Wax Super Hard Shell Silicone Car Wax
Westley's Acid Rain & Water Spot Remover (cleans,
    conditions surface for waxing)
ZEP Industrial Fallout Remover
ZEP Pro Finish (carnauba wax)

Polishes/Cleaners

Autoglym Exhibition Polish
Auto Wax All Weather Polish
Car Brite Super Seal
Clear Care
Eagle 1 Ultra Fine Scratch Remover & Polishing
    Compound
Finish 2001
Liquid Crystal Automobile Polish
Liquid Glass Polish/Finish
Meguiar's Deep Crystal Deep Gloss Polish
Meguiar's Heavy Duty Car Cleaner
Meguiar's Hi-Tech Cleaner No. 2 (clearcoat or
    conventional finishes)
Meguiar's Professional Machine Cleaner No. 1
No. 7 Auto Polish
Nu-Finish Liquid Car Polish
Nu-Finish Soft Paste Car Polish
PRO #1 Polish
PRO Progold
PRO Troubleshooter
3M Prep-Team Liquid Polish
Turtle Wax Pro Grade Condition #2 Professional
    Cleaner
Turtle Wax Pro Grade Condition #5 Professional
    Swirl Remover
ZEP Quick Gloss
ZEP Zeperfex

Finish Restorers

Turtle Wax One Step Color Back
Turtle Wax Clear Finish Restorer (for clearcoats)

One-Step Cleaners/Polishes/Waxes

Autoglym Super Resin Polish
Auto Wax Hi-Lite Cleaner-Wax
Blue Coral High Tech Auto Wax
Blue Coral Blue Poly One-Step Poly Sealant
Blue Coral Blue Poly One-Step Paste Poly Sealant
Car Brite Liquid Cleaner
Eagle 1 Five Minute Detailer
Meguiar's Car Cleaner Wax
Meguiar's Quik Detailer
Meguiar's Vibrant Paint Shield
Rain Dance Advanced Formula Polish
The Treatment Liquid One-Step Car Wax
The Treatment Carnauba/Wash N' Go
The Treatment Spray N' Glow
Turtle Wax One Step Carnauba Wash & Wax
Ultra Shine Clean 'N Polish
Westley's Auto Polish (cleans, polishes)

Tar and Bug Removers

CSA Tar & Bug Remover
Cyclo Bug & Tar Remover
McKay Tar & Bug Remover
No. 7 Tar & Bug Remover
PRO Bug Remover
Turtle Wax Bug & Tar Remover
Ultra Shine Tar Remover & Motor Degreaser
Westley's Bug & Tar Remover

Chrome and Metal Cleaners/Polishes/Protectants

Blue Coral Chrome Brite
Eagle 1 Aluminum Wash & Brightener
Eagle 1 Chrome Guard (protects against winter rust,
    corrosion and salt)
Eagle 1 Mag & Chrome Polish
Espree Everbrite Metal Cleaner/Polish
Meguiar's Professional Chrome & Metal Polish
No. 7 Chrome Polish
OxiSolv Aluminum Cleaner
Simoniz Chrome Cleaner
Turtle Wax Chrome Polish
Turtle Wax Silver Chrome Cleaner and Sealant
Westley's Espree Aluminum Cleaner

Leather Cleaners/Protectants

Armor All Leather Care
Autoglym Leather Care Cleaner
Blue Coral Leather & Vinyl Conditioner (cleans,
    restores, protects)
Connoisseur's Choice Cleaner
Connoisseur's Choice Protectant
Eagle 1 Creme Leather Care & Conditioner
Hide Food
Leather Clean
Leather Lotion

Lexol-pH Balanced Leather Cleaner
Lexol Leather Conditioner and Preservative
Meguiar's Vinyl/Leather/Rubber Cleaner/Conditioner
Scotchgard Leather Protector
Westley's Leather & Vinyl Cleaner

Vinyl Cleaners/Conditioners

Armor All Multi-Purpose Cleaner
Autoglym Vinyl and Rubber Care
Blue Coral Leather & Vinyl Conditioner
Car Brite Vinyl Beauty (vinyl interior/top)
Connoisseur's Choice Cleaner
CSA Premium Gold
Eagle 1 Spot Remover/Auto Interior
Mar-Hyde Rug, Upholstery and Vinyl Cleaner
Meguiar's Vinyl/Leather/Rubber Cleaner/Conditioner
Nu-Vinyl
PRO Wipe-On Vinyl Dressing
Turtle Wax Vinyl Top Cleaner
Turtle Wax Vinyl Top Wax
Westley's Clear-Magic
Westley's Leather & Vinyl Cleaner
Westley's Vinyl-Top Lustre

Plastics Cleaners/Protectants

Eagle 1 Plastic Polish & Protectant
Meguiar's Professional Plastic Cleaner (for plastic
    windows, windshields, etc.)
Meguiar's Professional Plastic Polish

Upholstery/Carpet Cleaners/Protectants

Armor All Multi-Purpose Cleaner
Autoglym Fabric Protector
Auto Wax E-Z Clean
Blue Coral Automotive Rug & Carpet Cleaner
Blue Coral Dri-Clean
Blue Coral Velour & Upholstery Cleaner
Car Brite Blue Max
Car Brite Nu-Look
Eagle 1 Spot Remover/Auto Interior
Mar-Hyde Rug, Upholstery and Vinyl Cleaner
Mothers Upholstery & Carpet Cleaner
PRO Aerosol Fabric Cleaner
PRO Heavy Duty Interior Cleaner
PRO Upholstery and Carpet Cleaner
Rally Upholstery/Carpet Cleaners
Scotchgard Carpet Cleaner and Protector
Scotchgard Upholstery Cleaner and Protector
Turtle Wax Carpet Cleaner & Protector
Turtle Wax Spot Remover
Turtle Wax Vinyl-Fabric Upholstery Cleaner &
    Protector
Turtle Wax Velour Upholstery Cleaner & Protector
Ultra Shine Upholstery Cleaner
Westley's Clear-Magic

Tire/Whitewall Cleaners

Armor All Tire Foam
Car Brite Whamo (whitewall tire cleaner)
CSA Silicone Tire Magic
Cyclo Whitewall Clean
Eagle 1 Tire Cleaner
Eagle 1 Tire Dressing & Protectant
Entire Whitewall and Wheel Cleaner
Kafko Brush White
OxiSolv Whitewall Cleaner
PRO Whitewall Cleaner
The Treatment White Lightning All-Purpose Cleaner
Turtle Wax Black & White Tire Cleaner
Ultra Shine All Purpose Cleaner
Westley's Bleche-Wite
ZEP FS/Formula 885

Tire and Bumper Treatments

Autoglym Bumper and Rubber Care
Auto Wax Bumper Magic
Cyclo Tire Shine
Mar-Hyde Bumper Black
Mar-Hyde Bumper Gray
Mar-Hyde Flexible Bumper and Plastic Patch
McKay Tire Black
Mechanics Tire Black
Meguiar's Professional Rubber Bumper Treatment
No. 7 Tire Black
Plasti-kote Bumper Black
Plasti-kote Bumper Chrome
PRO Black Bumper Paint
PRO Bumper Renewer
Rally Bumper & Trim (cleaner/polish for black and
     chrome bumpers and trim)
SEM Flexible Bumper Coater
Turtle Wax Black Chrome Cleaner/Sealant (for vinyl
     bumpers, rubber trim, moulding, etc.)
Westley's Black Magic
Westley's Black Tire Dressing
Westley's Just For Tires
Westley's Tire Shine

Wheel Cleaners

Car Brite Wire Wheel Cleaner
CSA Premium Gold
Eagle 1 All Finish Wheel Cleaner
Eagle 1 Wire & Chrome Wheel Cleaner
Eagle 1 Mag Cleaner
Entire Whitewall and Wheel Cleaner
Espree Mag Wheel Cleaner
Espree Mag Wheel Cleaner & Polish
Espree Wheel Magic (for painted, clearcoated, plastic,
     sculptured mag and wire wheels)
Espree Wire Wheel Cleaner
Mothers Mag & Aluminum Polish
Mothers Wheel Mist

OxiSolv Wire Wheel Cleaner
PRO Aluminum & Mag Polish
PRO Professional Wheel Cleaner
The Treatment Mag and Aluminum Wheel Cleaner
The Treatment Mag and Aluminum Polish
Turtle Wax Wheelbrite (for all wheels/hubcaps)
Turtle Wax Wheelbrite Wire Wheel Cleaner
Turtle Wax Wheelbrite Mag Wheel Cleaner

Top Cleaners, Treatments, and Dressings

Auto Wax Magic Dressing
Auto Wax Top Coat (for vinyl tops)
Car Brite Blue Magic (top/tire dressing; not
    recommended for interiors)
Car Brite Top Notch (vinyl top dressing)
PRO All Purpose Cleaner
PRO Wipe-On Vinyl Dressing
PRO Do-All Dressing
Westley's Convertible Top Cleaner
Westley's Vinyl-Top Lustre

Protectants (for vinyl, rubber, plastics, etc.)

Armor All Protectant
Autoglym Silicone Spray
Autoglym Vinyl and Rubber Care
Car Brite Super Kote
Clear Guard Protectant
Connoisseur's Choice Protectant
CSA Vinyl Protector
Eagle 1 Tire Dressing & Protectant
Mothers Protectant
PRO Clear Rubber Dressing
STP Son of a Gun Vinyl Protectant
3M Natural Gloss Vinyl and Rubber Dressing
Turtle Wax Protectant
Ultra Shine Protectant
ZEP All Around
ZEP Protect All

Sealers/Protectors

Autoglym Extra Gloss Protection
Car Brite Power Pak (sealer/color brightener)
Mar-Hyde Universal Autobody Sealer
McKay Stop Leak & Sealer
PRO Jiffy Seal
PRO Polymer II Sealant
Turtle Wax Clear Coat Paint Sealant
Ultra Shine Paint Sealant

Masking Tapes

Manco Auto Masking Tape
Manco Auto Seat Repair Tape
Shurtape
3M Masking Tape

Rust Removers/Converters

Mar-Hyde Rust Dissolver
Mar-Hyde One-Step Rust Converter Primer Sealer
OxiSolv Degreaser/Rust Remover
Plasti-kote Neutra Rust
SEM Rust-Mort
SEM Rust-Seal
3M Rust Avenger Rust Converter

Engine Cleaners/Degreasers

Auto Wax Motor Degreaser
Berryman B-33 Engine Cleaner
Car Brite All-Purp (water based engine cleaner)
Car Brite 10,10,10-The Perfect One
CSA Biodegradable Engine Cleaner
Cyclo Engine Clean
Gunk
KleanStroke All Purpose Cleaner
McKay Clear Magic
McKay Motor Shine
Mechanics Engine Degreaser
Mechanics Heavy Duty Degreaser and Cleaner
OxiSolv Degreaser & Rust Remover
PRO Engine Degreaser
PRO Red Devil Degreaser
Simple Green
3M Engine Degreaser
Turtle Wax Engine Cleaner
Ultra Shine Tar Remover & Motor Degreaser
Varsol Engine Cleaner

Battery Terminal Cleaners/Protectants

McKay Battery Terminal Cleaner & Protector Spray

High-Temperature Engine Paints

Mar-Hyde 1375-degree F High Heat Paint
Mar-Hyde Supreme 1500-degree F High Heat Paint
Plasti-kote Engine Enamel (500 degrees F)
Sperex VHT Engine Enamel
Zynolyte 1000F Hi-Temp Paint
Zynolyte VHT Engine Enamel

Aerosol Paints (body, chassis, wheels, touch-up, etc.)

Krylon Car Color
Krylon Van & Truck Spray Paint
Mar-Hyde Supreme Van & Truck Spray Paint
Mar-Hyde Supreme Roll Bar & Chassis Coating
Mar-Hyde Supreme Screamers (fluorescent colors)
Mar-Hyde Supreme Metal Flake
Mar-Hyde Supreme Chrome Aluminum
Mar-Hyde Supreme Silver & Gold Metallic
Mar-Hyde Touch-Up Paint
Mar-Hyde Lacquer

Plasti-kote Body Shop Paint
Plasti-kote Car Color Touch-Up
Plasti-kote Classic Lacquer
Plasti-kote Competition Colors (Metal Flake, Candy
    Apple, etc.)
Plasti-kote Import Car Color Touch-Up (also in
    bottles)
Plasti-kote Steel Wheels/Gold Wheels Paint
Plasti-kote Super Urethane
Plasti-kote Truck Color
Rust-Oleum Auto Primer
Rust-Oleum Zinc Chromate Primer
SEM Killer Color Fluorescent

Touch-Up/Striping/Repaint Aids

3M Imperial Wetordry Color Sanding Paper (micro
    fine grades, 1200–2000 grit)
3M Wetordry Sponge Pad (for hand sanding with
    Wetordry Color Sanding Paper)
3M Scotch Fine Line Paint Striping Tape
3M Scotch Fine Line Tape

Some Additional Detailing Aids

Car Brite Buffing and Polishing Pads
Car Brite Chamois and Sponges
Car Brite Detailing Brush
Grace Lee Whitewall and Vinyl Top Brushes
Grace Lee Detail Towel
Lake Country Car Wash Mitt
Lake Country Horsehair Detail Brush
Lake Country Waffle Foam Buffing Pads
Meguiar's Foam Polishing Pad
Meguiar's Hi-Tech Finesse Sanding Block
Meguiar's Hi-Tech Finesse Sanding Paper
OxiSolv Label Remover
Rally Big Sport Sponge
Rally Car Wash Sponge
3M Superbuff Buffing Pads
3M Superbuff Polishing Pads
3M Scotchcal Tailgate Replacement Letters (for most
    makes of trucks)
Wen Orbital Car Waxer

Detailing Adhesives/Adhesive Removers

Autoglym Tar & Adhesive Remover
3M Vinyl Trim Adhesive
3M Top and Trim Adhesive
3M Super Weatherstrip Adhesive

Trim Paints/Treatments

Mar-Hyde Black Satin
Mar-Hyde Gray Satin
SEM Trim Finishes
Westley's Black Magic

Fabric Paints

Car Brite Kolor Kote (for vinyl, carpets)
Mar-Hyde Fabric Color
Plasti-kote Ultra Vinyl
SEM Color Coat (for synthetic car fabrics)
SEM Plastic Prep (prepares fabric for Color Coat)

Vinyl Paints

Car Brite Kolor Kote
Car Brite Vinyl-Nu (for car tops, vinyl, leather)
Mar-Hyde Bri-Top
Mar-Hyde Vinyl Color Spray
Plasti-kote Ultra Vinyl
SEM Color Coat preceded by SEM Vinyl Prep
SEM Vinyl & Plastic Color Spray

Trunk Interiors

Plasti-kote Auto Trunk Paint

Pre-Painting Preparation Products

Mar-Hyde Total Prep

Glass Cleaners/Protectors/Windshield Washes

Car Brite Aerosol Glass Cleaner
Car Brite Klear
Clear Vision (windshield washer additive)
CSA Windshield & Glass Cleaner
Cyclo Glass Clean
Eagle 1 Automotive Glass Cleaner
Ice Away (windshield washer additive)
Mar-Hyde Professional Glass Cleaner
McKay Foam Glass Cleaner
Mothers Chrome & Glass Cleaner-Protector
National Liquid Ice Scraper
Rain Away (outside glass)
Super Stuff KlearStroke
The Treatment Glass Cleaner and Conditioner
3M Glass Cleaner
Westley's Glass Cleaner

Defogging Agents

No Fog
Rain-X Anti-Fog

Rubbing and Polishing Compounds

Autoglym Cutting Polish
Blue Coral Polishing Compound
Blue Coral Rubbing Compound
No. 7 Polishing Compound
No. 7 Rubbing Compound
Turtle Wax Polishing Compound
Turtle Wax Rubbing Compound
ZEP Tuff Buff

Undercoatings

CSA Rubberized Undercoating
Cyclo Under Coating
Mar-Hyde Undercoating
McKay Under Kote Spray
3M Underseal Rubberized Undercoating
Turtle Wax Super Seal
Westley's Rubberized Spray Undercoating
Westley's Spray Undercoating

Aftermarket Tinted Window Protection Film

Madico High Performance Window Film
Sunpro Sun Protective Tinting Film

Aggressive Means "abrasive." A detailing product that is "overly aggressive" is too abrasive, meaning it is probably harmful to car's finish or other surfaces.

Carnauba wax An extremely hard and highly protective wax made from the leaves of the Brazilian carnauba palm. It has a high melting point and is the polish wax preferred by most pro-detailers.

Clearcoat finish Hi-tech finish, sometimes called "clearcoat system." Among clearcoat finishes are those based on urethane, polyurethane, polyester, and fluorine resins.

Conventional finish Traditional auto paint, as lacquer, acrylic lacquer, enamel, and acrylic enamel car finish.

Detail stick A homemade crevice tool, usually a short length of ⅛-inch-diameter wooden doweling covered with a cloth; used to clean hard-to-reach places (for example, where windshield's interior meets the dashboard).

"English chrome" Chrome, common to some English-made cars, which is less shiny, more elegant, but usually more difficult to detail than chrome on many American-made cars.

Film Total film (paint) buildup from a car's bare metal to the surface of the top coat. On clearcoat finishes, this includes the phosphate coat (if used), primer, basecoat, and clearcoat. On conventional car finishes, film buildup includes the phosphate coat (if used), the primer, and the base (color) coat.

Finesse Name used on some detailing products that derives from automakers' "finesse" operations in which paint defects in newly produced cars are corrected.

Orange peel A disfiguring textured effect in car's finish that resembles the skin of an orange to the eye but usually feels smooth to the touch.

Oxidation The "chemical weathering" of a car's finish (if neglected) due to exposure to sunlight, atmospheric pollutants, and to air (oxygen). Unless oxidation has seriously deteriorated a car's finish, detailing can remove paint's surface oxidation and restore finish's color and shine.

Paint sags and runs Excessive paint buildup, resulting in runs and sags. Often due to paint being applied too thick, or to spray gun or aerosol spray can being held too close to surface being sprayed. Also can arise from spraying at too cold a temperature.

Prep Detailing slang for "preparation," which refers to any of several preliminary detailing steps. A "prep" product is one recommended for use before a final product is applied.

Rust converter Any of several products which convert rust to a hard, insoluble, but sandable and paintable surface. The chemical conversion usually produces a black surface which must be smoothed and painted.

Sandpaper grit   A sandpaper's abrasive particles. The higher a sandpaper's number (grit grade), the less abrasive it is. (In detailing car finish, extremely fine grit paper—from 600 to 3000 grit—is generally used.)

Topcoat   The top layer of auto paint, which is the color coat on conventional paint finishes, and the clear coat on basecoat/clearcoat paint finishes.

Vinyl vapor residue   An oily vapor, which becomes a residue, given off by some types of vinyl upholstery and other vinyl materials when subject to extreme heat—as during torrid summer days. Residue clings to most in-car surfaces, including the windshield.

Wet-sanding   Sanding out paint defects with water-lubricated, extremely fine (1200–3000 grit) wet-sanding paper. Also called "water sanding," "color sanding," and "flat sanding." Wet-sanding blocks or papers should be soaked in water for at least 30 minutes before using, and should be lubricated with water or a soap solution during sanding (to remove major paint defects).